*The Meaning of Existence in Contemporary Hispanic Literature*

Hispanic-American Studies No. 23

The Meaning of Existence in Contemporary Hispanic Literature

By Kessel Schwartz

UNIVERSITY OF MIAMI PRESS
Coral Gables, Florida

Designed by Bernard Lipsky

Manufactured in the United States of America

To my wife,
whose motto is
"And gladly write."

Contents

1

INTRODUCTION, *9*

2

POETRY, *37*
The Sea and Machado, *37*
García Lorca and Vermont, *52*
The Sea, Love, and Death in the Poetry of Aleixandre, *62*

3

NOVEL, *79*
Some Aspects of the Contemporary Novel of Ecuador, *79*
Alfredo Pareja y Diez Canseco, Social Novelist, *85*
Animal Symbolism in the Fiction of Ramón Sender, *99*

4

THEATER, *113*
Benavente and Shakespearean Drama, *113*
Benavente on Shakespearean Characters, *118*
Shakespeare's Influence on Benavente's Plays, *121*
Some Recent Works of Joaquín Calvo-Sotelo, *127*
Jacinto Grau and the Meaning of Existence, *133*
Reality in the Works of Alejandro Casona, *144*
Buero Vallejo and the Concept of Tragedy, *151*
Tragedy and the Criticism of Alfonso Sastre, *162*

5

ESSAY, *171*

Ortega y Gasset and Goethe, *171*
A Falangist View of Golden Age Literature, *183*
A Fascist View of Nineteenth-Century Spanish Literature, *191*
Culture and the Spanish Civil War, *197*
Madrid and Spanish Literature, *219*
The Pueblo, the Intellectuals, and the Civil War, *225*

Notes, *237*

Index, *252*

1

Introduction

I

EXISTENCE and preoccupation with its duality as represented by spirit-flesh, tradition-progress, Devil-God, and life-death have been leitmotivs in Spanish literature almost from its inception. Spain has concerned itself with the fusion of the human and the divine, the incompatible, the antithetical, and the paradoxical to such an extent that students of its philosophy, politics, and sociology have coined the concept of "las dos Españas."

Américo Castro believes that the characteristic qualities of Spain lie in its unique treatment of belief and human values, which stems from its experience and long contact with Arabs, Christians, and Jews. He contends that the contemporary Spaniard is in essence the one formed from about the year 1000 A.D. on. That which was most original and universal in Hispanic genius developed through the nine centuries of multi-cultural interaction. One of the primary aspects of the consciousness of being Spanish, says Castro, is that of existing as an essential man, with a vital rather than scientific system of values, and concerned for a constant "estar dentro de sí."

From medieval times on Spaniards viewed death as the road to eternal reward and punishment, democratically acknowledged in the Spanish version of the *Dance of Death* and poignantly portrayed and epitomized in the *Coplas* of Jorge Manrique who saw that our lives, indeed, are like the rivers which wind to the sea of death where all men, rich and poor, good and bad, must eventually end. The duality of a real and an ideal world, life and death, created the unique aspects of the Spanish Renaissance, the extreme humanistic and scholastic contention between learned and revealed truth, a duality so beautifully culminated in El Greco's "El entierro del Conde de Orgaz." In the first half of the sixteenth century Erasmianism defended interior religion, a return to a simple life, and a primitive form of Christianity. Its followers were later persecuted by the forces of reaction. In the second half of the century Spanish mystics sought a spiritual union with God in spite of their materialistic knowledge of life, and their direct contact and spiritual raptures were viewed with suspicion and were harassed by more orthodox church circles.

To a certain extent existence as the basis of philosophy and knowledge, summed up by irrationalism, takes over as a principle for Don Quixote, who tells Sancho that what he decides is reality is the truth, as he acts out the profound tragedy of the human comedy. The Golden Age dramas of Tirso, Calderón, Lope, and others treat of divine mercy or its lack, the theological implications of being a man, and the transitory nature of the things of this world. Another constant concern of Spanish literature is a democratic spirit and social preoccupation, revealed through the individual awareness of the anguish suffered by Everyman. Often done in an ironic and bitter vein, as by the stoic Quevedo, who did not bother to hide his hatred of sham and hypocrisy, social commentary involved Christian principles applied to the realm of men and its governors as exemplified in the works of Antonio de Guevara and Saavedra Fajardo and matched in turn by an extreme pessimism as reflected in *El criticón* of Baltasar Gracián.

The concept of "dos Españas" continued into the nineteenth and twentieth centuries. Krausismo, as preached by its practitioners, holds that we are all manifestations of the infinite body of an absolute God joined in the search of our Creator. Maintaining a balance among science, religion, and reason, krausistas promoted concepts of tolerance and good works. To know God logically one had to know his world, simply a finite part of an infinite divine essence. Bringing new vigor and polemics to university life, krausismo helped prepare the way for the "Generation of 1898." Francisco Giner de los Ríos started his Institución Libre de Enseñanza to create new men and help in the formation of future generations through teachers like Manuel Bartolomé Cossío, interested in the esthetic and spiritual reevaluation of the artist, and Joaquín Costa, historian and cultural devotee of Europe whose battle cry was "echar doble llave al sepulcro del Cid." These new winds of change did not go unopposed, and a number of the krausistas lost their positions and suffered other persecutions. Yet many of the greatest intellectual and political figures of the day, including Nicolás Salmerón, president of the first Spanish Republic, were krausistas. Later outgrowths from the Institución were the Junta para Ampliación de Estudios, first directed by Ramón y Cajal, and the Centro de Estudios Históricos through whose contacts, direct or indirect, Unamuno, Machado, Azorín, Ortega y Gasset, Navarro Tomás, and Américo Castro received a continuing inspiration. It is not accidental that many of the writers who followed the philosophy of the conservative Menéndez y Pelayo and Ramiro de Maeztu, and the Fascist supporters of the Franco rebellion, saw as their continuing enemies the krausistas, the Institución Libre de Enseñanza and its intellectual products like Antonio Machado.

We like to think that modern Spanish literature starts with the "Generation of 1898," first called "Generation of 1896" by Azorín, inventor of the sobriquet. If one follows rigidly the concepts of Julius Peterson about generations, it is difficult to consider its members as participating in a generation, literary school, or movement. The authors involved, each in his own way, examined the present and found it wanting, seeking through a variety of social, political, and literary reforms to change the context of Spanish life. Some through an emphasis on Spanish tradition and others through Europeanization sought Spanish rebirth and salvation. As Azorín said, these writers loved to make excursions in time and space, an insistence already felt among the krausistas, and they speak of living for life, man in his relationship to the universe, the fragmentation of the personality and the psyche, and the problem of the dehumanization of mankind.

Nietzsche, as Sobejano and others have shown and the authors themselves usually admitted, was of paramount influence in their development. Pío Baroja, according to Ernesto Giménez Caballero, 'El mejor nietzscheano español," questions traditional and absolute values, the relationships among beauty, truth, and goodness, and sees the individual as living affirmatively in the world through will and action; Azorín in *La voluntad* almost paraphrases Nietzsche and insists on the eternal recurrence, that everything which has ever existed must return unchanged; Unamuno, in spite of his expressed antipathy to the German, shared his ideas on eternity and willpower. Unamuno's philosophical starting point was the personal and historical situation in which he found himself; he determined his own dread and meaning of faith in the light of personal experience.

For the Generation, old concepts, values, and beliefs crumbled; they were either discarded or reevaluated, including the traditional one of a Christian God. New values had to replace the feeling of emptiness, and members of the Generation indulged in a desperate search for the reaffirmation of existence. Since neither rationalism nor Christianity could give them the reason for existence, they had to find a new definition of reality as well as a new esthetics and to seek a new way of being. Most of the writers decided to start from personal experience and base their ideas on the only reality they knew. They determined that one cannot infer existence from thought, and, courageously, these "bichos raros" abandoned security for self commitment. Unamuno, Machado, and other contemporaries evolved a philosophy, which was to receive its clearest exposition in the works of Ortega y Gasset, of life as a kind of drama to be lived, of destiny forged through will and action. They sought their role in life and, shunning abulia, tried to overcome the barriers which hemmed them in.

Whatever the tenets ascribed to the "Generation of 1898," such as love of old towns, new interpretations of history, tradition, and the Spanish soul, whatever the philosophical or idealistic preoccupations one encounters in the writings, one becomes aware that the meaning of existence is the one connecting theme which pervades the poetry, fiction, theater, and essay. One may argue that these writers, if they constitute a movement at all, form the first existentialist one in twentieth-century Europe. Man creates his own essence through his will or action and, faced by boundary situations including the final boundary of death, a nothingness which causes anguish, he wants to know who he is and where he is going. He questions the meaning of his existence, his relationship to his fellow man, to God, and to the cosmos. He cannot communicate, but he must face courageously the perils of an absurd world, from which neither resolve nor faith can save him. Even though man knows he will die, he must continue positively to decide at each moment what he is going to do and what he is going to be at the next.

The writers of the generation were somewhat prophetic about their culture, as were the romantics before them, but they substituted historical, philological, and philosophical trappings and the very scientific knowledge they pretended to scorn for a simple sentimental rebellion. They discovered that Spain had been living for any number of good reasons, moral, theological, or economic, but not for life; for culture, but not for human beings;

for the political or the economic man, but not, as Unamuno says, for the man of flesh and bone.

An artistic aspect of the philosophical inquiry, the related movement of modernism, was defined by Federico de Onís as the Spanish form of the universal crisis in letters and spirit which toward 1885 initiated the dissolution of the nineteenth century and was to be manifested in art, science, religion, politics, and gradually in all the other aspects of life with all the characteristics therefore of a deep historical change whose process continues today. Born as a negation against previous literature and its false values, accepting Nietzsche's distinction of Apollonian and Dionysian poetry, modernism has as many definitions as it has critics. The Nicaraguan Rubén Darío became its leader, himself inheriting and sharpening a legacy left him by José Martí, José Asunción Silva, and Manuel Gutiérrez Nájera. Cosmopolitan, exotic, esthetic, individual, aristocratic, pessimistic, amoral, and musical, modernism utilized sensations, explorations in time and space, pre-Colombian and Nordic mythology, and the inevitable dualism of life-death, virtue-sin, and spirit-flesh. In its broadest sense modernism goes beyond brilliance and pyrotechnics to considerations of universal concerns of existence and death.

Other movements after modernism sought elaborations of themes already present, consolidating, intensifying, and intellectualizing some of the previous elements. A number of elements such as futurism tried to reflect a dynamic new world. Creacionismo, which both the Chilean Vicente Huidobro and the Spaniard Gerardo Diego professed, dadaism, whose members were disgusted at the disappearance of their rational world, and surrealism, with its subconscious revolt against a discredited rationalism, played their part. New poetic generations questioned existence in a special way. The Spanish Civil War, a truly traumatic experience of cataclysmic proportions, sharpened the Spaniard's view of reality as anguished existence, not only philosophically but socially, creating a general crisis of human values and a renewed desperate search of man's relationship to God, to his own destiny, and to his fellow human beings.

Although the immediate impetus for twentieth-century poetic innovations undoubtedly came from modernism, Gustavo Adolfo Bécquer, the nineteenth-century romantic, influenced a number of twentieth-century poets. Dámaso Alonso sees Bécquer's hand in the best of García Lorca and Vicente Aleixandre, who like their precursor dealt in uncertain shapes.

Among early twentieth-century poets Rubén Darío assimilated the delicate rhythms and meters, combining catholic, pagan, decadent, and aristocratic elements in his experimental poetry, ornate and decorative in form but also pondering on life, death, and the eternity which awaits us all. Unamuno, meanwhile, rejected formal beauty for deeper themes in his philosophical, religious, and nature poetry, abstract and intellectual at times, but also human, warm, and anguished. His central theme is the fear of loss of being, a struggle to believe, and the eternalization of the moment. Juan Ramón Jiménez' poetry is one of flashing colors and interior music, a constant striving for an unattainable perfection. Passing through the phase of modernism to that of pure poetry, in his final stages he indulges in a never-ending search for God as a reflection of human love, life, and death. He writes poetry of solitude, anguish, mystery, and the transcendental and is often concerned with ontological structures of consciousness. In his best moments he seeks to become one with God, emotionally and intellectually, creating through Him a world of eternal beauty.

Antonio Machado, perhaps the most influential poet of the twentieth century and one of the half dozen greatest poets Spain has known, lived a life of solitude, although he knew two great loves, that of his wife Leonor and, after her death, years later, that of the mysterious Guiomar. Machado sees poetry as a problem. He disliked the baroque imagery, excessive adornment, and the aristocratic and artificial aspects reflected by some, seeking to express in his own work the essential intuition shared by all humanity. One aspect of Machado's work involves his ethical and social commitment as a historical man. Caught in a historical situation from which he cannot escape, he incorporates that historicity into his own existence, accepting his responsibility as a defender of the dignity of man. Machado clearly reflects what Octavio Paz calls the transformation brought about by poetry in the relationship between man and history from one of slavery and dependence to one of living essence which will never resign itself to die. Poetry cannot exist without history, but it serves to transmute history. Machado channeled his ethical concerns into a personal participation in the civil war.

In his *Campos de Castilla,* the telluric masterpiece of the "Generation of 1898" regarding the regeneration of Spain, and in his other poetry, he speaks directly to the human soul. Silent landscapes, solitude, compassion, existential anguish beyond his personal losses, a constant preoccupation with the inevitability and mystery of death, the deep palpitation of the human spirit, the secret places of man's soul, and a concern with God reflect his continuing considerations of the human condition. His three major themes: time, existence, and a search for God, are essentially fragments of a central existential unity. Machado professes an existential metaphysics in which time achieves an absolute value. He sees the future, past, and present as part of one integrated structure which is at the center of human "being," a philosophy very close to that of Heidegger's "ecstasies." His "being" involves future possibilities and a past which he must incorporate if he is to be in a factual and authentic present. In existing, Machado becomes a part of time itself, and his awareness of the temporal, his own existence and possibilities lead to anguish. He expressed many of these metaphysical speculations, garnered in part from an acquaintance with the thought of Nietzsche, Bergson, and Heidegger, through his poet-philosopher Juan Mairena.

As Machado faces the basic problem of existence, the flow of time, he seeks immortality in a God who will help him to survive. He tries to avoid an oversimplification of existence by ignoring what cannot be explained, but paradoxically recognizing the absurd gulf which separates man from the divine presence, and making love his road to communion with the absolute, he sets off on his quest. But a struggle for life and love inevitably ends in death, and man's natural instincts fight against an exterior reality which prevents him from realizing his full potential. As man faces his destiny on earth, suffering frustration, restlessness, fear, resignation, hope, and impatience as part of human conscience and being, he also must participate in the conflict against the destructive force of death which frustrates his entire existence. Machado, considering the enigmatic character of birth and death, views the latter as the end of the path which all must travel. Yet he also sees it as a challenge confronting man, and he cannot accept death as a final proof of the meaninglessness of life.

Probably the most individualistic of the poets who consolidated modernist innovations, León Felipe Camino y Galicia most clearly elucidated the political, moral, and ethical responsibility of man to his society and man's search for God. During the Spanish Civil War he published poetry of a savage intensity in which he indicted man's inhumanity to man, at the same time emphasizing the social aspects of the Christian message in an existentially anguished framework, in an irrational world without absolute values. Felipe specifically applies the themes of time, myth, God, and death

to man's miserable existence in a disintegrating and loveless world, hoping
through tears and suffering to obtain salvation. But even though man and
his existence are absurd and absolute values do not exist, man must manifest his responsibility to his fellow human beings and in a continuing tension and duality seek for meaning and God.

Shortly after 1920 the generation known as that of 1927 arose. In spite
of the contact of its members with the vanguardist movements, the generation represents a continuity of the existentially oriented poetry of Machado,
the abstract, intellectual, and yet human poetry of Unamuno, the pantheis-
tic and ever-changing quest for beauty of Juan Ramón Jiménez, and the
essentially moral and human poetry of León Felipe. For a time the poets
of this new generation concentrated on associative imagery and special
symbols such as the sea and ignored concrete realities. They resurrected
Góngora as their guide and took part in the great debates about the conflicting theories of pure poetry defended by Brémond and Valéry, but this
dehumanized poetry and rather formal and intellectualized period lasted
but a short time. Jorge Guillén, author of the intellectual, impersonal, and
beautiful *Cántico,* began to stress the need for rebirth, renewal, and harmony in a universe faced with annihilation. He substituted human preoccupations for songs to the joy of living, seeking human understanding
and courage in a world in flux. As he saw man's future narrowed by time's
onslaught, he realized that memory would not serve to delay or turn the
clock back because "Hoy no estás y yo no soy." Pedro Salinas abandoned
a refined intellectual poetry to reaffirm a faith in a world which nevertheless appalled him with its lack of divine guidance. He felt limited by his
exterior reality but realized its tragic, social, and significant aspects as part
of his adventure toward the absolute. Dámaso Alonso, who viewed poetry
as the nexus between two mysteries, also abandoned Góngora for religious
and metaphysical considerations of pain, death, cruelty, and man's individual essence in an unjust world. Emilio Prados, for all his surrealism, musi-
cality, and color, indulged in a suffering search for God. Luis Cernuda,
whatever the classic themes of his *La realidad y el deseo,* worried about
destruction and death, the abyss between man and society, and the struggle
between the soul and the body. Rafael Alberti, another master poet of this
generation, in his masterpiece *Sobre los ángeles,* seeks a lost love, religious
faith, and a way out of the darkness of a painful world of disintegrating

values. Like all the poets of his generation he writes of disorder, disillusion, and despair.

Federico García Lorca creates emotional sequences through recurring illogical imagery. His reality, a double one, seeks to know whether the moon on the water or in the sky is the true one. He transmutes ordinary objects and human beings, extracting their essence through a kind of deformation. In odd visual and sensory combinations he joins a childlike directness with a sophisticated examination of the dark recesses of the human soul. He passionately cries out for life, warmth, and meaning in a world of pain, sterility, and death. Much of his poetry concerns the conflict between cruelty and violence on the one hand and tenderness and love on the other. Primitive values, perhaps the real ones, and nature fight against a false civilization whose rejection in favor of a return to primitivism may solve the cares and hypocrisies endemic to modern life. In spite of the gaiety, enchantment, and magic of much of his poetry, Lorca is essentially a poet of dark strains, sudden silences, and sad solitudes, an integral part of his desire for a personal option in a depersonalized and technological world. His *Poeta en Nueva York* mirrors especially well this nightmarish world where Dionysian and Apollonian forces clash and where innocents, victimized by a cruel civilization, must face a sterile existence and an ever-present death. Lorca can make unconscious states assume a concrete reality in his portrayal of essentially simple people. He can identify with their tragedy and existence as they are persecuted by the forces of repression and evil. Lorca has a social conscience which can be seen in the I-thou relationship he immediately establishes. Yet one can know only his own reality, his own experience, his own existence. Thus Lorca can explain neither his life nor his poetry; he can only live them.

Lorca expresses a variety of attitudes toward religion, both accepting and rejecting traditional symbols. Tormented and searching for God, his principal concern is with the horror of facing nothingness. Passing time is measured by escaping blood and a ticking clock that places his own existence in doubt. At times the poet feels a complete void of self and also despair, one which he projects onto the world where only death makes sense. Yet he also accepts that world as his own, seeking authentic life and one worth living. In *Llanto por la muerte de Ignacio Sánchez Mejías,* perhaps the greatest elegy in modern Spanish literature, he mourns not only the death of his friend but ponders the meaning of death for everyone. The essential Lorca, then, as he plays with illusion and reality, is one haunted by death, who in life sees frustration, solitude, and pain, and searches for love and being through an identification with the primitive, the weak, and the helpless.

The "Generation of 1898" had animated objects; it gave them an existence and personalized old cities, landscapes, rivers, and hills. Vicente Aleixandre builds on this nature to convey a cosmic force, at first not modified by human spirit, but later he humanizes creation to make the flesh become spirit and the spirit flesh. His poetry, as it moves and transmutes, conveys feeling rather than logical sequence, a chaotic conglomeration with a cumulative vertiginous impact. Often hermetic, his poetry seeks trancendent heights, an all-pervading light, an obscure happiness, and a vision of universal life. His search is often voluptuous, sensual, and passionate, as he finds the substance of all things to be one. Carlos Bousoño, who has written perceptively on the poet, clearly shows the turn in Aleixandre from his early elemental vision of the world's reality to a concentration on man's existence in a temporal dimension of ethical implications. Aleixandre, starting with oneiric imagery and the collective unconscious, goes to the concrete, but his change is less a definite dichotomy than a development of his theme of man in a world of cosmic force which can create and destroy. The sea, in all its symbolic values of life and death, is but one of the many equations seeking to juxtapose a lost happiness and the agony of man as being lost in the universe, a despair tempered by the ethical and moral implications of being human. The poet seeks to fuse with the flesh of his beloved and capture the light of unattainable passion, since love is the beginning and end of all things. *Thanatos* means Eros, for only through death and a return to the earth can one destroy bodily limits which fully keep one from love, a final and perfect one.

In his early works man ranked last in the mineral, vegetable, and animal universe, but Aleixandre later realized the confrontation all mankind faces with an inevitable death. *Pasión de la tierra* examines the dark instincts of human existential forces, the total reality of mankind in a meaningless and hopeless world. *Espadas como labios* contrasts a constant longing to be with a fear of not being. *La destrucción o el amor,* an angry and even violent examination of nature, calls to the original forces of life in a world where mystery, darkness, frustration, and unchained telluric forces oppose man. In order to achieve fusion with the cosmos man must surrender his individual existence and his limiting structures to a love which destroys and becomes death itself. *Mundo a solas* portrays a world where man cannot take advantage of life and must lie enveloped in a dark forgetfulness. In the mystic, serene *Sombra del paraíso,* Aleixandre seeks escape from the cruelties of civilization in an innocent world beyond original sin and knowledge. He is as one with the creatures of the dawn and egotistically and narcissistically invents or remembers his own reality. He rejects his loss of innocence in a prehuman world against whose purity man committed original sin. *Nacimiento último* views death as birth because when man dies he finds his destiny.

Alexiandre's second period, beginning with *Historia del corazón,* sees death more stoically. The poet discovers man, his existential, social, historical, and temporal being. He now sings for everyone and not for telluric elemental creatures, longing now not so much for cosmic fusion as for unification with mankind. The poet, a man, becomes all men, destined to live and die. Since life is brief and time deceiving, one must make every moment of existence a meaningful one and live each day fully. Starting with the idea of cosmic fusion with the material universe through love, examining the childhood and fleeting existence of man, Aleixandre achieves a final reconciliation of man and creation in *En un vasto dominio,* as he postulates a universe composed of but one material, a formless creation awaiting fruition in time through the shaping and order of love. Man is a historical and spatial being within a temporal framework, but he is still the material of a shifting cosmos. José Olivio Jiménez views this work as the second volume of a two-part existential history. In *Historia del corazón* the poet sought salvation through a knowledge of man's temporal and historical existence. He finds the answer now in "the vastest of dominions," the temporal existence of man as the expression of a single material into which everything is irrevocably integrated. The poet fuses substance and time and gives us his clearest statement of man's existence and his almost becoming.

A number of fine poets of the "Generation of 1936," like Luis Rosales, Felipe Vivanco, and Dionisio Ridruejo, after their neo-Garcilaso revolt of graceful poetry and counted syllables, suffered the profound humanization which the tragedy of modern life brings. A sharp break can easily be seen between the early vague love poems of Ridruejo and his concern with human flesh and agony after his experiences with the Blue Division on the Russian front. Existential aspirations fill Leopoldo Panero's search for God, and he cannot avoid his horror at the thought of approaching death. Miguel Hernández, who really belongs to no generation, continued the fusion of the popular and cultured and, abandoning dehumanized and artificial forms, agonizes over a tormented love and at the thought of man's inevitable death. A strange mixture of violence, tenderness, and despair, he sees man's inhumanity toward man as an impediment toward the attainment of man's true potential. The poetic group known as "La juventud creadora" reflects the spiritual dejection caused by the Spanish Civil War, and one can see an increasing preoccupation with existential finality. About 1946 a sharp anti-formalistic tone and a return to the humility, fraternity, and human preoccupations of Machado become obvious in the poetry of Eugenio de Nora and Gabriel Celaya, as they insist on human essence and seek salvation in collective despair. In the 1950s and 1960s poets more and more strove for authenticity in human and social reality. José Hierro, in both his hallucinatory and documentary styles, writes of death, solitude, and fleeting being in a senseless world of death. Yet he refuses to agonize or despair completely, because life can be beautiful. José Angel Valente, Angel González, and Claudio Rodríguez record the crisis of the individual, the religious and philosophical problems of man, human solidarity, social and political preoccupations, and the meaning of human liberty. Passing through a Gongoristic and Garcilaso revival, living through the despair of a fratricidal war, seeing a new naturalism, the new poets keep returning to the historical, temporal, existential, and God-oriented perspectives, seeing man as a seeker for salvation, and absorbed by human injustice and human solidarity.

II

It was not until the nineteenth century that Spanish writers began to view American literature as a unique entity. Spanish American romanticism considered political freedom and public service as aspects of literary aspiration. The authors emphasized nature more, also, in seeking to create a new and autochthonous literature. Human dignity was an early concern for a number of authors, such as Esteban Echeverría and José Mármol in Argentina, who fought against the tyranny of Rosas. Cirilo Villaverde, Anselmo Suárez y Romero, and others deplored the evils of slavery. Social concern continued to be reflected in *Enriquillo,* by Manuel Jesús Galván, who viewed the Indian as the symbol of human freedom, and in *Aves sin nido,* by Clorinda Matto de Turner, who saw the Indian as a victim of his society. A number of realists, whatever their picturesque concerns, explored the social conflicts of their society. Naturalism, too, reflected a new interest in the life of the poor and unfortunate, and even the modernists attempted to define the national soul of the country in which they lived, whatever their Hellenic or Renaissance explorations.

With the advent of *criollismo* and its total reflection of telluric and autochthonous elements, authors examined man and his values in a new way. In the jungle, in the haciendas, in rural areas, and in the city, miserable human types suffered and died as part of America's social tragedy. The criollistas drew upon their natural surroundings to present a colorful reality of a changing society, a reality at times cruel but also warm and sensitive in its acceptance of the tragedy of existence. Four classic writers, Mariano Azuela, José Eustasio Rivera, Ricardo Güiraldes, and Rómulo Gallegos, all essentially criollistas, concerned themselves with the tragic destiny of man, at times finding a scapegoat in nature as a terror-inspiring force and at others pessimistically commenting on the social degeneration brought about by humanity's moral imperfections. In *Los de abajo* and other novels, Azuela bitterly outlines the lack of utopian goals achieved by the Mexican Revolution. Believing firmly in the pueblo, he felt keenly what he considered to be the betrayal of its aims and in the process documented the very fabric of revolution and revolutionaries in works which expressed the instinctive and inarticulate fight for human dignity. In his novel *La vorágine* José Eustasio Rivera examines man, overwhelmed by cosmic forces and a victim of an unjust society, whose human desires are frustrated both by human and nonhuman powers. Cova, idealistically moved by the sight of the human condition, cannot bear the terror and grief inherent in that life or survive the sweeping force of nature. Ricardo Güiraldes in *Don Segundo Sombra* details the relationship of man and nature and the need in human affairs for both tradition and new insights to forge a viable future. The combination of fatalism, stoicism, and freedom reflects the national personality of Argentina. Rómulo Gallegos also provides an epic portrayal of man against nature and injustice. Man must fight to survive, kill the evil within his own soul, and find himself and his destiny.

Novels of indictment, of politics, of racial prejudice, and a host of similar themes mark the attempts to change political and social environment by using fiction as an instrument for the transformation of society. The novelists relate the horrible living conditions of unfortunate wretches, seeking to wound the reader spiritually and make him aware of the suffering of the everyday world. As Jean Franco says, ". . . the true originality of Latin American art . . . has kept alive the vision of a more just and humane form of society and continues to emphasize these emotions and relationships, which are wider than the purely personal." The fanatical priest, the political lieutenant, and the rapacious hacendado were but symptoms of an agony sweeping twentieth-century man, but in the 1930s and 1940s economic and political exploration replaced the moral preachments of an earlier age. The Ecuadorian campaign for redemption of the people was matched by Bolivian and, especially, by Peruvian authors like Ciro Alegría and José María Arguedas, who examine the existence and culture of the Indian, his telluric relationships, and his superiority, as a natural product of his environment, to the white man.

In the twentieth century, novelists sought a new view of reality and man, and Spanish America began to reflect the new technical and philosophical aspects of the European novel of Joyce, Kafka, and Proust. Mythology, life as a present existence, alienation in an absurd world, magic realism, the relationship of spiritual and sexual experiences, the destruction of chronological time, and self-sufficient characters show the new mood. Eduardo Mallea and many others combine the theme of existence with a search for justice and liberty, the praxis or project for all mankind. The novelists sought spiritual fulfillment but gradually abandoned hope that they could modify their society. Feeling impotent in a fatuous world of cosmic nothingness, they show us characters caught in inflexible situations without solution, as they desperately search for human value. The question is no longer that of a choice between civilization and barbarism but of a rebellion against rational reality as an infringement on the independence and right to choose of every individual. The amazing new techniques—superimposed new structural levels, multiple personalities and perspectives, the disintegration, at times, of novelistic structure itself, the deformation of reality, the mixtures of fantasy and reality, the confusion of temporality, the poetic vision where fable, fancy, and nightmare fuse—do not disguise the individual hopes and dreams common to all humanity, and the search in which all men are "I." The characters, in their internal agony, are entangled and involved with other characters, but they abandon logical consistency as they suffer an increasing intensity in their impotence and futility.

Salvador Garmendia of Venezuela in *Día de ceniza* shows the inability of man to accept his reality. In Colombia, Eduardo Caballero Calderón creates an absurd world lacking in moral values where man turns his back on Christ. Gabriel García Márquez, the chronicler of Macondo, details a world of dreams, sex, and death. He examines the appearance and reality of everyday life, man's ability to come to grips with the theme of his existence, and the inevitable, universal, and painful solitude in which we all live. His *Cien años de soledad* mirrors the concerns shared by many, among them the Uruguayan Juan Carlos Onetti, whose lonely protagonists live through the remembrance of things past in an alienated and isolated existential world. In novels such as *El astillero* his obsessed characters, seen through strange mirrors, seek truth and fear death in senseless surroundings from which only death can free them. Carlos Martínez Moreno and Mario Benedetti respectively detail the death and decay of society and the metaphysical anguish of man who cannot escape from his closed circumstance. The Guatemalan Miguel Angel Asturias comments on antiquated social structures, human devastation, and man's despair, mixing science and sorcery, allegory and sex, in an attempt to penetrate the mind of the Indian. In Cuba Alejo Carpentier shows man's quest for authentic existence by a return to his starting point and examines the impact of primitive magic and various categories of realities in novels like *Los pasos perdidos* and *El siglo de las luces*. José Lezama Lima writes hermetic works about the role of the sexual encounter in modern existence, and Guillermo Cabrera Infante attacks the Bohemian nightmare of Cuban life and characters living in a nonsensical environment.

The idea of gamesmanship, one of the constants of the new novel, has its precursor in the fiction of Jorge Luis Borges and his labyrinths, paradoxical realities of dreams within dreams, the eternal return, and the intellectual chess game of life. Even greater gamesmanship is used by Julio Cortázar, also from Argentina, who builds and rejects the ontological investigation.

Leopoldo Marechal, in novels such as *El banquete de Severo Arcángelo,* examines the complex allegory of existence. But the existential agonies of Mallea, Sábato, and others continue to reflect the solitude and anguish, the meaning of true existence as distinct from unauthentic living, the replacing of objective reality by a subjective one, and the role of death. It may be argued that Cortázar, whatever his fantasy and grotesque parodies, seeks the fulfillment of self in a mystic labyrinth where existence is a puzzle. His protagonist Oliveira in *Rayuela* wants life in the present and rejects both past and future, but he also destroys the present as a kind of joke where each character invents the reality which pleases him. A number of novelists, Augusto Roa Bastos of Paraguay, Carlos Fuentes of Mexico, and Mario Vargas Llosa of Peru, each in his own way, allegorically, poetically, and symbolically, focus on human longing for a new and meaningful reality in a gray and negative life where even the concepts of tragedy and existence themselves have become a bore in an uncaring, indifferent, and irrational universe.

The twentieth-century Spanish novel is more sharply concerned with the problems of existence. Miguel de Unamuno deals with themes of love, death, envy, and eternity, and in representative novels, *Niebla* and *San Manuel Bueno, Mártir,* he stresses the idea that one finds life as one becomes life. His agonists (he refuses to call them protagonists) face his own central problem of the search for immortality and the need to find faith and belief in eternal life. His characters cannot escape their anguish at their own temporality. Life is inconsistent and illogical, but man struggles against his destiny, lives each moment, craves the completing power of love, and seeks answers to his torment at the thought of termination. Valle-Inclán also talks of the tragic sense of life, which he believes can be conveyed only through a deformed esthetic to match the grotesque and ridiculous aspects of the Western values which he rejects. Pío Baroja seeks to solve the problems of existence through a kind of inconclusive action, for he sees the plague of modern Spain as a lack of willpower. Man is condemned to a sad and irrational reality where only the strong have the right to survive in an indifferent and illogical universe where human beings use nobility to disguise their animal instincts and where moral values are delusive. His heroes seek absolute liberty to form their own morality, for each person is his own radical reality. His characters long for life but cannot circumvent the boundary situations they face. In *Camino de perfección*

Baroja shows the spiritual crisis of the Spaniard; in *Paradox Rey,* the futility of dreams of utopia; in *La busca,* the search for life in an uncaring and hypocritical world where hunger, sickness, and human degradation are accepted as the norm. Gabriel Miró indulges in a number of pagan-Christian combinations and examines the love of each person for his consciousness and feelings about his own existence. Finally, in his generation, Ramón Pérez de Ayala documents the relationship between life and art, the tragic implications of being human, man's difficulty in solving problems of reason and faith, thought and action, and in trying to shape his essence. Pérez de Ayala believes that man must be the master of his destiny, but he is both cruelly and compassionately aware of human folly. He tempers his metaphysical yearnings by his intellectual approach to life, his use of abstractions, and his burlesque of the sexual habits of his people. For most of his life he was opposed to corrupt politics and militarism as practical depressors of liberty, for him, along with dignity, the supreme goal of humanity. He tries to analyze Spain's individual and collective crisis of conscience and through his characters, Belarmino and Apolonio, the conflict between philosophy and action, reason and faith.

After the "Generation of 1898" Ramón Sender best fits José María Gironella's dictum that "lo primero que hace falta para ser novelista es ser un hombre." Sender insists that he is an ordinary man who documents crude realism but cannot fully identify with bourgeois or proletarian aims. Yet he resists definition because of his belief that the one who defines us kills us—"el que nos conoce nos limita, el que nos comprende nos domina." He accepts for himself part of the universal guilt for what happened in Spain, a country which for him no longer exists. He lives on, but he does not know who he is: "I travel along the road of life, but I know not whither, but I am content to be and to travel."

Among the problems of existence he discusses, he devotes a goodly space to the horrors of war and the brutality practiced by human beings against each other. He has a continuing compassion for the underdog, a respect for human dignity, tolerance, and love for fellow human beings. In seeking a primitive type of Christianity he at times, by individualizing himself sufficiently, seeks to dilute himself so that incoherence and violence may make him more tolerant of self. He contends that until all men in ages to come can awaken to the potentiality of their true being, to the meaning of duty, God, and neighbor, some will always have to sacrifice themselves to light the way for new generations. Sender identifies himself with collective needs. He is not so much concerned about the immortality of the individual as about the immortality of mankind, for human personality, more apparent than real in this temporal world, will die, but human nature will survive.

Sender ponders man's fate and existence, believing that we escape from one situation to fall into another. We are at the mercy of coincidence, but we must love and be loved as part of humanity. We may hope for regeneration and faith in the face of existential despair as we travel life's unknown path, a road which leads through injustice to death. Although Sender's protagonists are aware of death, they prepare for it by making their existence in this life meaningful, for death serves as a challenge to make the most use of the temporal flow given to each person. In novels like *Imán,* Sender shows us the disillusion, death, and cruelty of war. *Mr. Witt en el Cantón*'s despairing protagonist indulges in retrospective uneasiness at the approach of old age. In *El lugar del hombre* Sender examines man's experiences, hopes, dreams, the problem of good and evil, and the need to find meaning and dignity in life. Here the individual is extremely important, his dignity untransferable and the empathic responsibility of all humanity. In *El epitalamio del prieto Trinidad* Sender offers us a metaphysical view of the human condition where man must choose between ethical self and freedom. When man's spiritual nature is liberated, he will be free truly to love. *La esfera* shows us a search for absolute justice and offers us a microcosm of human life. *El verdugo afable* concludes that only two kinds of human beings, hangmen and victims, exist. Few men can face the truth of their complicity, and only hangmen have taken upon themselves the responsibility for the social order and the incurably evil nature of man. In *Los cinco libros de Ariadna* Sender postulates the creation of man's essence through freedom, assertion of will, and action, and the need to live dangerously at times in the expression of that will. Man moves in an irrational world without guidance, but he is responsible for what he will make of his life and the values he chooses to create. Whoever has no God has no self, and he who has no self is in despair, yet God can only get man to understand himself, and to the degree that we do so, we are authentic. Sender's man may be saved through his love for humanity or for a God who offers us light and silence so that with them we may "poblar la nada y redimirle a él en cierto modo del horrendo caos de los orígenes." *Requiem por un campesino español* explores the true meaning of conscience and what the Spanish Civil War did to a generation of men and their beliefs. Finally, *Crónica del alba,* which he wrote over and over during a period of more than a quarter of a century, explores the nature of reality and the human personality and reveals the moral awakening of the protagonist, his realization of the impossibility of pure love, and the meaning of identification with the needs of other humans. In the ninth and last part of man's journey, *La vida comienza ahora,* he expresses his longing for the ideal destroyed by the ugly reality of the civil war.

After Sender, the next important name is that of Camilo José Cela, who assaults the reader with the smells, sounds, sorrows, and colors of Spain. He rejects absolute values of any kind and shows us men who lead lives of desperation, caught by the forces of destiny. The ontological being of man's existence concerns him, but he offers us violence and cruelty as a kind of esthetic equation of existence. In *La familia de Pascual Duarte,* a man, driven by forces he cannot understand, performs acts beyond good and evil. Cela chooses primitive elemental violence as weapons in a false world, one of many in man's anguished attempt to escape from his desperate spiritual crisis. His protagonist's progressive frustration, unable to know and to find God, bears out Cela's conclusion that the normal relationship among men is one of conflict, violence, and hate.

Most of the other novels of contemporary Spain comment on man's problems of communication, the futility and emptiness of life, people hemmed in by situations with which they cannot cope, and study an age where faith in absolute values has been replaced by a search for authenticity in the face of nothingness. Carmen Laforet shows us the anxieties of our times, the disillusion of frustrated and unhappy individuals, the lack of fulfillment, and the inevitable death awaiting us all. Ana María Matute and Miguel Delibes reflect the unhappiness and difficulties of tormented children and young adults. The angriest of the angry young novelists, Juan Goytisolo, is preoccupied with the false values of Spanish civilization. He is still haunted by civil war memories and, remembering the crimes, contrasts sordid reality with the fairy-tale world of fable. His adolescents lack the positive goals needed to satisfy their anxieties. Sick members of a sick society, they reveal their maladjustments through their emotionalized attitudes and social values. They perceive vaguely the barriers placed on them, but they are paralyzed by guilt feelings and by their own inadequacies and past failures. They have neither the wish nor the will to cure their alienation, but, impelled by unknown forces which limit the implementation of their desires and possibilities for self realization, they are unauthentic members of a society where human values have been brutalized and desecrated and where true communication is impossible.

Goytosolo's adolescents in *Juegos de manos* attempt to justify their existence, but, uncertain, anxious, and disoriented, they inevitably fail. *Duelo en el Paraíso* tells of the tragic destruction of youthful innocence, the last refuge in a world of beasts. *El circo* shows us men as grotesque actors in an empty environment where security can be had only at the price of conformity to a schizoid dream world. *Fiestas* concerns the isolation of solitary people and the social injustices practiced against them by "religious" men. *La resaca* and *La isla* show us that man has lost his spiritual and political illusions. In most of these novels death, a principal protagonist, is used as a means for evading reality, as a reflection of Spain's spiritual death or as a search for personal freedom. Goytisolo's latest novel, *Señas de identidad,* strives to find a lost identity and illusion, impossible in the Franco dictatorship, which has destroyed both lives and human dignity. The hero, Alvaro Mendiola, searches in his reveries for himself to complement Spain's pursuit of its own soul—a country and a man lost in limbo, suffering in a world where essential human qualities have disappeared, where man is insufficient and hopeless. The hero, thus, suffers unforgettable memories that lack a viable purpose.

III

Spanish drama in the twentieth century was dominated by Jacinto Benavente in the first quarter of the century, by Alejandro Casona and García Lorca in the thirties and forties, and by Antonio Buero Vallejo and Alfonso Sastre from the fifties to the present. Contributing a link with the current theater of the absurd and a special concept of reality, Ramón del Valle-Inclán provided the *esperpento*, a grotesque twisting of reality to find its true shape in relationship to man and his world. Jacinto Benavente was a primary renovating force in his early elegant works where he pitilessly attacked a succession of types who emphasized the hollow and hypocritical criteria of Spanish society. In satirizing the middle and upper classes, he gave us a pessimistic and skeptical view of human nature. Yet in these ironic and elegant comedies of manners and in later works he also showed a continuing compasion for and understanding of human society and the effects of absurd conventions on defenseless human beings. Benavente believes that in every human being there burns a spark of divine spirit, but he also claims that the motives we so piously profess serve largely to hide the essential nature of our own vanity and false values. Very little happens in Benavente's dramas, and he is not endowed with great perceptivity or power of observation, but he copies human life with realistic fidelity. In some of his plays, like *El dragón de fuego,* materialism and idealism vie for control; in others, like *La princesa Bebé,* the individual is faced with the choice of escaping society or conforming to it; in still others man wants to live his life through the determination of his own will and energy. In his masterpiece, *Los intereses creados,* Benavente uses grotesque masks to show the hidden threads of existence, the passions, ambitions, vanity, and concerns which move man to triumph over his own soul through the glorification of love. Benavente confronts the idealist with the cynic. Idealists like Leandro come to accept truth, goodness, and beauty as ultimate goals, but his morality springs from love. Crispin's strength lies in believing to be true only that which meets his needs, and his truths change with changing conditions. Benavente seems to be saying that morality is relative, that man has both good and evil potentialities, that goodness is difficult to maintain but opportunism need not always triumph. We cannot avoid moral contradictions and conflict in individual decisions where love is a deciding force.

Miguel de Unamuno wrote skeleton-like dramas about the essence of human beings, unsatisfied maternal instincts, and the problem of reality and personality. In *El otro, La esfinge,* and other dramas he documents the Cain and Abel theme and portrays the same agonists and frustrated searchers for existence and eternity we find in his other works. Valle-Inclán shares Unamuno's concern for personality. Viewing existence as an absurdity, he presents us with his personal vision of the miserable life of Spaniards and the irrational existence of all mankind. His esperpentos are the aesthetic but grotesque filters of a vulgar reality, a composite picture of Spanish circumstance whose reality and fictional distortions are reversible because fundamentally they both have a grotesque identity.

Jacinto Grau's dramas, whatever their symbolic or allegorical framework, concern human passions and emotions, the power of love and the power of death. His protagonists exhibit a faith in human ability to save man from his own errors through affirmation and love, an insatiable appetite to know God and to seek resurrection and affirmation of their own being. In this existence the inability to communicate, to know God, to love humanity, and to have immortality leads to guilt and anguish, but one must try to use will to determine the future and strive constantly for an I-thou relationship. Man is responsible for his own actions. At times, like the don Juan of *El burlador que no se burla,* he is a God who chooses for himself and for the moment, without belief in morality, in human values, or in transcendental concerns. He acts beyond good and evil. At others, like Pigmalión of *El señor de Pigmalión,* man must accept responsibility because as an individual he decides for the entire race he has created, and he has qualms about his total involvement. Many times Grau awards a second chance, but like Sartre he accepts man's facticity, his finiteness, his mortality, and his limited choices. But, within the limits of his human condition, Grau's creations can make choices and modify, by new actions and through a new awareness, the effect of a former act.

García Lorca's dramas are replete with themes of life and death, man's desires and the forebodings of the human heart. His characters are daily companions to death. Yerma cannot give life but returns to her husband the death which he, in a sense, had given to her. In his other plays he deals with lost hope, lost youth, and the brooding passions of a tragic humanity which cannot face the absurd, empty, and death-filled society in which it lives. Lorca's characters cannot communicate in a world where communication is not favored and where love cannot penetrate the closed minds of a closed society.

Alejandro Casona tried to bring beauty into life, and compassionately he constantly affirmed the meaning of living and love. His characters often weave a fantastic world as a defense against the real world of truth which we must all face, including that profoundest of truths, expressed in *La dama del alba,* that death herself is a tragic victim of her own destiny, one which nobody can escape. In other dramas, such as *Siete gritos en el mar,* the dramatist examines the meaning of reality, of sensuality, of avarice, and of human indifference. His conclusions, as in *El caballero de las espuelas de oro,* seem to be that we need a balance between faith and reality. Casona deals with spiritual crises. Rejecting the materialism and rationalism of the nineteenth century, he sees man as having a positive dignity in a depersonalized world. His protagonists face spiritual and moral responsibilities and, whatever their guilt or anxiety, make their own positive decisions. The basic choices confronting the individual may or may not be associated with political implications, but they often involve all mankind and enjoin escape into an unreal world because of humanity's metaphysical interdependence. Man, then, cannot hide from his own reality, his own responsibility, or his need for others.

Casona adopts a moral tone and a Christian ethic in viewing his spiritual crises. His characters face life bravely and optimistically in spite of exposure to disillusion, disappointment, and death. They seek spiritual salvation in a sordid everyday world where they consistently affirm the power of love and understanding. Charles Leighton concedes that Casona is nonetheless somewhat existentialist in his concern with concrete metaphysical and moral problems. Casona defends the individual overwhelmed by a society which drives him toward self-destruction, and he needs certain principles to be able to make a positive choice in favor of life in any given situation.

Antonio Buero Vallejo, a peripheral member of the "Generation of 1936," suffered the scars of the Spanish Civil War, but, noting the despair and disillusion in his country, he believes in positive human action and responsibility to help create a better world. His heroes are quite often unhappy at their own limitations and blind to the truth of their own existence, but the tragic sense of his plays is always attenuated or sharpened by some hope for the future such as an ultimate alleviation of human misery or a life after death. As he examines the human condition, his strong moral and ethical sense shines through. He tries to elevate the sordid through illusion and hope, refocusing the conflict as one between illusion and reality, certainly aspects of the human condition of our time. In overcoming the barriers imposed on them by life, by the unknown, or by society, and often through suffering, his characters achieve insight into the meaning of their existence. *Hoy es fiesta,* by no means his best play, is typical in its reflection of the lack of communication between people, the guilt and suffering which can be man's fate, the despair and desolation in which contemporary man lives; but it also shows man's dreams, his hopes, his honest compassion, his understanding, and the triumph of love. As Buero's protagonists seek truth, they must overcome their own incomprehension of self, their isolation, their inability to communicate, and they must try to develop their best qualities as human beings. His picture of human existence has both its misery and its grandeur, its anguish and its hope. Whatever the uncertainties of life Buero portrays, there can be little doubt about his affirmation of faith against doubt and hope against cynicism as part of the human comedy.

Alfonso Sastre opposes to Buero's open tragedy of another chance, comprehension of the problems of our age, and faith and hope for the future, a closed situation of anguish. In Sastre's theater man is an anguished being living in a closed situation, seeking a happiness which is denied to him. His unhappy creatures reflect on their destiny and on the unknown sin for which they are being punished. Among his plays are those involving David Harko, the puritanical Communist forced to denounce his own mother and to face the realization that utopia does not exist (*El pan de todos*); a strike for the improvement of working conditions and its circumvention by the owners (*Tierra roja*); a woman driven by forces she cannot control to an untimely end (*Ana Kleiber*). There are no happy endings, and his protagonists are always disillusioned or frustrated.

Sastre, distressed by what he considers Buero's conformity, feels that only socially oriented theater is meaningful. Historically, a dialectical position is difficult to distinguish from accommodation. Not too long before 1960 the very attempt to give to the Spanish stage a true tragic dimension, whatever the theme, was in itself a kind of *"oposición dialéctica"* which many confused with accommodation. Given the dialectic contradiction of an artist with his society and the obfuscation involved in any kind of acting in certain circumstances, it is easy to make a mistake and write a theater of accommodation while sincerely believing that one is developing subtle dialectic differences. He faults Buero for fearing to present tragedy as immutable and without remedy. Sastre continued to view tragic incidents as involving destruction, pain, and agony. He praised the unhappy ending and the closed situation, and he also persevered in his attack on Buero's theater as a kind of accommodation and self-censorship. Buero acknowledges the need to be *engagé*, but he states that his choices are to write plays and postpone their production for a happier day or write plays in a masked manner in the hope of being understood. Buero thinks he has adopted moral positions and fought the good fight in the current Spanish tragedy, and undoubtedly both he and Sastre strive always to ameliorate the Spanish tragedy which they and ordinary Spaniards are forced to live.

IV

We have already seen that the "Generation of 1898" tried to solve the problems of man in the modern world. Among the essayists Angel Ganivet believed that his country should reject science, invention, and European culture, which had no real significance for Spain, and seek Spain's future in its spiritual qualities and true essence, promoting them through willpower and the reaffirmation of the essential Christian message. One must be a man before he can be anything else, act in life and not contemplate it. Ganivet constantly examines the moral implications of being a man but always asserts his faith in the individual. Unamuno seems always to be following the admonition in Hebrews 2:14-15 as he looks on existential man held in bonds by the thought of death (his devil) from which Christ or God may free him through his victory. In his hunger to exist, Unamuno creates God, rejecting empirical thinking to take the somersault of faith from denial to affirmation of the existence of immortality. Unamuno is not satisfied to find eternal life through remembrance, his children, or his writings, for only a belief in the possibility of a personal survival gives meaning to this life.

Beyond his personal religious experiences and his agony at being unable to solve the incompatability of reason and faith, Unamuno accepts the historical as valuable. He wants to know not only his destiny but his origin and what he is in the present. Unamuno coined a concept of intrahistory which accepts the world of present exterior reality but only as a temporal fragment of an eternal inner day-by-day history of the soul, an eternalization of a series of presents already gone by. In his works he treats the meaning of language, tradition, social thought, will, and rejuvenation, and interprets Spanish culture, the essence of its soul, and its eternal traditions. But the essential Unamuno is the man of flesh and bone who wrote *Del sentimiento trágico de la vida.* A man who does not know where he is going but does not want to die, he sees the conflict between faith and knowledge, eternity and time, the spiritual and the secular. Since he cannot solve the problem of existence and immortality rationally, he must turn to faith as a sustaining force in his tragedy, anguish, and struggle. Through will, faith, and action he may resolve the contradictions inherent in the problem and come to terms with the inevitable extinction and nothingness he faces. But man can never be certain of his fate in the universe, and if that is all there is to life, to live for a moment and disappear into the void of nothingness, then life is without value. Still one should live it in such a way that to disappear into nothingness will constitute an injustice.

José Martínez Ruiz (Azorín) sought the essence of Spain through his feeling for the countryside, but he fused its sadness and melancholy onto the existence of the eternal Spaniards. Time was the great destroyer and individuals had to die, but Azorín believed that to live is to see return and also that if time could be slowed down, fleeting existence might be prolonged. Although he played with time and space, the meaning of reality and the meaning of death, he suffered silently and sadly beneath his calm exterior. A sensitive of history, he saw life as a contradictory series of fragments, a distillation of what had been, and his disillusioned participants in the conflict between sentiment and reason, culture and life, reflect a petrification of the past into the present. Yet, as he revitalized the past, he achieved a kind of life through his ideas of eternal recurrence and cosmic time. He feared the passing of time and the approaching end, but he continued positively to face existence, not so much through grand passions but through the humble details of everyday life.

José Ortega y Gasset claimed that in *Meditaciones del Quijote* he anticipated Heidegger in almost all his principal points: "Apenas hay uno o dos conceptos importantes de Heidegger que no pre-existían, a veces con anterioridad de trece años, en mis libros." Man cannot avoid the present or past, but the essence of human life is to determine the future. Man does not have a nature but he has a history, and the past, a form of having been, is what we are because it is our own past, and man has only that nature and existence and being which he has performed. He is in essence the sum total of his acts and a "project" towards the future. Although Ortega's concept of living is the same as that of Heidegger, anguish and nausea are not a part of his existential philosophy. In his other works Ortega also anticipated essentially all the ideas later to be used by Sartre in his *L'Etre et le Néant*. Rejecting Cartesian philosophy, Ortega holds that man is himself and his circumstances. *El tema de nuestro tiempo* sharpens the focus of his *razón vital* as a form of life and human reality which makes itself. In *La rebelión de las masas* Ortega stresses the moral need of man to invent and adopt a vital project, to submit himself to its exigencies and to become engagé. In *En torno a Galileo* and especially in *Historia como sistema* he views existence as a series of possibilities among which man must choose, and his liberty is the liberty to choose: "Soy por fuerza libre lo quiera o no."

Ortega's ratio-vitalism sees the center of rationalism as life, a problem from which all others stem, for reality is the struggle between reason and life, and an infinite number of realities may exist, dependent on the individual point of view. For Ortega, man's essence lies in his existence, as distinguished from that of objects which have a different set of largely rigid possibilities. In a stone, essence precedes existence and determines its nature in a fixed manner. In man, reason is only a part of existence, for concrete life is always evolving and living comes before theorizing. At each moment man must choose what he will be at the next one. He acquires "being" at the cost of becoming exterior to himself, by not identifying with nature or intelligence, but rather by finishing his unfinished personality. Existence involves a continuous interplay between the individual and his circumstances (things and other men who surround us but only as we become aware of them). We live in an uncertain and hostile universe against which we must struggle, and we work with things to realize our program of existence. Yet man's task is conditioned by his ideas and beliefs, for he must arrive at a system of convictions which will enable him to act in and on his circumstances. In the final analysis Ortega in his theory of life and *razón vital* is completely existential and anti-phenomenological, but he also clings to the belief of his admired Goethe that only among all men can one live as a human.

Pedro Laín Entralgo, among others, continued to discourse on hope, despair, and existentialism in his *La espera y la esperanza*. But the existence of Spain in the twentieth century involved a unique event, the Spanish Civil War, although all countries were inevitably involved in its results. Through an examination of the journals of the war years, one can come to understand the special shade of meaning given to the word "existence" in Spain, to human values, and to the concept of sacrifice and salvation. Many of the intellectuals sought through a kind of social realism the rejuvenation of society, hoping that the present civil struggle might presage a future spiritual unity of Spain's dual vision of life. These journals give us insight into the thoughts, hopes, and daily despairs of the war years which in one way or another have continued to determine almost all contemporary Spanish literature and existence. As one reads some of the criticism and philosophy of these journals some three decades later, they at times appear didactic in attempting to determine a work's validity through demonstrating its truth or degree of compliance with reality. Most of the writers tried to convey insights, whether reasoned or intuitive, into the effects and the emotional nature of a war experience. Most of the entries are not sharply definitive or perceptive in their stressing of circumstantial, external, and symbolic values as a logical unity, and they claim that the Republican intellectual is the voice of the people. Concern and conviction, passion and nostalgia, and a conflict between reasoned and instinctive judgments provide constant emphatic satisfaction. For the most part the writers avoid an irrational accretion in support of an identity of interest, and we can see the conscience and the intellectual resources of men, neither despondent nor indifferent, who helped determine the entire course of contemporary Spanish literature. We also receive a reminder of a continuing commitment and the fruitlessness of trying to forget what cannot be forgotten.

Juan Goytisolo, born in 1931 and representative of his generation, laments the disappearance of the Spaniards' positive virtues with the arrival of a new industrial religion. Even the pueblo, in the present, must accept responsibility for its government. Present-day Spaniards have created a caricature of reality, ambiguous and without character. The myths of a preindustrial nation offer only romantic escapism to the modern nonconformist intellectual without freedom of action. Men of his generation prepared themselves for events which did not occur, and they are now growing old without having known either youth or responsibility. Writers and intellectuals, says Goytisolo, unaware of the organic transformation of Spanish society, tilt at windmills in a universe populated by ghosts. In Spain the mercantilization of human relations, an inferiority complex, idle imitation, self-satisfaction, and exploitation of so-called ancient virtues, have created a country which, if it is not yet Europe, in any event is no longer Spain. Before Spain can recreate itself it must be willing to face its reality, uncover the cowardice, hypocrisy, and egotism beneath its masks of pride and nobility, and reinforce the cause of human aspiration in its populace which has deteriorated into the "shadow of a people." In a Spain where a struggle for a more valid existence seems futile, the writer involved in a fight for man's transformation must strive for the fusion of personal experience, emotions, and ideas to achieve a necessary tension which, as Juan Goytisolo said, "will illuminate a new reality, not just a dead copy or simple prolongation of the emotions or ideas but an evident . . . truth for the one who communicates it and for the one who receives it."

2 | Poetry

The Sea and Machado

WATER IMAGERY and symbolism have always played a large part in the world's literature. The ancient belief that the earth arose from a chaos of which water constituted the principal element was reinforced by the description of creation in the Book of Genesis. The Greeks stressed the existence of water gods, nymphs, and nereids, and saw in fresh and salt water varying symbolic virtues such as youth, immortality, and fertility. Horace and other poets used the sea to inspire the entire gamut of human emotions and to symbolize every aspect of human existence from life to death.

Spain has produced poets inspired by the sea from the Galician-Portuguese School to the contemporary period. In the twentieth century Unamuno, Juan Ramón Jiménez, León Felipe, Jorge Guillén, Gerardo Diego, García Lorca, Pedro Salinas, Vicente Aleixandre, and Rafael Alberti have stressed water and sea imagery. León Felipe uses the sea to sum up human suffering, ambition, life, and death. His sea is "amargo e infinito" and represents not only the poet, but all mankind, as he wishes to go "solo otra vez como principio! el llanto . . . el mar." [1] Juan Ramón Jiménez faces an immense sea which he can never fathom but which makes him aware of his creator. He also creates a sea in his thematic improvisations to convey different moods and emotions such as love. Vicente Aleixandre's works abound in sea imagery.[2] To him the sea represents the love of virgin sirens, childhood innocence, a receptacle of truth where simple creatures obtain a fusion with the world impossible for man, and his well-known love-death equation.[3] Pedro Salinas equates the sea with love, happiness, and interdependence. "Ahora te quiero/como el mar quiere a su agua," [4] for perfect love lies in complete union such as a mixture of water with water. The sea is in harmony with the rest of nature (pp. 311–313) and fits within its limits as naturally as the soul fits the body (p. 299). In it resides idealism and hope and perhaps the only order possible in a chaotic world. Its unfathomable mystery symbolizes his faith: ". . . oh Contemplado eterno! / . . . Y de tanto mirarte, nos salvemos" (p. 329). Rafael Alberti, as Concha Zardoya points out, uses the sea as "tema unitario y elemento que relaciona libros de concepción diversa." [5] In *Marinero en tierra* he begins with "la nostalgia del mar," [6] views the sea as his entrance into a world of childhood and in later works as the vehicle for a return in spirit to that same childhood. The sea may be good or bad, Spain, freedom, love, life, or death, but it is basic to an understanding of his poetry. As he himself said in *Baladas y canciones del Paraná,* "Ocho sílabas son muchas para cantar./Me basta una que tenga por dentro la mar." [7] Azorín, perhaps, summed up best of all what the land and sea mean to twentieth-century Spaniards. "El paisaje somos nosotros; el paisaje es nuestro espíritu, sus melancolías, sus placideces, sus anhelos, sus tártagos." [8]

Antonio Machado also concentrated on sea imagery in his poetry. As Alice McVan states: "The sea as his wonderful and all-encompassing symbol, charged with multitudes of meanings . . . came to signify God, hope, life, death, and all things intangible." [9] Yet, surprisingly enough, although McVan, Ramón de Zubiría, Laín Entralgo, and others mention the importance of the sea in Machado, no study of his use of the sea has appeared. Almost every other aspect of his work has been thoroughly examined: Richard Predmore,[10] Ricardo Gullón,[11] and Juan López-Morillas[12] have studied time in his poetry; Bartolomé Mostaza,[13] Predmore,[14] and others, the *paisaje* in his works; Dámaso Alonso,[15] Julián Marías,[16] Luis Rosales,[17] José Maria Pemán,[18] and Ramón de Zubiría,[19] the *fuente;* Ramón Ruiz,[20] the *camino;* and Alejandro Ramírez,[21] the *tierra.*

Machado, in a poem dedicated to Julio Castro, voiced his early admiration for the sea, "que yo también de niño, ser quería/pastor de olas, capitán de estrellas." [22] This early esteem came to be a poetic preoccupation, as the sea eventually came to represent his destination, an objective, and symbolic end. Laín Entralgo points out: "No es infrecuente que la muerte reciba en sus versos el nombre de 'mar.' " [23] Pradal-

Rodríguez states that the sea "representa en Machado a la vez la soledad y la muerte." [24] Like Unamuno, whom he ardently admired, Machado expresses dread at the loss of identity and the fear of nothingness, becoming as it were a drop of water in the vast sea, an idea which he repeats in many of his poems.

> *¿Qué es esta gota en el viento*
> *que grita al mar, soy el mar?* (p. 664)

> *. . . que ha de caer como rama que sobre las aguas flota,*
> *antes de perderse, gota*
> *de mar, en la mar inmensa.* (p. 667)

> *Morir . . . ¿Caer como gota*
> *de mar en el mar inmenso?* (p. 830)

Man is a drop in the ocean, the immensity from which he came and to which he must return. The sea gave him life and claims him again as part of its substance in death, or as he says:

> *Cantad conmigo en coro: Saber, nada sabemos,*
> *de arcano mar vinimos, a ignota mar iremos . . .* (p. 822)

This idea occurs from his earliest poetry:

> *Apenas desamarrada*
> *la pobre barca, viajero, del árbol de la ribera,*
> *se canta no somos nada.*
> *Donde acaba el pobre río la inmnesa mar nos espera.* (pp. 663–664)

Alice McVan explains that "every man must blaze his own trail, and, in the end, must accept the fact that the pathway was opened upon the sea." [25] Machado, through Juan de Mairena, claims that death is our constant companion; "ella es, por de pronto, cosa de nuestro cuerpo. Y no está mal que la imaginemos como nuestra propia 'notomía' o esqueleto que llevamos dentro, siempre que comprendamos el valor simbólico de esta representación" (p. 1073). This double image or life-death relationship occurs throughout. Is it better, Machado asks, to have

the conscience of a visionary who sees live fish in the deep aquarium
which cannot be caught or to have the cursed task

> *de ir arrojando a la arena*
> *muertos, los peces del mar?*   (p. 828)

Man can adopt a positive or negative attitude toward life and death, for
the meaning of both is summed up by the sea. One man thinks of life
as an illusion of the sea which must one day end, whereas the dreamer
thinks perhaps the final boundary of the sea may be overcome:

> *El otro mira al agua. . . .*
> *Y piensa: "Es esta vida una ilusión marina*
> *de un pescador que un día ya no puede pescar."*
> *El soñador ha visto que el mar se le ilumina,*
> *y sueña que es la muerte una ilusión del mar.*   (pp. 834–835)

Again and again in contemplating life and at times love, he finds death:

> *Como yo, cerca del mar,*
> *río de barro salobre,*
> *¿sueñas con tu manantial?*   (p. 903)

One must resign oneself for life represents but a fleeting moment before the final existential boundary which is death:

> *Caminante, no hay camino,*
> *sino estelas en la mar.*   (p. 826)

and again:

> *Todo pasa y todo queda;*
> *pero lo nuestro es pasar,*
> *pasar haciendo caminos,*
> *caminos sobre la mar.*   (p. 830)

Laín Entralgo sees the continuing image of the sea as "imagen de la
muerte y del término indefinible." [26] Machado wonders at the meaning
of life and goodness when confronted with inevitable death:

Mucho importa
que en la vida mala y corta
que llevamos
libres o siervos seamos;
mas, si vamos
a la mar,
lo mismo nos han de dar.   (p. 805)

The sea serves, too, as the vehicle of death. He learns of the death of
Rubén Darío, "ruiseñor de los mares," as the news "nos vino atravesando
el mar" (pp. 851–852). The sea or death may be something to fear,
but the sea may soothe man, too, or at least give him peace. Jorge
Manrique fascinated Machado (pp. 959–961, 1073, 1076, 1103), and
the latter glosses the former's famous poem:

Nuestras vidas son los ríos
que van a dar a la mar,
que es el morir ¡Gran cantar!
Entre los poetas míos
tiene Manrique un altar.
Dulce goce de vivir:
mala ciencia del pasar,
ciego huir a la mar.
Tras el pavor del morir
está el placer de llegar.   (p. 703)

And Machado in his *Retrato,* in spite of all existential fears at the
final boundary, feels he will be ready to arrive:

Y cuando llegue el día del último viaje
y esté al partir la nave que nunca ha de tornar,
me encontraréis a bordo ligero de equipaje,
casi desnudo, como los hijos de la mar.   (p. 734)

But if the sea is death, is there nothing beyond? Machado's religious
preoccupations are as bound up in the sea as are his existential ones,
and at times they appear to be one and the same. According to McVan,
"The sea and God are Antonio Machado's ultimate symbols and the two
are not only interchangeable, they are opposites and they are one." [27]

Machado constantly preoccupied himself with the thought of God's existence (pp. 1040 ff.), God's justice (p. 1077), and the possibility of faith in Him (p. 1109). The question of God the creator, according to Juan de Mairena, gives "anchura de velas, si hemos de navegar en los altos mares del pensamiento" (p. 1180). In Machado there appears almost always a play on the meaning of the word God: "Un Dios existente —decía mi maestro— sería algo terrible. ¡Que Dios nos libre de él! " (p. 996). God, then, may take many shapes. He may be the path of salvation from life to death. He may be "Dios sobre la mar camino" (p. 740). He may represent vengeance, or he may represent love, "con doble faz de amor y de venganza" (p. 740), something which Machado found difficult to accept: "Amar a Dios sobre todas las cosas . . . es algo más difícil de lo que parece" (p. 999). Leonor, nevertheless, had brought him close to the loving God, and his heartrending cry at her loss inspired the poem which José Luis L. Aranguren calls "quizá el más religioso de todo Antonio Machado." [28]

> Señor, ya me arrancaste lo que yo más quería.
> Oye otra vez, Dios mío, mi corazón clamar.
> Tu voluntad se hizo, Señor, contra la mía.
> Señor, ya estamos solos mi corazón y el mar.   (p. 794)

Luis Felipe Vivanco claims that these verses form but the first strophe. "Y el resto de las estrofas se queda sin decir—expresado, tal vez, y no dicho—dentro de la palabra mar." [29] One might go further and affirm that the sea sums up his complete feeling about God. The sea is the substance from which all else, even God, is born. God is the sea, for it is the universal and unfathomable element which contains all meaning. Thus God may lie hidden in the depths of the sea, never revealing himself except as reflected light, like the moon on the water.

> Dios no es el mar, está en el mar; riela
> como luna en el agua, o aparece
> como una blanca vela;
> en el mar se despierta o se adormece.   (p. 835)

Yet at the same time:

> *Creó la mar, y nace*
> *de la mar cual la nube y la tormenta;*
> *es el Creador y la criatura lo hace;*
> *su aliento es alma, y por el alma alienta.*
> *Yo he de hacerte, mi Dios, cual Tú me hiciste,*
> *y para darte el alma que me diste*
> *en mí te he de crear.* (p. 836)

Thus man through the sea's essence created God in his mind, sensing the outward manifestations of His existence as one may realize the greatness of the ocean depths by observing the surface. God and the sea are one and the same, born of each other. The sea is created by God, but it also creates the Creator. Existentially, much as in Unamuno's *Del sentimiento trágico de la vida,* man may create his God, "el Dios que todos hacemos" (p. 836). Yet one continues always the anguished search for that same God, "El Dios que todos buscamos/y que nunca encontraremos" (p. 836). This God whom Machado seeks is not a symbolic wooden statue of Jesus but the one "que anduvo en el mar" (p. 808). Man must fight the existential battle with life, with death, with God, as he struggles with the faint promise of a salvation he does not comprehend. Often God may appear in a dream (pp. 824, 827, 831), but "En sueños lucha con Dios;/y despierto, con el mar" (p. 826) and "soñó caminos en los mares/y dijo: 'Es Dios sobre la mar camino'" (p. 740). Nevertheless, if God appears in dreams, may not Machado in turn be but a product of a dream of God? Is he to die and become one with God, the immense sea, or, deprived of God's knowledge, will he be:

> *uno, sin sombra y sin sueño,*
> *un solitario que avanza*
> *sin camino y sin espejo?* (pp. 830–831)

The conclusion would seem to be that "Todo el que camino anda,/como Jesús, sobre el mar" (p. 820), that, as he writes Grandmontagne, God and the sea, interwoven, offer salvation, ". . . Que Dios os dé su mano,/que el mar y el cielo os sean propicios, capitán" (p. 915), and that through religion many may escape a kind of death which perhaps Machado himself will not escape. He writes to Julio Castro:

> Dios a tu copla y a tu barco guarde
> seguro el ritmo, firmes las cuadernas,
> y que del mar y del olvido triunfen,
> poeta y capitán, nave y poema.   (p. 917)

The ship metaphor to symbolize a safe passage through a dangerous sea occurs in numerous poems dealing with the sea. The latter represented peril
and adventure, much as the garden, which Machado also employs symbolically, often represented a feeling of normality and safety.

Religion and existence are inseparable, and Machado constantly seeks
life's meaning and his own identity, for life may be simply

> . . . una ilusión marina
> de un pescador que un día ya no puede pescar.   (p. 835)

To understand life one must seek to know the meaning of death and its
significance. Using his drop symbolism once more, he asks:

> ¿Qué es esta gota en el viento
> que grita al mar: soy el mar?   (p. 664)

His struggles with God, his search for immortality, and man's endeavor on
earth may be fruitless, for his attempts to make roads on the sea are immediately erased.

> Todo pasa y todo queda;
> pero lo nuestro es pasar,
> pasar haciendo caminos,
> caminos sobre la mar.   (p. 830)

Nevertheless, the sea symbolizes life or existence in a variety of aspects.
Man must continue to create his own world and his own directions, and by
his mere passage through life create or make his own life. In this changing
world there is no outlined and predetermined path but only "estelas en la
mar" (p. 826). Machado, as a student of Bergson and a reader of Heidegger, concentrates on the temporal and fleeting aspect of human existence:

> *Agua del buen manantial,*
> *siempre viva,*
> *fugitiva;*
>
> .   .   .   .
>
> *Bogadora,*
> *marinera*
> *hacia la mar sin ribera.* (p. 804)

Zubiría points out that water symbolizes the "fuga de lo temporal." [30] For Machado life and youth are like a river winding to the sea. This lost youth, however, is not necessarily something to be lamented, for age may bring a realization of life's reality.

> *Mis viejos mares duermen: se apagaron*
> *sus espumas sonoras*
> *sobre la playa estéril. La tormenta*
> *camina lejos en la nube torva.* (p. 671)

In youth, for national and other reasons, the youth sees life as filled with gloomy forebodings, as he seeks the elusive dream, "mientras la mar dormía ahita de naufragios" (p. 846). Youth leaves the sordid galley in port and attempts to sail in a ship of gold

> *hacia los altos mares, sin aguardar ribera,*
> *lanzando velas y anclas y gobernalle al mar.* (p. 847)

Youth's duty is to make a positive act of will and live one's life. In many of his poems Machado superimposes youthful dreams on mature disillusion: the youth dreams his illusions; the adult voices his anguished disillusion. Machado intertwines the river of time and man's destiny so skillfully that he creates a poetic world of unchanging time in which the transitory and sempiternal are fused to create a timeless world, or as the poet says, "Hoy es siempre todavía" (p. 887).

The sea may represent a new life and freedom for Spaniards living in a decadent country. As the great leveler of all men, the sea may serve as a release for "atónitos palurdos" who, finding the land a dead and dying thing,

> *. . . van, abandonando el mortecino hogar,*
> *como tus largos ríos, Castilla, hacia la mar!*   (p. 735)

These poor sons of the soil who work, suffer, and sometimes die on the cursed land, abandon their homes "por los sagrados ríos hacia los anchos mares" (p. 737). Machado's grandfather, Antonio Machado Núñez, had gone to Guatemala, as had other members of the family including Machado's brother Joaquín. Perhaps, says McVan, Antonio wished to go and envied Joaquín. "It has been surmised that this remained a thorn in Antonio's conscience." [31] It is the youngest brother, Miguel, in "La tierra de Alvargonzález," who "fue más allá de los mares/y hoy torna indiano opulento" (p. 776). This idea of seeking one's fortune overseas is repeated in "A Don Miguel de Unamuno": "y que el oro busco tras de los mares" (p. 855). In "El Viajero" Machado mentions his sea dream:

> *¿Sonríe al sol de oro*
> *de la tierra de un sueño no encontrada;*
> *y ve su nave hender el mar sonoro,*
> *de viento y luz la blanca vela hinchada?*   (pp. 650–651)

But the poet's dream was not fulfilled. As he somewhat wistfully says, "Mas no es tu fiesta el Ultramar lejano,/sino la ermita junto al manso río;" (p. 673). After his dreams of adventure "en el mar, de cien veleros" (p. 927), his heart returns to its task "con néctares del campo que florece/ y el luto de la tarde desabrida" (p. 928). For although the poet says "he navegado en cien mares/y atracado en cien riberas" (p. 651), like Grandmontagne,

> *Tras de mucho devorar*
> *caminos del mar profundo,*
> *vió las estrellas brillar*
> *sobre la panza del mundo.*   (p. 914)

Machado constantly identifies the sea with the earth:

> *decrépitas ciudades, caminos sin mesones,*
>
> . . . .

> *como tus largos ríos, Castilla, hacia la mar!* (p. 735)

> *¿Acaso como tú y por siempre, Duero,*
> *irá corriendo hacia la mar Castilla?* (p. 743)

> *la tempestad llevarse los limos de la tierra*
> *por los sagrados ríos hacia los anchos mares;* (p. 737)

> *abiertos los jazmines, maduros los trigales,*
> *azules las montañas y el olivar florido;*
> *Guadalquivir corriendo al mar entre vergeles;* (p. 790)

> *tras leguas y más leguas de campos amarillos—,*
> *por esta tierra, lejos del mar y la montaña.* (p. 817)

Machado contrasts Extremadura and the sea, Soria and the sea, La Mancha and the sea, and above all Castilla and the sea. Azorín, to whom Machado had dedicated two poems for the former's *Castilla* (p. 791, p. 843) and on whom he has a poem (pp. 911–912), in speaking of Machado's landscapes of Soria, claimed that these "no están trazadas por una mano carnal, sino que son tan sutiles, tan aladas, tan etéreas, y al mismo tiempo tan reales y tangibles que diríase que es el propio espíritu del poeta—no su cuerpo—el que alienta en esos paisajes." [32] Another critic states: "Machado se ve a sí mismo, se siente a sí mismo en el paisaje. O se le extiende el paisaje por los espacios infinitos de su alma." [33] The sea, too, reflects Machado's soul states and is an integral aspect of his *paisaje:*

> *Castilla la gentil y la bravía;*
> *la parda y la manchega.*
> *Castilla, España de los largos ríos*
> *que el mar no ha visto y corre hacia los mares.* (p. 843)

> *Junto a la sierra florida,*
> *bulle el ancho mar.* (p. 879)

Often the land symbol is the garden:

Érase de un marinero
que hizo un jardín junto al mar,
y se metió a jardinero.
Estaba el jardín en flor,
y el jardinero se fue
por esos mares de Dios.   (p. 835)
Que el caminante es suma del camino,
y en el jardín, junto del mar sereno,
le acompaña el aroma montesino,
ardor de seco henil en campo ameno.   (p. 910)

Yet in the final anaysis, though the sea may offer consolation or a path
through life, Machado the poet of Castile and his poetic heart turn to the
land from the seashore "y en tierra labradora y marinera/suspiro por los
yermos castellanos" (p. 924).

Machado saw great inspiration in the sea:

De la mar al percepto,
del percepto al concepto,
del concepto a la idea
—oh, la linda tarea!—,
de la idea a la mar.   (p. 837)

He uses the sea-art image to advise the artist to wait until flood tide and not
to be overly anxious to set sail, for he who waits will win the victory, as life
is long and art a plaything. However, if life is short:

y no llega la mar a tu galera,
aguarda sin partir y siempre espera,
que el arte es largo y, además, no importa.   (p. 835)

He views the achievements of others as stemming from the sea and
bringing glory to Spain. Rubén Darío is

. . . peregrino
de un ultramar de Sol, nos trae el oro
de su verbo divino.

. . . . `

> *La nave bien guarnida,*
> *con fuerte casco y acerada prora,*
> *de viento y luz la blanca vela henchida*
> *surca, pronta a arribar, la mar sonora;*
> *y yo le grito: ¡Salve! a la bandera*
> *flamígera que tiene*
> *esta hermosa galera,*
> *que de una nueva España a España viene.*   (p. 851)

Others addressed in similar terms are: Narciso Alonso Cortés, whose fortress opposes time as the bridge opposes its stem to the river's force, "bajo ella el tiempo lleva bramando su torrente,/sus aguas cenagosas huyendo hacia los mares" (p. 853) ; Azorín, "Oh, tú, Azorín, que de la mar de Ulises /viniste al ancho llano" (p. 845) ; Xavier Valcarce, ". . . abrí con una diminuta llave/el ventanal del fondo que da a la mar sombría?" (p. 841) ; Ramón Pérez de Ayala:

> *Gran poeta, el pacífico sendero*
> *cantó que lleva a la asturiana aldea;*
> *el mar polisonoro y sol de Homero.*   (p. 912)

Francisco Grandmontagne:

> *calma le dió el oceano*
> *y grandeza;*
> *y de un pueblo americano*
> *donde florece la hombría*
> *nos trae la fe y la alegría*
> *que ha perdido el castellano.*   (pp. 914–915)

and Julio Castro:

> *En cada verso tuyo*
> *hay un golpe de mar, que me despierta*
> *a sueños de otros días.*   (p. 917)

The sea, which separates him from them, reminds him of his loves:

> *De mar a mar entre los dos la guerra*
> *más honda que la mar. En mi parterre,*
> *miro a la mar que el horizonte cierra.*
> *Tú asomada, Guiomar, a un finisterre,*
> *miras hacia otro mar, la mar de España . . .* [34]

> *Me embriagaré una noche*
> *de cielo negro y bajo,*
> *para cantar contigo,*
> *orilla al mar salado.*   (p. 685)

He recalls Leonor whose river of life was swept out to sea, but the past, seared in his memory, brings also hope for the future, and her name will be forever engraved in his heart:

> *Pero aunque fluya hacia la mar ignota,*
> *es la vida también agua de fuente*
> *que de claro venero, gota a gota.*   (p. 929)

Nevertheless his later comfort and love will be for Guiomar:

> *Por ti la mar ensaya olas y espumas,*
> *y el iris, sobre el monte, otros colores,*
>
> . . . .
>
> *Por ti, oh, Guiomar! . . .*   (p. 985)

And finally, the sea may give rise to objective descriptions of moods and emotions. The sea may reflect joy, sunshine, merriment, and an ideal.

> *El mar hierve y canta . . .*
> *El mar es un sueño sonoro*
> *bajo el sol de abril.*
> *El mar hierve y ríe*
> *con olas azules y espumas de leche y de plata,*   (p. 688)

The sea may represent bitterness and sadness in its gray waves roughened by the wind.

> *Palpita un mar de acero de olas grises*
>
> .   .   .   .
>
> *... Sopla el viento norte*
> *y riza el mar. El triste mar arrulla*
> *una ilusión amarga con sus olas grises,*
>
> .   .   .   .
>
> .   .   .   .
>
> *Cierra la tarde el horizonte*
> *anubarrado. Sobre el mar de acero*
> *hay un cielo de plomo.*[35]

Machado views the sea as great poets have viewed it from time immemorial, as a primitive place of potential power, as an alluring call which is difficult to deny, as unfathomable, desolate, mysterious, terrible, as life and death, God and eternity. Machado's sea serves for every mood and occasion and it may be smiling, sonorous, somber, salty, fierce, tranquil, bitter, or loving.

[From *Hispania,* vol. XLVIII, no. 2, May, 1965]

García Lorca and Vermont

CRITICS who have written about Lorca in America feel that New York had little influence on his work and that his opinion of the United States was almost completely negative. For Angel del Río, "whatever significance *Poet in New York* may have does not spring from any genuine contact with actual American life, which the poet saw only from the outside." [1] Gil Benumeya quotes Lorca as having said: "Fuera del arte negro no queda en los Estados Unidos más que mecánica y automatismo." [2] Conrad Aiken says: "He hated us, and rightly, for the right reasons." [3] Yet in August 1929, Lorca spent ten days in an unspoiled section of colonial New England and came away from his experience enriched and understanding its way of life.

Some two or three years before he came to the United States, García Lorca had met Philip Cummings, a young American poet-student at the Residencia in Madrid. Lorca and Cummings became friends and Cummings invited him to stay at his parents' cabin at Lake Eden, Vermont. In the following letter, written some six weeks earlier, even though Lorca calls New York "babilónica, cruel y violenta ciudad," he mentions that it is "llena por otra parte de gran belleza moderna."

Querido amiguito mío
Recibí tu carta con gran alegría. He encontrado ya un sitio en New York. Deseo verte muy pronto y pienso constantemente en ti pero me he matriculado por consejo de Onís, el profesor en la Universidad de Columbia y yo no puedo por esta causa ir contigo hasta dentro de seis semanas. Si entonces tú sigues queriendo, yo iré a tu lado encantado.
Si para entonces tú no estás en tu casa, te ruego vengas a verme a

New York. ¿Te parece bien? Escríbeme con toda confianza si esto puede ser.

Estoy confundido por tu gran amabilidad enviándome el dinero para el billete y desde luego si no se arregla mi viaje dentro de seis semanas te lo devolveré guardándote siempre gratitud y lealtad hidalga que es todo lo mejor que puede dar un español.

Escríbeme enseguida querido amigo y dime si te parece bien el retraso de mi viaje. Yo debo hacer, ya que estoy matriculado, este curso de inglés. Luego yo pasaría unos diás contigo y serían deliciosos para mí.

Espero que tú me contestarás y no te olvidarás de este poeta del Sur perdido ahora en esta babilónica cruel y violenta ciudad, llena por otra parte de gran belleza moderna.

Vivo en Columbia y mis señas son éstas.

Mister Federico G. Lorca,
Furnald Hall,
Columbia University
New York City.

Espero que tú me contestarás enseguida. Adiós queridísimo. Recibe un abrazo de Federico.

Saluda con todo respeto a tus padres.[4]

Cummings was Lorca's only contact with a native creative writer in this country. Lorca spent a good part of the day at Eden scribbling away on an overturned boat, and he and Cummings pursued the subject of poetry for hours on end in the cool dusk of the northern Vermont lake shore. At night they would lie awake arguing about words, religion, life, and death. Cummings translated Lorca's *Canciones* while the latter sat beside him with his legs dangling over the porch railing. Although Lorca officially knew no English, he would argue constantly over the exact shade of meaning to be conveyed by a word. Thus, the *Canciones,* as translated by Cummings, regardless of its intrinsic poetic worth, is the only personally approved version of a translation of Lorca's poetry into English. Lorca later sent him an autographed copy as a "recuerdo cariñoso de la estancia en mi cabaña de Vermont," as well as an autographed copy of the *Romancero Gitano*.

Lorca had undergone a grave personal crisis, which need not be commented upon, but his suffering and loneliness were well known. Lorca's dislike for his family, stemming from more than his father's reservations about his son's spending more time with his poetry than with his studies, contributed somewhat to this melancholy, as did his feelings about Spanish Catholicism. It would appear ironic that the very poetic contributions which made the name of Lorca great were opposed as foolishness by those who have since profited so much by their relationship to him. In Lorca's poems the conflict between impulse and constraint is with us constantly, but he found a partial, if temporary, alleviation for his sorrow in the calm and friendly atmosphere of the Cummings' menage.

In a letter to his friend, Angel del Río, from Eden Mills, Lorca called it, "Un paisaje prodigioso pero de una melancolía infinita. Una buena experiencia para mí. . . . No cesa de llover. Esta familia es muy simpática y llena de un encanto suave, pero los bosques y el lago me sumen en un estado de desesperación poética muy difícil de sostener. Escribo todo el día y a la noche me siento agotado. . . . Ahora cae la noche. Han encendido las luces de petróleo y toda mi infancia viene a mi memoria envuelta en una gloria de amapolas y cereales. He encontrado entre los helechos una rueca cubierta de arañas y en el lago no canta ni una rana. . . . Esto es acogedor para mí, pero me ahogo en esta niebla y esta tranquilidad que hacen surgir mis recuerdos de una manera que me queman." [5] Vermont was the first real "earth" Lorca had experienced since leaving his own country, and though his restlessness and uncertainty were ever recurring, Vermont was an interlude of peace which helped him regain his emotional equilibrium.

Although not overgiven to physical exercise, he and Cummings tramped all over that part of Vermont. Federico had a special love for old tree stumps, left over from lumbering operations, and he called them Moorish castles to be attacked. He was fascinated by stone walls, which for him were the castles of men's minds. He claimed that man has always built with stone. "In Europe they built castles; here they build walls." An examination of Vermont painters reveals the same love of stumps, walls, and fence posts. When not composing, Lorca would sit for lengthy periods on the white kitchen stool and watch Mrs. Cummings make doughtnuts—which he adored. He talked to her in Spanish while she talked to him in English, and in spite of the barriers they somehow understood one another.

Two ladies named Tyler, one a school teacher, had a nearby cabin, and Lorca would pick flowers for Dorothea and Elizabeth. In the afternoons he would drink tea, "una desesperación de te," in their house which he called the "casa del arco iris." Even in the brief time he was there he grew to know the woods and farms of the district. He liked the way the "pueblo" lived and played concerts for the farmers and their wives at a dance hall, since burned down. Everything interested him, even the outhouses which he called "rincón de los sacerdotes." He reserved his special dislike for the constantly noisy frogs and their "fanfarronada."

In the minds of most of the Spaniards or Spanish Americans who wrote about Lorca, there is no norm for Vermont or New England. Yet on his long walks in the woods, his visits to the stone quarry, his trips for milk, or while sitting at the lake or playing for the farmers, Lorca was next to the real earth and spirit of America. As Cummings says, "I suspect—with me—maybe a little through me—Federico knew the traditional heart of America —at least of Colonial New England." [6] Lorca was familiar with Whitman, at least, and it is doubtful that he could have experimented so significantly without some awareness of the traditions within which he was working. In New York, even in the country, he felt he was in a *tertulia* atmosphere on display for his friends, and not one with the earth. Vermont for him was a refuge as it was for "todo lo que huye de la tierra" ("Tierra y luna," *O.C.,* p. 557).

Which are the Vermont poems of *Poeta en Nueva York?* Lorca composed dozens of verses, inspired by Vermont, which he never wrote down but which he recited to his friends. Of his written work, usually, "Poemas del Lago Edem Mills," section IV of *Poeta en Nueva York,* are the only poems assigned to Vermont inspiration. Although "Poema Doble del Lago Edem" and "Cielo Vivo" are the only poems specifically dated at Lake Eden, "Tierra y Luna" and "Vaca" also belong to his Vermont stay. "Vaca," listed in all editions as belonging to section V, "En la Cabaña del Farmer," stems from a real experience well remembered by Cummings. Section VI, "Poemas de la Soledad en Vermont." though written later in New York, depend on Vermont for much of their symbolism.

In "Poema Doble del Lago Edem" (*O.C.,* p. 426) Lorca calls for his ancient voice of love and truth, his former poetry, as he recalls older emotions and sorrows. The poet seeks to find himself, and he needs to cry "como lloran los niños del último banco," because he is not all man, poet, or leaf, but only a wounded pulse that explores the things of beyond. Nevertheless, through his crying he will blurt out his "verdad de hombre de sangre, matando en mí la burla y la sugestión del vocablo." Lorca, in Vermont, attempts to define and recover his personality, almost lost "entre la multitud que vomita" ("Paisaje de la Multitud que Vomita") in New York. He feels the negation of the mysterious forces with which he works. Inwardly he is gnawed by a primitive nostalgia which would lift his eyes to the heavens, to Paradise where Eve eats ants and "Adán fecunda peces deslumbrados," but the poet is torn from the heights where he finds no support. He then sorrows at the unending anguish which pursues him along with "el sueño y la muerte" which seek him, as he looks for an escape from the infernal reality in which he has lived. In New York only "the murdered dogs, the interminable milk trains, the cat's paw smashed by the motorist" answered his cry. He could only offer himself there "a ser comido por las vacas estrujadas cuando sus gritos llenan el valle donde el Hudson se emborracha con aceite" (*New York Oficina y Denuncia*). But Vermont, "allí donde mugen las vacas que tienen patitas de paje," offers the possibility of another direction, a temporary escape through genuine contact with the earth. Lorca's poetry is far from simple as he dislocates language into his complex meaning. He uses the imagery of everyday life, but he elevates and intensifies it so that it represents the reality as it is and yet much more.

"Cielo Vivo" (*O.C.*, p. 428) was inspired by a night of brilliant aurora borealis activity as the lake reflected the lights against a pitch black Mount Norris. Lorca claimed the light was held prisoner by Lake Eden, and he referred constantly to the "misticismo del lago" and the "lodo eterno del lago" in his discussions with Cummings.

In this poem, also dated August 24, 1929, the poet, through nature, is trying to obtain a spiritual tranquility which the multitudes of the cities cannot have. They have lost their battle to dominate and possess nature through inventions and science. "La luz es sepultada por cadenas y ruidos en impúdico reto de ciencia sin raíces" ("La Aurora"). They cannot come to grips with the anguish of their inner being and in New York, when dawn arrived, there was nobody there to receive it, for "no hay mañana ni esperanza posible. A veces las monedas en enjambres furiosos taladran y devoran abandonados niños" ("La Aurora"). Lorca felt abandoned, isolated, in New York, but in Vermont, newly born, he returns to a clean and fresh landscape to try to understand himself. "Pero me iré al primer paisaje de choques, líquidos y rumores que trasmina a niño recién nacido y donde toda superficie es evitada, para entender que lo que busco tendrá su blanco de alegría cuando yo vuelo mezclado con el amor y las arenas." It is true that the poet may not find what he seeks, but he continues the search as he goes "al primer paisaje de humedades y latidos." Guillermo Díaz-Plaja clearly sensed the struggle in Lorca between the dramatic clash of the two worlds: the artificial in New York and the natural in Vermont. "Entre Nueva York y la casita de madera de Vermont en que residió el poeta se da plásticamente y en sus formas supremas el choque entre la naturaleza y la civilización." [7] Hope and despair, life and death are inextricably meshed in the coruscation and darkness of his total work, but in the Lake Eden poems expectation outweighs despair.

Díaz-Plaja places the poem, "Tierra y Luna," with the Vermont group. "Es una obra representativa todavía de su etapa americana. El dramático choque entre lo instintivo y lo racional, según la simbología repetidamente estudiada (Vida-Tierra; Muerte-Luna), se da en este poema de aire dionisíaco que el poeta fecha en plena selva americana—en la Cabaña de Dum Kunium, Vermont, agosto de 1929." Lorca again seeks "another time's voice," where he will find "en el niño y en las criaturas que pasan los arcos," the idea of earth, "tierra alegrísima." There is, of course, the continuing contrast with the "niño desnudo que pisotean los borrachos de Brooklyn," for he has not shed the anguish of modern living, but it is "tierra lo que vengo buscando." In the clash of the double world of "Ciudad" and "Naturaleza" as Guillermo Díaz-Plaja puts it, "Nuestro poeta nos presenta constantemente . . . el choque dramático de estos dos mundos: el de la naturaleza y el de la artificiosidad; . . . Y no hay que añadir que el poeta se resuelve siempre con un empuje biológico, a favor de las cosas vitales y libres." [8]

"Vaca" (*O.C.*, p. 431) also belongs to the Lake Eden series of part IV. The two friends had gone to a neighboring farm for milk. A cow had been hurt and the farmer had sent for a veterinarian. Lorca, astonished at the thought of a doctor for a cow, remarked, according to Cummings, that in Spain, "We don't even have doctors for people."

Perhaps the real background for his inspiration is not always the vital factor in Lorca's poetic creation, but the sensory impact is so vital here that we receive the spontaneous sentiment and sensation without loss of intensity. Lorca stresses organic tangibility in portraying the hurt cow with her bleeding muzzle. "Se tendió la vaca herida. Árboles y arroyos trepaban por sus cuernos. Su hocico sangraba en el cielo." He makes us feel the atmosphere of the "honey of stables" and the "cows bawling with half-opened eyes." In Lorca's work concrete reality and the visionary fuse in typical

Spanish fashion, but in this poem the realistic and external elements seem to predominate. Yet even here the reality is touched by the startling imagery and subtle genius which never desert him as he tells us that the "cow of ashes has departed and gone bawling through the debris of a motionless sky where the drunkards lunch on death."

The poems of section VI, "Poemas de la Soledad en Vermont," reflect on the ever-present Lorca concern with death. But his death is not the one found in the desolate and divided cities of Rilke, nor the "unreal city under the brown fog of a winter dawn" of Eliot's *The Waste Land,* nor yet the ant-heap city "ou le spectre en plein jour raccroche le passant" of Baudelaire's "Les Septs Vieillards." Death in these forms waits for Lorca in New York. In Vermont his death is closer to Whitman's "knowledge of death as walking one side of me, and the thought of death closewalking the other side of me" ("When Lilacs Last in the Dooryard Bloom'd"). Often a memory in retrospect is more vital and intense than the subjective immediate expression of an experience, and although these poems were written later, their contemporary analysis of death makes use of American symbols as well as of his Mozarabic heritage and clearly reflect the Vermont background.

In Vermont he had sought to escape his pain and sublimate his hate through the power of love. In a new symbolism, Lorca returns to death, which for him is love's companion. He weaves new rhythms in his pursuit of death and one discovers a biology of death in his lyric world. Death paradoxically enables him to understand life, as in the life of the rose, for example, one finds the components of its destruction:

> ¡Y el caballo,
> qué flecha aguda exprime de la rosa!
> qué rosa gris levanta de su belfo!
> ¡Y la rosa,
> qué rebaño de luces y alaridos
> ata en el vivo azúcar de su tronco! ("Muerte," *O.C.,* p. 434)

Honig insists that Lorca feared "that what is precious in each passing moment will be eternally lost as soon as one has allowed himself the luxury of believing that the flux has stopped." [9] In nature Lorca found an incessant and eternal conflict shared by living things which must undergo change and even disappear.

¡Qué esfuerzo del caballo por ser perro!
¡Qué esfuerzo del perro por ser golondrina!
¡Qué esfuerzo de la golondrina por ser abeja!
¡Qué esfuerzo de la abeja por ser caballo!
    ("Muerte," *O.C.*, p. 434)
    Para ver que todo se ha ido,
para ver los huecos y los vestidos,
dame tu guante de luna
tu otro guante perdido en la hierba,
amor mío. ("Nocturno del Hueco," *O.C.*, pp. 435–437)

Lorca had mentioned as some of the principal images of death in Spain, "La cuchilla y la rueda del carro, y la navaja y las barbas pinchonas de los pastores, y la luna pelada, y la mosca, y las alacenas húmedas, y los derribos, y los santos cubiertos de encaje, y la cal, y la línea hiriente de aleros y miradores . . ." ("Teoría y Juego del Duende," *O.C.*, p. 42). He adds to these symbols in "Nocturno del Hueco" the imprint of bloody branches, dead snails, mummified arm, deserted square, the cry of the grasses, the dagger-struck moon. Man's efforts seem futile for only nothingness, the void, and death wait for him in his contact with the universe: "No hay siglo nuevo ni luz reciente./Solo un caballo azul y una madrugada."

"Paisaje con dos tumbas y un perro asirio" continues the images of the cold moon, the warm blood found in *Romancero Gitano* and other works, and combines them with that of the howling dog. In "Impresiones y Paisajes" Lorca had commented on the impact of the "aullidos . . . que les salían de lo más hondo de su alma . . . es la muerte inevitable que flota en los ambientes en busca de sus víctimas, es la muerte el pensamiento que nos inquieta al conjuro diabólico del aullido . . . con la voz profunda que mana de muy hondo, con la cual el espanto tiene fastuosidades asiáticas" (*O.C.*, pp. 1467–68). In this poem the howl of the Asiatic dog is "una lengua morada que deja hormigas de espanto y licor de lirios."

The last two poems of the Vermont section, "Ruina" (*O.C.*, pp. 438–439) and "Luna y Panorama de los Insectos" (*O.C.*, pp. 440–442), recombine death symbols with the earth. Earlier Lorca had contemplated clouds, the rocks, the waters, the shores of the lake, the insects, as escapes from the slavery of man and machine. The sky was a manifestation of nature's beauty and peace, although amidst the lowing of the cows, death was seeking the author: "La muerte me estaba buscando" ("Poema Doble del Lago

Edem"). Even though the author did not find a permanent refuge from the
city, he listened to the flow of water and felt the freshness of the breeze.
But in this section the grasses are the servants of death. "Yo vi llegar las
hierbas y les eché un cordero que balaba bajo sus dientecillos y lancetas"
("Ruina"). The moon is a "guante de humo" ("Luna y Panorama de los
Insectos") as in "Ruina" it was "una calavera de caballo," images of death.
In the Lake Eden poems the manifestations of nature were usually symbols
of hope. Here they are symbols of death.

Lorca's earth continues to be populated with plants, animals, insects, the
grass, the horse, as he adds further dimensions to his concept of death, but
even here, occasionally, a simple, even fresh, lyrical note intrudes: "Las
nubes, en manada, se quedaron dormidas contemplando" ("Ruina,") and
"Si el aire sopla blandamente mi corazón tiene la forma de una niña"
("Luna y Panorama de los Insectos"). They are quickly overwhelmed,
however, by the "saliva swords," for the law of life has become that of
death.

Alfredo de la Guardia relegates Eden Mills to an insignificant role in
Lorca's life: "A orillas del lago Edem Mills no se siente captado por la
tierra inmensa y joven, por el continente que recorre el planeta de un polo
al otro polo, entre los dos más grandes océanos. Porque, sin embargo,
América ha servido para abrirle los ojos a la angustia de la humanidad, a la
miseria del mundo." [10] The theme of social protest can be read into many
parts of the volume, it is true. Lorca, as one who had suffered in his own
life, and with a poet's insight, understood and sympathized with the mis-
eries of the "pueblo," but while we need not deny his understanding and
sympathy for any man imprisoned by the "river of oil," to read his work as a
social document is in this writer's judgment an error. In examining his stay
at Lake Eden with people close to nature, one reaches the conclusion that
Lorca came away with more than his oft-quoted Gil Benumeya interview
would indicate.

The sadness of *Poeta en Nueva York* and Lorca's preoccupation with
death stem from sources deeply interwoven into the fabric of the poet's
personality and subconscious. New York and Vermont are simply new
facets of the eternal considerations for Lorca, life and death. In nature he
found both. At Lake Eden he saw both. With a true poet's imagination
and inspiration, in poems written at Eden, and in others drawing upon the
storehouse of memory in Vermont, he transformed reality, reconceived it

in his imagination, and gave it a purer and more essential if more complex meaning. Honig, in comparing *Poeta en Nueva York* with Rimbaud's *Saison en Enfer,* comments that both works were "an attempt to escape . . . from a traditional poetic inheritance. . . . In the release of imagination both poets sought . . . a deeper truth in the experience of nature. . . . *Saison en Enfer* and *Poeta en Nueva York* are a surrender to death at the same time that they mark the beginning of a new life for the writers . . . Lorca found himself a surer, more responsible artist in consequence of the momentary deviation." [11]

[From *Hispania,* vol. XLII, no. 1, March, 1959]

The Sea, Love, and Death in the Poetry of Aleixandre

WHILE it is true that a psychoanalytic interpretation, where applied, may not be clinically valid without the cooperation and interpretation of the poet himself under expert analysis, and although in dealing with half-conscious remote associations, shifting illusions, and confusing images the recurring themes may not give definitive answers, an examination of the sea symbolism in Aleixandre's poetry reveals the neurotic motivation behind and preoccupation with the equation that love equals death. As Freud points out, love and death instincts fuse and blend with one another and reveal themselves in an ambivalent attitude towards various objects: "for the opposition between the two classes of instincts we may put the polarity of love and hate. There is no difficulty in finding a representative of Eros; but we must be grateful that we can find a representative of the elusive death instinct in the instinct of destruction to which hate points the way. . . . In lower animals some die in the act of reproduction because after Eros has been eliminated through the process of satisfaction the death instinct has a free hand for accomplishing its purposes." [1] Melanie Klein has shown that in this tension "destructive and libidinal instincts are fused together; but its effect of causing anxiety is referable to the destructive." [2]

Whereas Jung's theory of the artist insists on the separation of his personal life and his impersonal creative process,[3] Freud views the artist as one who compensates, through his creativity, for his inability to lead a satisfying personal life. Imagination, according to Freud, is a refuge which provides a substitute pleasure for narcissistic wishes which the artist had to abandon in real life. In a sense the poet resembles the neurotic who rejects reality for the world of fantasy which he disguises and distorts to avoid confrontation with strong repressions; he shares these fantasies with the audience as reflections, possibly of subconscious wishes possessed by all mankind. "An artist is originally a man who turns away from reality because he cannot come to terms without the renunciation of instinctual satisfaction which it at first demands and he allows his erotic and ambitious wishes full play in the life of phantasy. He finds the way back to reality, however, from this world of phantasy by making use of special gifts to mold his phantasies into truths of a new kind, which are valued by men as precious reflections of reality." [4]

Many psychoanalysts have interested themselves in the relationships between art and neurosis, symbols and illness. Freud himself analyzed *Gradiva*,[5] by the Scandinavian writer W. Jensen, and wrote a psychoanalytic biography of Leonardo da Vinci, shedding light on the relation of his sexuality to his creative work. Freud felt that such knowledge enhanced rather than detracted from the enjoyment of a work of art.[6] As Lawrence Kubie has shown, creativity and illness are not mutually dependent.[7] It is nevertheless equally apparent that a man who suffers grave illness has time to daydream and think of death. Dr. Kubie admits: "Wherever unconscious influences play a dominant role the creative process in science or art becomes almost identical with the neurotic process—merely transmitting unconscious conflicts into some socially and artistically acceptable symbolic form." [8] Flanders Dunbar shows "Freud . . . never lost sight of the essential unity of psyche and soma and he often dealt with somatic symptoms." [9]

In April of 1925 a serious illness caused Aleixandre to retire to the countryside for two years. This illness left an indelible impression on his poetry, which concentrated on an evasion of reality and a preoccupation, at least in part, with his own physical necessities. Juan José Domenchina phrases it as "el poeta dolece de una enfermedad que le sume en un apartamiento casi absoluto—es una poesía biológica." [10] For Max Aub, "La vida enfermiza de Vicente Aleixandre marca indeleblemente sus poemas, cantos desesperados de amor insatisfecho . . . poesía de un hombre acostado que ve pasar por los cielos las fantasmagorías de su imaginación." [11] Dámaso Alonso saw in him a poet whom God "tocó como toca lo que quiere afinar; con el dolor. Dolor físico que dejó huella en el cuerpo y en el alma." [12] Luis Cernuda recalls Aleixandre as "Enfermo y solo, vive allá en el suelo/Que fuera el mío." [13] Aleixandre refers to his own illness and its effect on his career: "Puntualizaré que la iniciación de una conciencia de poeta—conciencia de una vocación decidida y posible—afloró con el cambio que años después una enfermedad larga y grave imprimió al rumbo de mi existencia. Edad: veinti-tantos años. Campo y soledad . . . Este cambio total decidió mi vida." [14]

In 1932 a new illness which proved to be almost fatal struck him, and he had to have a kidney removed and spend a long period of convalescence.[15] Sickly, alone, withdrawn, a man who fought death constantly and sought life instinctively,[16] Aleixandre wanted a refuge from a world indifferent to his pain and found it in a dream world of the unconscious where he might escape the reality of his impotence. In his poetry, orgiastic Dionysian efforts to recreate a reality through imagery struggle with Apollonian tendencies to control his subconcious fantasy world. Aleixandre was never able nor willing to give an adequate explanation of his poetry, but he recognized it as a necessity based on subconscious desires. "No sé lo que es la poesía y desconfío profundamente de todo juicio sobre lo siempre inexplicable . . . Y que no hago más que vivir cuanto puedo y lo que puedo, escribiendo poesía porque es mi necesidad todavía." [17] Sáinz de Robles, sensing Aleixandre's struggles and tensions, feels he writes as do very few poets "exclusivamente para sí mismos, sin otra necesidad que la de eliminar de sí una presión que acabaría por ahogarle, sin otro interés que 'verse fuera de sí,' como quien busca un espejo sólo para 'recobrarse' en lo exterior." [18] The poet, then, is only one more object of nature which reflects in its total reality his personal problems and anguish, as Aleixandre seems to imply throughout his work.

Whatever the unconscious fantasies and their intensification through Aleixandre's illness, he consciously admitted the direct influence of Freud's works. "Sé que sin la impresión de Freud, *Pasión de la tierra* no hubiera tomado la forma que tomó, aunque yo entonces no tuviera conciencia de ello." [19] "He de confesar la profunda impresión que la lectura de un psicólogo [Freud] de incisiva influencia me produjo en 1928, y el cambio de raíz que en mi modesta obra se produjo." [20]

In *Ámbito* (1924–1927), Aleixandre sets the stage for the sea as the battleground between Eros and Thanatos. "Mar y Aurora" [21] shows us the sea as a living entity whose timid waves and passive foam awaken with the dawn. Gradually the sun's rays disperse the shadows, and the sea becomes more active as the sunlight and the sea renew their daily symbolic relationship, "lento, diario, culto/bebedor de las ondas." A primitive belief held that the sea had previously swallowed the old sun and like a woman gave birth the following day to a new sun.[22] "Mar y noche" (pp. 102), the counterpart of the life force of the previous poem, reveals a dark and threatening sea viewed as a mouth, throat, and gullet waiting eagerly to devour the night: [23]

> *Boca—mar—toda ella, pide noche;*
> *noche extensa, bien prieta y grande,*
> *para sus fauces hórridas, y enseña*
> *todos sus blancos dientes de espuma.*

Seeking to swallow its enemy, the sea, chained to its black bed, vainly strains its muscles to free itself.

> *Torso y miembros. Las duras*
> *contracciones enseñan*
> *músculos emergidos, redondos bultos,*
> *álgidos despidos.*
> *Parece atado al hondo*
> *abismo el mar, en cruz, mirando*
> *al cielo alto, por desasirse,*
> *violento, rugiente, clavado al lecho negro.*

"The moment before falling asleep (when the sense of being engulfed is strongest) . . . there is a pool or lake which will 'swallow her up,' or there is a yawning or gaping chasm or canyon. More elaborately the dreamer may be threatened by the jaws of death . . ." [24] In these two poems Aleixandre produces a kind of primal relationship and reciprocal cannibalism as the day drinks the sea and the sea attempts to devour the night, again implying that the drive for life and the impulse to destruction are mutually independent factors.

More clearly in *Pasión de la tierra* (1928–1929) the poems emphasize a combination of death and sexuality. "Ser de esperanza y lluvia" (pp. 158–159) reveals a dying poet who does not know if "el fondo del mar puede encontrarse en un anillo. Porque tengo en la mano un pulmón que respira y una cabeza rota ha dado a luz a dos serpientes vivas." Aleixandre here and in future sea imagery, in extrarational and compulsive symbolism, stresses his need for loving and being loved, and his impotence, and thus in a sense death state, at fulfilling that need. According to Ernest Jones "Themes of death and castration . . . are extremely closely associated and . . . anxiety concerning indefinite survival of the personality constantly expresses the fear of a punitive impotence." [25]

"Ansiedad para el día" (pp. 200–201) implies death, breast, and castration fantasies. Aleixandre misses a finger of his hand which he does not wish to recognize in the beak of a sea gull. The poet feels "perdido en el océano" against the background of a giant wave made up of handfuls of umbrellas, and wants to wet his tongue in the ecstatic blue of heaven. Both the pleasurable and the unhappy are conveyed in the screen memory which seems to be equated with a primitive wish to sleep and to join the mother. Being one with her at the breast and in sleep means also to lose one's individual consciousness or ego, and thus in a sense to die. To merge or be lost in the ocean clearly reflects this loss of individuality, characteristic of going to sleep. The poet is both buoyed up and supported by the waves and yet he is threatened, a typical reaction of anxiety dreams.[26] But the earless monster will carry "en lugar de su palabra una tijera breve, la justa para cortar la explicación abierta." The defenseless poet delivers himself up to the powerful shears. He is also threatened by the "gargantas de las sirenas húmedas." The poet then indulges in a kind of autocannibalism: "lloro la cabeza entera. Me rueda por el pecho y río con las uñas, con los dos pies que me abanican," while a dried-up girl demands whether he has enough skin left for two arms. Sinking and smothering sensations, or the loss of consciousness, are found in fantasies of oral incorporation or being eaten. A baby treats the breast as it does its own fingers or other parts which it stuffs into its mouth, indulging in a kind of autocannibalism. This type of anxiety comes from childhood fantasies about the prenatal state, an aspect of which is the child's imagining it entered into the mother by being swallowed.[27]

"El amor padecido" (pp. 211–212), the last poem in this collection, shows phallic and oedipal fantasies. "Prefiero ese ala muscular hecha de firmeza, que no teme herir con su extremo la cárcel del cielo, la cerrazón de la altura emblanquecida. No son dientes esos limites de horizonte . . . para amar la forma perpendicular de uno mismo." "No grité aunque me herían. Aunque tú me ocultabas la forma de tu pecho. Sentí salir el sol dentro del alma. Interiormente las puntas del erizo, si aciertan, pueden salir de dentro de uno mismo y atraer la venganza, atraer los relámpagos . . . que penetran y buscan el misterio, la cámara vacía donde la madre no vivió aunque gime, aunque el mar con mandíbulas la nombra." Karl Abraham shows that the sun may be a symbol of the father's phallus. He continues: "I might briefly mention that in many neurotics the father is not represented by the sun, but by lightning . . . Lightning furthermore especially represents the punishing (killing) powers of the father.[28] The breast, the empty room associated with the mother, and the sea with jaws help support such a meaning. In Aleixandre's sea symbolism what is commonly called a castration complex, in a sense psychological death, recurs constantly.[29]

Espadas como labios (1930–1931) continues the fantasies. "El más bello amor" (pp. 243–244) rejects the false love of women. "Falsa hasta la sencilla manera con que las muchachas/cuelgan de noche sus pechos que no están tocados." Sexual passion and outlet can only be satisfied in a sexual fantasy of copulation, the wish to be devoured ("una boca imponente como una fruta bestial/ . . . un mordisco que abarcase todo el agua o la noche") which smacks of the hallucinatory.[30]

> *Pero me encontré un tiburón en forma de cariño;*
> *no, no: en forma de tiburón amado;*
> *escualo limpio, corazón extensible, ardor o crimen,*
> *deliciosa posesión que consiste en el mar.*
>
> .   .   .   .
>
> *Así, sin acabarse mudo ese acoplamiento sangriento,*
> *respirando sobre todo una tinta espesa,*
> *los besos son las manchas, las extensibles manchas*
> *que no me podrán arrancar las manos más delicadas.*
>
> .   .   .   .
>
> *Te penetro callando mientras grito o desgarro,*
> *mientras mis alaridos hacen música o sueño,*
> *porque beso murallas, las que nunca tendrán ojos,*
> *y beso esa yema fácil sensible como la pluma.*

The poet's psyche appears to reject reality for a regression to the past where his sexual instinct operated freely. The fish inhabiting the life-giving seas represent a vital sexual force of destructive capacity. One finds unacceptable, in this connection, the criticism of Bousoño and Dámaso Alonso. The former insists that, "sin embargo moral es la raíz del panteísmo erótico que tantas veces ha sido señalado como característico del primer Aleixandre" (*P.C.*, p. 21), and the latter that Aleixandre's animals are primitive, uncorruptible beings who love in intimate union with all the elemental forces of nature.[31]

In "Playa ignorante" (pp. 279–280) the poet comes from the exhausted world and desires to become one with the sea. He is buoyed up, rocked by heat, pierced by the water, as the sea with which he has fused strikes his unmovable body, a sea which in "Formas sobre el mar" (pp. 291–293) represents death or sleep and the unknown frontier to which life, "el mundo es lo no partido," leads one, "mientras pasa ya el tiempo como nuez,/ como lo que ha desalojado el mar súbito a besos." Aleixandre shows that through dying symbols of detumescence a life may ensue. The creatures which inhabit his seas, then, may be "peces sordos," "peces podridos," "pez que se ahoga," "pez que se pudre," "peces como piedras," "peces regalados," "peces que anidan," and "peces colorados con el rubor de vivir." [32]

The poems of *La destrucción o el amor* (1932–1933) continue Aleixandre's sea imagery. In "La selva y el mar" (pp. 299–300), the human ego is overwhelmed by elemental forces of fantasy, represented by a variety of fierce animals who show their swords or teeth,

> *al descubierto en los cuellos allá donde la arteria golpea,*
> *donde no se sabe si es el amor o el odio*
> *lo que reluce en los blancos colmillos.*

> .   .   .   .

> *El tigre, el león cazador, el elefante que en sus*
> *colmillos lleva algún suave collar,*
> *la cobra que se parece al amor más ardiente,*
> *el águila que acaricia a la roca como los sesos duros,*
> *el pequeño escorpión que con sus pinzas sólo aspira*
> *a oprimir un instante la vida,*
> *la menguada presencia de un cuerpo de hombre que*
> *jamás podrá ser confundido con una selva,*

. . . .

Todo suena cuando el rumor del bosque siempre virgen
se levanta como dos alas de oro,
élitros, bronce o caracol rotundo,
frente a un mar que jamás confundirá sus espumas con
las ramillas tiernas.

Aleixandre views the instinctive attack of primitive animals as a form of love, but the implied sexual force may also represent a passive masochistic gratification or even a passive homosexual implication, for he both loves and fears these symbols of masculine virility, the lion, the cobra, and the eagle. To wish to be eaten by menacing animals often represents a death fantasy equivalent to a fear of castration,[33] or as Melanie Klein has shown, the neurotic dread of death is primarily related to the fear of being devoured.[34] The fear of death may also be an "anxious transmutation of the original pleasure of falling asleep. The idea of oral impregnation includes not only the active eating process, but the passive 'being eaten' as well." [35]

As Bousoño has shown, Aleixandre establishes an inverse hierarchy in which the non-living triumph over the living, the mineral over the vegetable, the vegetable over the animal, and the animal over man (pp. 21–22). He welcomes life and love as a longed-for enemy which he fears but which will nevertheless relieve his own dammed up sexuality. Thus the forest is viewed as virginal and untouched by the impregnating sea, and the powerful claws of the animals, "el amor que se clava," cannot fertilize,

. . . por más que el surtidor se prolongue,
por más que los pechos entreabiertos en tierra
proyecten su dolor o su avidez a los cielos azules.

His exploding sexuality, "la sangre ardiente que brota de la herida," is impotent against the rejecting virgin forest, which must be punished, "amor o castigo contra los troncos estériles," as it faces the far-off withdrawing sea of life.

The fierce attacks of and identification with the long list of animals which the poet projects outward against the world may also serve as a father substitute onto which the fear of a father, a derivation of the Oedipus complex, has been displaced.[36] Otto Rank's idea is that a fusion through primitive life with animals may be "a rationalization . . . of the wish—through the desire to be eaten—to get back again into the mother's animal womb." [37] Monroe Meyer points out "there does not exist in the mind of the little child the flattering if somewhat fictitious gulf that adult man places between himself and other species." [38]

"Después de la Muerte" (pp. 303–304) equates the sea, filled with threatening tongues and furious foam, with both life and death; a sea which is "ladrón que roba los pechos,/ el mar donde mi cuerpo estuvo en vida a merced de las ondas." This death is both good and bad, for the sea may represent a kind of timeless afterlife which deletes the distinction between annihilation and immortality.

In "Mar en la tierra" (pp. 379–380) death may be a happiness, "la oscura dicha de morir," which will triumph over life and a world which is merely a dissolving grain born for a divine water, "para ese mar inmenso que yace sobre el polvo." According to Freud, water or the sea symbolizes the original fountain of birth or the genesis of the individual either in association with the concept that the sea is the vital element from which all animal species came or in simple relation to the uterus of the mother, where the child originated in liquid. Fantasies and unconscious thoughts relating to life in the womb contain "the profoundest unconscious reason for the belief in a life after death, which represents only the projection into the future of this mysterious life before birth." [39] Aleixandre's pseudo-animistic theory holds that man returns in death to the place from which he came, to the sea which gave him birth, and thus a dark happiness.

> La dicha consistirá en deshacerse como lo minúsculo,
> en transformarse en la severa espina,
> resto de un océano que como la luz se marchó,
> gota de arena que fue un pecho gigante
> y que salida por la garganta como un sollozo aquí yace.

The state of sleep bears a marked resemblance to the prenatal state, and it is easy to postulate an intrauterine regression, the dark joy of dying, of fusing with the sea, that is, returning to the womb. "La Muerte" (pp. 414–415), the last poem in the collection, stresses the poet's search for life against a powerfully threatening sea.[40] He wants "el color rosa o la vida," but the sea offers him a love which must end in death, "un amor que con la muerte acaba," for which the poet is prepared. "Ah, pronto, pronto; quiero morir frente a ti, mar," but the sea, both love and death, withdraws, and the poet is drained and empty. In death he seeks surrender to his beloved nature, his final and greatest act of love; only thus can he achieve freedom.

> *Muerte como el puñado de arena,*
> *como el agua que en el hoyo queda solitaria,*
> *como la gaviota que en medio de la noche*
> *tiene un color de sangre sobre el mar que no existe.*

Mundo a solas (1934–1936) repeats Aleixandre's idea of an elemental world in which the sea plays a prominent part. "No existe el hombre" (pp. 423–424) stresses that "Un mar no es un lecho donde el cuerpo de un hombre puede tenderse a solas./ Un mar no es un sudario para una muerte lúcida." [41] The sea is nevertheless a death, "una caja siempre,/ que es un bloque con límites que nadie, nadie estrecha." "Pájaros sin descenso" (pp. 429–430) shows human life which lives and dreams at the edge of the nonhuman sea. "No, no confundáis ya el mar, el mar inerte, con un corazón agitado." Even though man may choose to ignore it, the sea is there, eternal and waiting. In "Al Amor" (pp. 441–442) the sea has many faces, sweet and warm or cold and burning, threatening or promising. The sea is man's traditional enemy untroubled by man's weakness. It is "el duro, el terso, el transparente, amenazante mar que busca orillas, . . . y que rueda por los pies de unos seres humanos." This transitory, impetuous, furious, loving sea is nevertheless "Mortal enemigo que a cuerpo me venciste,/ para escapar triunfante a tu ignorada patria," an image repeated in "Mundo inhumano" (pp. 449–450) where there beats a sea where man does not exist. In "El amor iracundo" (pp. 455–456) the poet offers himself like an awaiting beach to the sea, but the latter is one which has escaped its calcareous bed, a proud abyss where fish rot, "roca pelada donde sueña la muerte." In "Nadie" (pp. 457–458) the sea is a love which man can never really possess,

> *la desesperación de tropezar siempre en el mar,*
> *de beber de esa lágrima, de esa tremenda lágrima*
> *en que un pie se humedece, pero que nunca acaricia.*

"Los Cielos" (pp. 459–460) repeats that love and life are to be found in
the sea,

> *En medio de los mares y en las altas esferas,*
> *bajo los cauces hondos de la mar poderosa,*
> *buscad la vida acaso como brillo inestable,*
> *oscuridad profunda para un único pecho.*

But even though the sea offers itself and its love, "Robusto el mar se eleva
sin alas por amarte," man is incapable of reciprocating. Man may return
to the primitive sea to be with nature and life, but his sterility and inca-
pacity for loving cause his own destruction.

Sombra del paraíso (1939–1943) contains some of Aleixandre's most
provocative sea imagery. Aleixandre lived in Málaga between the ages of
two and nine, and as Bousoño has pointed out, "El mar, azul y enorme, era
quizá lo que mas amaba: cielo, arena, espuma." [42] Dámaso Alonso feels
that Málaga represented for Aleixandre "la infancia azul del propio poeta
elevada a andaluz paraíso. El cansancio del hombre le hace mirar a su infancia remota como hacia un paraíso lejano. Y ya en el libro ambas simbo-
lizaciones corren entremezcladas." [43]

Aleixandre himself stresses the importance of the temporal in contemporary Spanish poetry. "De ahí la frecuencia con que aparece en sus obras
el tema del 'tiempo perdido,' de la edad humana, y con ella en primer
término, como representación de temporalidad, el tema de la infancia tras-
cendida y mitificada, ya se trata de una niñez que el poeta evoca para sim-
bolizar a su través el 'fugit irreparibile tempus.' " [44] Aleixandre views his
childhood world as Eden in mythopoeic fashion. "El poeta" (pp. 463–
464) reveals that he is no longer the victim of an impassioned sexuality
represented by the sea.

> *. . . es una playa*
> *donde la mar embiste con sus espumas rotas,*
> *dientes de amor que mordiendo los bordes de la tierra,*
> *braman dulce a los seres.*

Rather in the sea and in himself he sees a need for affection and identification with nature.

> *Un pecho robusto que reposa atravesado por el mar*
> *respira como la inmensa marea celeste*
> *y abre sus brazos yacentes y toca, acaricia*
> *los extremos límites de la tierra.*

This is not to say that the psychological interpretations of earlier works are no longer germane. On the contrary, the poet's return to his youth gives ample opportunity for continuing interpretations. "Destino trágico" (pp. 470–472) presents a silent but loved sea, as Aleixandre tries to define that sea. It is not foam, the wind, a bird, a stone, or a fleeting kiss. Under the ocean he sees a forest and birds in the trees. The waves are the wind which moves the branches as he listens to the song of the birds. The sea still recalls an animal, but it is now tranquil and "sus dientes blancos visibles en las fauces doradas,/ brillaban ahora en paz." But this peace is not what it appears, for he falls,

> *. . . espumante en los senos del agua;*
> *vi dos brazos largos surtir de la negra presencia*
> *y vi vuestra blancura, oí el último grito,*
> *cubierto rápidamente por los trinos alegres de los*
> *ruiseñores del fondo.*

The poem may symbolize union with the mother, her triumph as she summons one back to the earlier, simpler state of primitive or prenatal life, in a sense, non-life or death, and thus "destino trágico."

"Poderío de la noche" (pp. 481–483) represents the sea as the noise of life, "un pecho tendido a la postrera caricia del sol," which the poet searches for to rekindle his old indentification with nature and his former love relationship. The sea was youth and joy of life, but those days are far away. Although still beautiful and kindly, the sea now has another face, for the passing of time stills life and love, just as night puts an end to the day .

> *Otro mar muerto, bello,*
> *abajo acaba de asfixiarse. Unos labios*
> *inmensos cesaron de latir, y en sus bordes*
> *aun se ve deshacerse un aliento, una espuma.*

The loving sea nevertheless of "Primavera en la tierra" (pp. 501–503)
symbolizes his youth:

> *En ese mar alzado, gemidor, que dolía*
> *como una piedra toda de luz que a mí me amase,*
> *mojé mis pies, herí con mi cuerpo sus ondas,*
> *y dominé insinuando mi bulto afiladísimo,*
> *como un delfín que goza las espumas tendidas.*

Aleixandre, through the sea's generative force, kindles his memory and
thus evokes an emotion previously felt. He enjoyed and suffered his
youthful memories through the sea, and there he had the pleasure, youth,
love, and things of far more value than the empty reality in which he now
lives.

> *Gocé, sufrí, encendí los agoniosos mares,*
> *los abrasados mares,*
> *y sentí la pujanza de la vida cantando,*
> *ensalzado en el ápice del placer a los cielos.*

The sea in "Mar del paraíso" (pp. 516–518) represents the most positive
identification of the sea, as life, and the realization that one can manage
to live in spite of the worst that can happen to one; a person can con-
valesce from his impotence and manage life on new terms. The poet dreams
of happiness and love, "vasto mar sin cansancio,/ última expresión de un
amor que no acaba." In his youth, the first vision of life included the sea.
In maturity the poet still faces the sea with the hope of regaining his lost
desire, even though dimmed by adult experience.

> *Por eso hoy, mar,*
> *con el polvo de la tierra en mis hombros,*
> *impregnado todavía del efímero deseo apagado del hombre,*
> *heme aquí, luz eterna,*
> *vasto mar sin cansancio,*
> *rosa del mundo ardiente.*
> *Heme aquí frente a ti, mar, todavía . . .*

In "Destino de la carne" (pp. 562–563) [45] Aleixandre shows that man is born for a moment to be a spark of light, consumed with love, and then he becomes one with nothingness. The poet sees tired gray bundles of human bodies who retain at the shores of the sea the consciousness that life never really ends. The bodies continue to pile up neverthless in mountains of flesh, endlessly and apparently hopelessly, at the sea which is both the origin of life and also the end of life in an ever-recurring process.

> *Cuerpos humanos, rocas cansadas, grises bultos*
> *que a la orilla del mar conciencia siempre*
> *tenéis de que la vida no acaba, no, heredándose.*
>
> . . . .
>
> *¡Siempre carne del hombre, sin luz! Siempre rodados*
> *desde allá, de un océano sin origen que envía*
> *ondas, ondas, espumas, cuerpos cansados, bordes*
> *de un mar que no se acaba y que siempre jadea en sus orillas.*
>
> . . . .
>
> *Sobre ese mar de cuerpos que aquí vierten sin tregua, que*
> *aquí rompen*
> *redondamente y quedan mortales en las playas,*
>
> . . . .
> . . . . hacia el origen
> *último de la vida, al confín del océano eterno*
> *que humanos desparrama*
> *sus grises cuerpos. Hacia la luz, hacia esa escala ascendente*
> *de brillos*
> *que de un pecho benigno hacia una boca sube,*
> *hacia unos ojos grandes, totales que contemplan,*
> *hacia unas manos mudas, finitas, que aprisionan,*
> *donde cansados siempre, vitales, aún nacemos.*

The unconscious identification of the state after death with the state before birth is one of widespread occurrence, as is the conception that at death we pass away by the same road that we traveled when we entered into life at birth. Thus the sea may be especially identified with both birth and death.[46] Otto Rank stressed that the earliest place of abode, the "mother's body, where everything is given without even asking, is Paradise. To be born is to be cast out of the Garden of Eden. And the rest of life is taken up with efforts to replace this lost Paradise as best one can and by various means." [47]

In *Nacimiento último* (1927–1952), the far-off sea reflects a continuing desire for love and life as well as death in poems such as "La estampa antigua" (p. 597) and "Eternamente" (p. 598), where young girls wait for strong men "que arrebatadamente desemboquen con ellas/ en la mar ...," and "Junio del paraíso" (pp. 649–651) which considers the sea as an eternal life symbol which gives the world a constant rebirth.

> *El mar ... No es que naciese el mar. Intacto, eterno,*
> *el mar sólo era el mar. Cada mañana, estaba.*
> *Hijo del mar, el mundo nacía siempre arrojado*
> *nocturnamente de su brillante espuma.*

This sea brings passion with its "hirviente resplandor," as human beings love one another along the beaches. But the sea also promotes purity, as the graceful roe deer on whom no hand has yet set its love finds its fruition through the sea. For age does not destroy the contemplation of life and love, and through the sea one may find eternity and life, a death and love which are but fleeting moments in the eternal scheme of things, "y sentir el fuego sin edad de lo que nunca naciera,/ a cuya orilla vida y muerte son un beso, una espuma."

In *Historia del corazón* (1945–1953) the poet seeks his real human existence, unable to rediscover the certain constants of the past in fusion with love or nature. Nevertheless, the sea appears still in its psychological and spiritual aspects, as it recalls memories of his infancy, youth, and maturity.

The idea that love equals death is the leitmotiv of almost all Aleixandre's poetry and not exclusively an aspect of his sea imagery. Since the sea meant so much more, however, both consciously and unconsciously to Aleixandre, the man, and since the sea as the origin of life and a place of death have been universal constants in man's inheritance, it is through its symbolism that his ideas become clear. In addition to a repressed sexuality common to many poets, a neurotic and somewhat limited group of fantasies recur throughout. Aleixandre's youth in Málaga impressed the sea on his consciousness so that it became for him the symbol of that youth which he equated with innocence, happiness, and his mother. In psychoanalytic literature the sea and ocean in dreams often symbolize the mother. His desire to return and merge with that happiness and all it represents implies his death as an individual, as he is absorbed by a larger unit.[48] Intrauterine life, being premortal, except for the Church, is easily equated with postmortal life; so that life before birth equals, as a fantasy, life after death.[49] Aleixandre's sea, then, is pathognomic, as it reflects the anxieties and fantasies of his unconscious conflicts, which he artistically conveys in symbolic form.

[From *Hispania,* vol. L, no. 2, May, 1967]

3 | Novel

Some Aspects of
the Contemporary Novel
of Ecuador

FROM 1918 on, a series of disasters affected the cacao crops from which Ecuador's revenue was largely derived. Economic distress furthered political agitation and on July 9, 1925, army officers led a Socialist revolution which the young novelists visualized as a promise of a better future for their traditionalist country. Workers in the city, however, and on the large estates continued to exist under intolerable conditions without adequate food, shelter, or medical care, the political boss supported the rich landowners, and the government, in the name of greater production, encouraged the landowners to produce by whatever means.

The contrasts between wealth and poverty were black enough, but the authors, reacting violently to the extreme conservatism of their country, sought to improve upon the facts and offered revolution as an answer. Almost all the Ecuadorian novelists were Communists or Socialists seeking to do away with the quasi-feudal system of their country, and inspired by *La Reforma Universitaria*,[1] they issued manifestoes calling upon the students to take part in the revolution in order to realize a platform of social betterment.

The young novelists admired Manuel González Prada as an anti-Catholic defender of the Indian, saw a reflection of Ecuadorian exploitation in José Eustasio Rivera's work, and were impressed by Alcides Arguedas and Mariano Azuela for their treatment of the Indian and revolt. José Vasconcelos stimulated the new novelists when he visited Ecuador in 1929, and one of them, Alfredo Pareja y Diez Canseco, claimed: "Había ejercido en mi corazón de dieciocho años una influencia definitiva." [2] But of all Spanish American influences, that of José Carlos Mariátegui was the most important. His literary journal *Amauta,* started in 1926, which dealt also with the redemption of the Indian, influenced contemporary Ecuadorian reviews like *Savia* and *América,* and his *Siete ensayos de interpretación de la realidad peruana,* 1928, which insisted on the Indian's need for socialism, left a lasting impression on the Ecuadorian novelists who considered him, as Benjamín Carrión says: "Dentro de nuestra generación, el hombre apasionado y fuerte." [3]

The young Ecuadorian writers accepted ideas from heterogeneous sources, many of them from older literary periods. Frank Norris' *Octopus* contains scenes almost duplicated in the work of Adalberto Ortiz and Joaquín Gallegos Lara, and Upton Sinclair's *The Jungle* also proved influential. The Ecuadorians interpreted the works of Dostoevski, Andreyev, and Gorki in the light of their own needs, seeing in Dostoevski, for example, an enemy of capitalism and a defender of the poor. Andreyev's *Sashka Jigouleff,* from which Pedro Jorge Vera quotes and obtains the title for his *Los animales puros,* was read avidly in Ecuador and touched the young writers deeply. Gorki's *Mother,* about a woman who awakens and goes from dumb submission to Socialist idealism, reflects the symbolism loved so dearly by the Ecuadorians. Emile Zola and Henri Barbusse also excited interest, the former because his scenes of class struggle and pictures of sexual lusts appealed to the Ecuadorians who were attempting to bring about a rebirth of naturalism, the latter because of his exhortations to fight for a better society. Enrique Terán calls Barbusse, "el más grande de los escritores de la vanguardia revolucionaria mundial . . . vuelve a sentir y escuchar la sensibilidad que se conmovió antes; profundizando hoy la veneración que tuvimos para el maestro." [4]

The new polemical attitude first appeared in Ecuadorian poetry. The modernists, Arturo Borja, melancholy poet of delicate tones, and Medardo Angel Silva, a morbid copy of the pathetic and musical French symbolist, Albert Samain, gave way to a new school headed by Jorge Carrera Andrade and Gonzalo Escudero, who created poetry as an expression of their feelings about society. Ecuadorian anthologies published between 1920 and 1925 show selections from both schools, but it was evident that primitive and indigenous elements and social revolution were replacing the artificial worlds of Greek gods.

The literary journals followed the poets in a declaration of war against the old art. Many of these fugitive reviews had familiar titles: *Claridad,*

Germinal, and *La Vanguardia. América,* the best known review, was founded August 10, 1925, just one month after the Socialist revolution, and almost all the contemporary novelists were contributors. Other novelists directed publications: Demetrio Aguilera Malta, *Ideal;* Alfredo Pareja y Diez Canseco, *Voluntad;* and Gerardo Gallegos, *Savia.*

The contemporary Ecuadorian novel is the final historical development of an attempt to fuse local and European influences, or as Luis Alberto Sánchez phrased it: "Anhelo de crear literariamente en el ambiente feudal de la sierra ecuatoriana las mismas realidades que en los medios industriales de Europa." [5] All the Ecuadorian novels emphasize a definite European political ideology, although the novelists offer individual solutions for the problems they present. They insist that abnormality must be considered a vital and significant factor in the new novel, and all of them include sexual aberrations, multiplying instances and accumulating naturalistic detail. One sees a deliberate and consistent attempt to combine what the novelists termed Freudianism with Marxian struggle, and many of the novelists sought to link psychoanalysis to acts of depravity. The tendency to extremes grew because of the vehement opposition of the conservative elements in Ecuador, and the writers attacked the sexual taboos of the bourgeoisie as part of their revolt. The writers emphasize descriptions of the customs and habits of the different regions and races, marriages, wakes, fiestas, local superstitions, and natural setting in an attempt to give the essence of the local scene.

In addition to naturalism and regionalism, a symbolism often overdone and a violation of theme is forced upon the reader. Most often this takes the form of a final vision or moral into which is injected a false note of courage. The solutions presented are incompatible with the material, for the scenes are negative and pessimistic and the conclusions affirmative and optimistic. In Jorge Icaza's *Cholos,* 1938, Guagcho and his half brothers, symbolically united, go off into the sunrise to seek a new future for Ecuador; in *Huairapamushcas,* 1948, the cholos use their telluric symbol as a Jacob's ladder to a higher social class. Joaquín Gallegos Lara's masses in *Cruces sobre el agua,* 1946, float crosses on rafts over the graves of the victims of government brutality. In almost every novel there is a speech at the end about the hope for the future: Francisco in Icaza's *En las calles,* 1935, Serafín in his *Media vida deslumbrados,* 1942, Balón in Pareja y Diez Canseco's *Hechos y hazañas de Don Balón de Baba,* 1939, and many more. Autocthonous symbols are used in an odd combination with European ideology. In José de la Cuadra's *Los Sangurimas,* 1934, the *matapalo,* in Aguilera Malta's *Don Goyo,* 1933, the *manglar,* and in *Huairapamushcas,* the *yatunyura* trees are thus used. The *matapalo* digs its roots deep into Ecuadorian soil as does the Montuvian; the *manglar* should be preserved and possessed by the cholos and not by the foreigner; the *yatunyura* reflects the Indian soul. Although many of these symbols are without subtlety, the authors feel they must be included, and although they cannot avoid describing situations as they exist, futile and hopeless, they are aware of the need to discover some hope and are forced to invent the artificial solution.

The novelists' exposition is often short, choppy, and simple in an attempt to reflect the new sensibility. By stripping their prose of nonessentials they seek to maintain the shock status they desire through stylistic as well as thematic changes. "Vino de improviso. Como un aguacero en día de sol. Comía cerezas jugosas bajo un árbol. Estaba echado cerca de la orilla." [6] They cram a long series of episodes and incidents into the confines of one story to allow them freer range in discussing several problems, and in their novels they use several subplots or series of short stories about a central theme. Together with simplicity of prose they seek a complication of episodes which overloads the superstructure of the novels or splits them into several short stories. Aside from the ideological motives, the authors feel more at ease when attempting that form. As Mariano Latorre says: "En la técnica del cuento, los actuales escritores del Ecuador son artistas acabados. Les tocó nacer, sin duda, cuando la novela corta no tenía ya secretos en la historia literaria." [7]

The language of the contemporary novel is full of colloquial forms, many of which occur in the popular Spanish spoken everywhere. Along with the universal popular speech, constructions and words peculiarly Ecuadorian or derived from Quichua emerge to give the language a distinctive flavor. Some critics have objected to what they feel are stylistic and grammatical exaggerations. "Estos autores desconocen las leyes sintácticas del idioma, se burlan de la puntuación, y en general escriben un castellano tan abigarrado y extraño que sería un verdadero martirio para los académicos de la lengua si los académicos se preocuparan de la literatura hispanoamericana." [8] Upon examining these works carefully one finds some disregard of grammatical decency, but the authors seek to maintain unity between the form and concept of their work and use the vulgar and un-grammatical in specific situations to produce a colorful whole. The language used in description or narrative has almost none of the corrupted Spanish or Quichua vocabulary, which occur consistently only in dialogue.

Although the principal authors of mountain and coastal regions are united in a general political and social philosophy, each major author emphasizes certain aspects of the contemporary scene. José de la Cuadra concentrates on the deep passions of a primitive people, attacks the sexual taboos of the Ecuadorian middle class, and forms his plots in terms of the contemporary interpretations of abnormal psychology and psychoanalysis. Since his experience had been in criminal law, he portrayed rape, murder, and violence of all kinds and analyzed criminal psychology with uncanny subtlety. His irony and humor help relieve the drabness of the morbid and repellent in his descriptions of psycho-sexual phenomena. Demetrio Aguilera Malta's objective depiction of the sordid in Ecuadorian life does not prevent the inclusion of scenes of inhibited human grandeur, and he gives lyric expression to the elements which make up his native Guayaquil in an attempt to put the reprehensible in Ecuadorian society in its proper relationship to the whole pattern of Ecuadorian and foreign society. While Cuadra's emphasis lies primarily on primitive sex, Aguilera Malta has a few appalling pictures of promiscuity, but he emphasizes more the relationship of primitive man to nature. He thus retrogresses to a period in the development of the Latin American novel where the symbolic struggle against nature was the characteristic theme (*La Vorágine, Canaima,* and others). Pareja avoids the narrow selection of substantiating material used by some Ecuadorian novelists to imply that sexual perversion is a national pastime. He portrays national defects, but he does not accept them as the whole truth. In dealing with sorrow and disaster, the pathetic, disgusting, and grotesque, he also insists on the noble and heroic. Jorge Icaza, in considering the mass problem, has often created characters incidental to the novel, serving to illustrate the social aspects of the theme of the moment. Since most of his Indian characters merely repeat the same individual from novel to novel, Icaza finds himself in the odd position of objecting to the dis-individualizing actions of the exploiters while insisting on the anonymity of the Indian. His use of horror to awaken sympathy fails, for the pain seems to be inflicted on mechanical rather than human beings. If Icaza's Indians are the brutes he seems to think they are, little purpose would be served in having a social revolution to obtain their redemption. The hopeless situation described throughout most of his works seems more convincing than the facile solution in the last few pages of his novels. Icaza, in painting the blackest reality and the whitest hope, is the most unrealistic of all the writers. Enrique Gil Gilbert, in addition to his masterful physical descriptions, offers an ethical message, but he does not thrust his problem at the reader. In his devotion to a cause he indulges in a passionate search for a way to improve the fate of the Ecuadorian peasants. A warm and human writer, he seems to say that beneath the squalor and misery, the coarseness and cruelty of Ecuadorian life, there exists the beautiful and good.

The contemporary novelists have campaigned in the hope of redeeming the Indian, Negro, and other downtrodden elements from an old slavery. In their emphasis on the social problems they form a part of a general Ecuadorian movement in art, sculpture, and literature, and they have absorbed a conflicting mass of foreign influences in an attempt to bring a foreign culture into the Ecuadorian tradition, and especially to graft European socialism on that tradition. Each writer has a slightly different definition of socialism and uses the word to cover all sorts of the vague and indefinite schemes to improve or revolutionize society. In their hatred for the men who rule they too often show us the oppressors as completely evil and the oppressed as completely good. Within this stereotyped system, collectively, the characters live. Taken as a whole the school is fundamentally homogeneous in the description of cruder experiences as it has attempted to translate the Ecuadorian environment into the raw material for fiction. Published in very limited editions in Ecuador, where the cultural level of the masses is such that the demand for theoretical, socialistic literature is almost nonexistent, the novels have been more eagerly read in other countries. The novel as an instrument for remedying the social ills has proved somewhat ineffective, and the ideal of the common man capturing control of his own destiny and abolishing servitude and cruelty is remote from fulfillment in Ecuador, but the novelists have continued to oppose strenuously the forces disrupting Ecuador and in the process have published some excellent novels.

[From *Hispania,* vol. XXXVIII, no. 3, September, 1955]

Alfredo Pareja y Diez Canseco, Social Novelist

ALFREDO PAREJA Y DIEZ CANSECO (1908) belongs to the Socialist generation of twentieth-century Ecuador, a country of violent conflicts between conservative and liberal elements. Pareja lived through the hectic political turmoil of the twenties, his formative years, and soon reached the conclusion that Ecuador's salvation lay with the left-wing ideologies.

Pareja visited New York in 1930 and worked on the docks for a year. In Ecuador he held various positions: professor of history, professor of Spanish and Spanish American Literature at Colegio Vicente Rocafuerte, superintendent of Secondary Education, and Guayas Province deputy. In 1937, persecuted by Federico Páez, he was first jailed and then exiled to Chile where he worked for the Ercilla publishing house. From there he went to Bolivia before returning to Ecuador. In 1938, Aurelio Mosquera Narváez dismissed the Assembly of which Pareja was a member and jailed him for thirty days, and this experience later formed the basis of one of his novels. Pareja bought some drug stores but sold them in 1946 to travel around South America, especially in Argentina, Uruguay, and Paraguay, and in that same year he served as special UNRRA representative in Montevideo. In 1948, after a brief trip for UNRRA through Peru and Panama, he returned to Quito, where, with the exception of short trips to the United States and elsewhere, he has since lived.

Pareja has demonstrated what he would call ethical sympathies in his work, but he has insisted that he does not wish to use his art as an instrument of propaganda. He desired, he said, only to show the realities which cried for justice, as he denounced the corrupt and unjust. Pareja has denied being a left winger, but his best novels have a socialistic goal. Un-like most of the contemporary Ecuadorians, however, emotional considera-tions do not destroy his objectivity in some of his portrayals of the pro-letariat. He has traveled so much that he knows, not only his local scenes, but also how a good part of the rest of the world lives, and this cos-mopolitan background has allowed him to analyze various levels of society. One critic has said of him: "The Paris of 1920 has laid its hand upon him. It is far easier to picture Pareja in the company of Gertrude Stein or Guillaume Apollinaire than in that of Maxim Gorki or Sinclair Lewis." [1]

Pareja's early works contain surrealistic elements which detract from the vigor of his work. As Torres-Rioseco has said: "Alfredo Pareja y Diez Canseco es, hasta su novela *Río arriba*, 1931, un escritor superficial en quien el suprarealismo se limita todavía al florecimiento del disparate." [2] *La casa de los locos*, 1929, satirizes Ecuadorian politics. Indeed, Pareja attacked so many real people in his work that he was unable to publish it for some time. Adolfo Simmonds, in an overly kind critique, calls it: "Una producción de extraordinario mérito. Un corte orginial, un estilo nuevo, un lenguaje sobrio y, entre líneas todo el espíritu del siglo . . . La casa de los locos . . . manifestación espontánea de una mentalidad joven, hijo de su tiempo." [3] Simmonds saw the influence of Ehrenburg, Gide, and Proust in the work and felt it to be the first modern Ecuadorian novel. Among the many real people mentioned in his novel dedicated "a los niños i a los viejos de mi patria infantil," one finds José Vasconcelos, who for him "Había ejercido en mi corazón de dieciocho años una influencia definitiva. Cambió el rumbo de mi vida." [4] Pareja declares here that the left wing ideologies offer the only hope for the future against the dictator-ship and corrupt government, and his youthful diatribe in defense of jus-tice, while lacking in literary merit, has a freshness which is, at times, appealing.

La Señorita Ecuador, 1930, a mixture of fantasy and realism, exhibits little artistic preoccupation. Pareja wrote a "frivolous" novel that he felt everyone would enjoy, as he narrates the life story of Sarita Chacón, beauty contest winner. Even here, however, there appear serious themes, as he discusses the Montuvian in city and country and contrasts his agility and grace in his native environment with his torpor and stupidity in the city.

Pareja makes certain that Sara (proletariat) wins over Blanche (aristocracy), a superficial symbolism much used in the contemporary Ecuadorian novels. He speaks of the abuse of the poor by the rich and the attempts of the latter to maintain the former in poverty and ignorance. Pareja insists that if he were an aristocrat "me daría vergüenza de la pobreza espiritual que esta clase tiene en mi país, de su estupidez, de su suciedad podrida." [5] Finally Pareja attacks those who dare say there is no social problem in Ecuador and points out the sufferings of the *cholo,* the excesses of the *gamonales,* and the effects of a medieval feudal-barbaric system.

Río arriba, 1931, turns to Freud, sex, and abnormal psychology, as Pareja indulges in a long series of philosophical discussions. He relates the inconsequential loves of one student and the neurosis of another. The neurotic commits suicide when he learns that his mistress is in reality his sister, and his friend becomes crazy. The characters spend the major part of the book discussing Schopenhauer, Dante, and Freud. One must agree with Neftalí Agrella as he insists, "esta novela de Pareja y Diez Canseco es una obra truculenta en cuanto a novela y mal lograda en cuanto a obra." [6] Pareja discusses the problem of illegitimacy, but his theme, especially in the love between sister and brother, recalls *Aves sin nido,* and hardly resembles a contemporary problem. Pareja's idealism and love for justice triumph over his artistic talents here.

El muelle, 1933, is the first novel in which, without denying his social consciousness, he makes it an important element of rather than a substitute for his art. Pareja shows us the tragedy of the dock worker, his daily life, his hates, loves, and contacts with other human beings. Juan Hidrovo, cacao worker, married to María del Socorro, loses his position because of the economic crisis. He decides to go to New York to work on the docks and while there, he takes part in a union strike. During a police battle, his best friend, Claudio Barrera, is killed. Juan finally returns to Ecuador where María has been trying valiantly to earn her daily bread as a cook and laundress. Angel Mariño, a rich contractor for whom she works, seduces her, but she rejects him when she learns that Juan is returning, and loses her position. Juan is unable to find work and María becomes tubercular. Mariño receives the contract for a new Guayaquil dock and Juan works there until Mariño sees him there one day with María and fires him. The overall impression of *El Muelle* is not lacking in force and is at times a moving and complete picture of Ecuadorian life. The ending hints at the tragedy to follow and in that sense is simply another beginning of a degrading chapter of Ecuadorian life.

María is a brave and generous although somewhat ingenuous and ignorant woman. She is honorable but lacks the moral stamina to refuse Mariño. Juan, a strong but rather unintelligent worker, is full of the spirit of adventure, and like his creator travels over the oceans in search of a better fate. Pareja treats Jacinta and Florencia, the two old "beatas," and Mariño, the ugly and unscrupulous contractor, with irony rather than with indignation. Mariño is what one critic calls "un personaje continental que lo encontramos en el Ecuador como en Bolivia, en Chile como en el Perú." [7] Claudio Barrera, who dies in his struggle for justice, symbolizes freedom in Pareja's work.

Benjamín Carrión, who wrote the prologue of the first edition, considered *El Muelle* one of the greatest Latin American novels, and Antonio Montalvo has emphasized the obvious sociological and social aspects of the novel. "Alfredo Pareja y Diez Canseco, con agudo y hondo sentido sociologizante primero y social después—social por una corriente subterránea, silenciosa, pero fuertemente impregnada de amor y comprensión humanos, que corre en su novela se adentra en el alma misma de sus personajes—que él tipifica maestramente—pertenecientes a los humildes fondos de nuestra sociología." [8]

Pareja blends issues like unemployment, prison corruption, and political fraud into the action of the novel without apparent vehemence, but while he occupies himself with external forces, he implies effectively the character, the squalor, and the theme upon which he insists. Pareja compares workers in New York with those in Ecuador and describes the effects of imperialism on Ecuador's semi-colonial civilization. The U.S. Standard Iron Corporation, like its Ecuadorian counterpart, becomes the symbol of that oppression.

Antonio Montalvo saw in the work "the cosmic, crude, and brutal emotion of human sorrow." Other critics have seen it as a "gran novela americana que puede parangonarse a las mejores del continente," [9] "una de las mejores novelas de Hispanoamérica," [10] "una de las raras novelas específicamente americanas," [11] and "de las mejores novelas que se han escrito en esta América, novela sin novelistas." [12]

El muelle, then, was one of the first mature productions of the Ecuador-

ian novel. It has depth, pace, and meaning and coordinates scattered reflections about social injustices as it reveals the character of the Ecuadorian
half-breed. In spite of its photographic realism, it has a universal flavor
which carries it beyond the geographical limits of Ecuador. It shows us
the dignity, courage, and honesty of ordinary men and women who face
the fearful odds against them, human elements which are surely an important part of fiction.

Parts of *El muelle* are similar in tone to *The Harbor* of Ernest Poole,
published in 1915. Poole's novel, published in several editions, impressed
Pareja, interested in the sea, docks, and harbors. Like *El muelle, The Harbor*
emphasizes the struggle between capital and labor, and the strike scene
and battle against the police symbolized by the struggles of *The Harbor's*
Francesco Vasca and *El muelle's* Claudio Barrera parallel one another. "Se
lanzaron sobre él los policías . . . a garrotazos cayeron los primeros. Los que
fugaban por el claro que se abrió, sintieron un golpe en las piernas, un
crujido seco y se doblaron . . . y los tiros de pistola coreando, los gritos
enardecidos." [13] "Quickly their clubs rose and fell, and men dropped all
around them. But furious hundreds kept rushing in . . . came under the
clubs and went down with the rest, and still the mass poured over them
. . . after that the pistol shots. Then more in a sharp, steady crackle . . .
Only a few men here and there turned . . . to shout back frenzied, quiver-
ing oaths." [14]

La beldaca, 1935, reaffirmed Luis Alberto Sánchez' opinion that "Pareja
está llamado a ser uno de los primeros novelistas del continente, vale decir
del idioma." [15] In this history of a boat and the man whose life was inextricably bound to it, Pareja dwells at length on the countryside as a descriptive and colorful medium. The author evokes for us the fishermen, water
sellers, coconut peddlers, and all the life and color of the small villages
near Guayaquil.

The characters lack the stature of those of *El muelle.* Armando Vélez is
the standard villain who deceives Parrales, bribes the political boss, and
cheats the *cholos.* The one appealing character is Jesús, the man who was
never to achieve his simple heart's desire of owning his boat completely,
and whose simple love for his boat and the sea was to determine the course
of his entire life. Unlike Stevenson or Conrad, Pareja sees more than the
eternal struggle of man against the sea, and he has interwoven in symbolic
context the struggle of the poor and ignorant *cholos* against a system of

tyranny which affords them no redress. Pareja refrains from obtruding his personality but manages to convey his sense of horror to the reader. Ricardo Latcham, comparing it to the other Ecuadorian novels, feels that "no tiene la frase desarticulada, la gesticulación barroca, el desaliño excesivo." [16]

La Baldomera, 1938, deals with the famous strike of November 15, 1922. Pareja, fourteen years old at the time, was vividly impressed by the murder of his fellow citizens and writes with the warmth of the horrified eye witness, though the years have dulled the first hot flush of indignation. He subtitles his work "la tragedia del cholo sudamericano," and the symbol of that tragedy is Baldomera. She fights against the exploitation of human resources by a small privileged class and is for Pareja the explosive material beneath the rigid social strata of Ecuador which would offer hope for reform if properly educated and channeled. An ugly mulatto of the lowest social class, shrewd, uncouth, huge, and aggressive, she turns to crime as one of the have-nots of the world, but in spite of her drawbacks she is not a completely unsympathetic figure, and her warm heart and courage help atone for her occasional lack of moral scruples. Her qualities of humanity and sentiment reveal themselves as she sacrifices herself for her people and her son, and she seeks her salvation, at times unknowingly, but always without fear. The other characters, Lamparita, famous cuatrero who rides Escorpión, the horse no one else can ride; Polibio, who flees the city for the country; Inocente, the son who betrays his own people and his mother, but who, too, finally revolts against injustice; and Honorio Paredes, the factory boss, are the more typical symbols of the contemporary Ecuadorian novel. More interesting is the Guayaquil full of surviving traditions, the savor of the vernacular, the authentic color of the life of his native city. In a colorful local background he gives his reader a whole world of Ecuadorianisms.

The standard introduction of Acevedo, the labor agitator who suggests revolution as a solution for ills, is artificial, and upon reading the novel one wonders why Pareja introduced him, since the impression which he sought to convey, that such a solution is inevitable, arises from the situations themselves. La Baldomera, in spite of its creation of a magnetic character, fits all too closely the pattern of proletarian novels described by Carl Van Doren: "The action was likely to come to its head in a strike, and it took for granted an essential class conflict between the owners and the landless propertyless workers. The heroes, in a time of unprecedented unemployment, were men desperately looking for work or trying to keep their

jobs. The strongest virtue celebrated in the novels was proletarian solidarity." [17]

The usual catalogue of ills appears. Lamparita's old sweetheart, Can-
delaria, finds that prostitution is all a country girl can expect in Guayaquil.
The Ecuadorian poor starve while the rich throw food into the river to increase product demand. Pareja's *cholos* may not seem as sordid as those in
Jorge Icaza's novels, but they are all slaves in the same situation, hated by
the white, despising themselves, and wanting a small bit of the world's
goodness which they feel they have earned. The evils pictured conform
fundamentally to characteristic acts of human beings silhouetted against
the background of the author's ideals. Richard Latcham, sensing in *La Baldomera* a veritable explosion of life, labels it "el más compacto y anatómico
. . . el más vertebrado y consciente de su instrumento creador . . . lleno de
hombres desaforados y grandes hembras de pasión." [18] Powerful and intense at times, *La Baldomera* lacks a profundity of concept, although one
must agree with Jorge Díez who sees it as "el clamor, el grito de una clase
cuya vida es un permanente anochecer en medio día." [19]

Hechos y hazañas de don Balón de Baba, 1939, failed to achieve the
success of his previous works. Composed under uncomfortable conditions
and in haste to meet an advanced deadline, it portrays a man with ideals,
beliefs, and longings. Balón overindulges for the purposes of fiction in
his passionate purpose of reshaping the new Ecuadorian world, but he
refuses to follow mechanically a political imperative.

Balón is mad only in his dream of remaking the world. Duped by friends,
he is at times a ludicrous figure, but his sincere love for the common man
and his desire for social change ennoble him. His whole life was full of
energy and agitation in his desire to "hacer bien." Inocente, the Ecuadorian Sancho full of proverbs and maxims, is at times as mad as his master.
Bound to the latter by his devotion, he found himself unable to busy himself only with the practical necessities of life, and only through helping
Balón does he find himself. The dreamer and the materialist fuse, and in
this fusion is one hope for the future.

Pareja again portrays the injustices of his land, and his tirades against
the aristocrats are more vigorous than ever. Illiterate and ignorant workers toil from morning till night, must buy goods at company stores, and are
the victims of a vicious slave system as their debts are inherited by their
children and grandchildren. Balón cries out: "Yo veo a gente morirse de

hambre, y he visto a padres que no tienen con que enterrar a los hijos que murieron por falta de alimentos . . . Ah! Inocente, Inocente, qué crueles son los capitalistas. ¡Y todavía creen que haciendo caridades se remedia todo!" [20]

Pareja through Balón insists that an outsider, unless he were ignorant or perverse, would realize that only a social revolution can save Ecuador, and waxing more enthusiastic over a cause to which he has since cooled somewhat, claims: "Bien sé que soy idealista, un ideólogo, pero también soy un realista y la humanidad me necesita. El socialismo revolucionario avanzadista tiene que triunfar en el mundo entero." [21]

His next novel, *Hombres sin tiempo*, 1941, originally called *Penal García Moreno*, stemmed from his imprisonment in that "den of sordid and icy terror." Ostensibly it was written in praise of Oleas Zambrano, one of the few enlightened prison directors in Ecuador. Angel F. Rojas fails to see any social orientation in the novel. "Llama la atención que, no obstante ser una obra concebida en la prisión y en plena tormenta política, busque desarrollarse en un terreno tan alejado de ella . . . No hay la transcendencia social que el relato ecuatoriano contemporáneo busca tener en *Hombres sin tiempo*." [22] Yet Pareja dedicates the book as a symbol of his faith in the young generation of Ecuador who, "hagan de este dolor geográfico una Patria con sentido nacional y grande, con voz y sangre de indios y de cholos arrancando de nuestra atormentada vida ecuatoriana tanto odio, tanta desvergüenza, tanta hojarasca de falsa norma convencional." [23] Dishonest lawyers sell out to the man with money. Judges have separate standards of justice for rich and poor. The tortures in jail include hanging by the thumbs, electric shocks, and sadistic beatings.

Nicolás Ramírez, a teacher imprisoned for a sexual attack and murder, is the focal point around which the story revolves. In jail he meets a series of characters whose life stories we hear, among them that of a woman imprisoned for killing her false lover. She is released before he is, and failing to find an honest position, becomes a prostitute. When freedom comes to Ramírez, he seeks out Margarita only to discover that both of them, without realizing it, have grown old and their life no longer has a purpose. The minor characters are interesting from a social point of view. Gabriel murders both for pleasure and revenge against the society which frees the guilty and convicts the innocent. He resents the society that could have helped him when he was young but refused to do so. Jaramillo, the Negro, hides his inward inferiority feelings by an outward show of violence. Sebastián Casal, silent on other subjects, talks fluently only about man's exploitation of man.

In structure this novel is a series of stories loosely connected by a principal theme. Technical experimentation in the art of counterpoint makes for a certain ambiguity of content. Pareja delves into the subconscious writhings of his characters, and it is difficult at times to follow the series of tales within tales. Narrated in the first person as a diary of an ex-convict, in spite of political innuendos, it concentrates also on the spiritual needs and fears of its characters and reflects the growing maturity of the Ecuadorian novelist.

Las tres ratas, 1944, was to be his last published novel for many years, as he turned to other kinds of writing. Prepared for the Farrar and Rinehart contest, the novel finished just below Gil Gilbert's *Nuestro Pan,* which later finished second to *El mundo es ancho y ajeno* of Ciro Alegría. The committee said of the novel in 1942, when it was submitted: "que se trataba de una novela de acabada estructura en el género, notable por el verismo de sus personajes y la sostenida emoción que circula a través de sus páginas." [24] Structurally it is probably the best of his works though it lacks the force of *La Baldomera* or *El muelle.* It traces admirably the rise and fall of the liberal family and the liberal movement in Ecuador and investigates once more the sufferings and doubts of man, but the author abandons direct denunciation of the social structure in order to tell a good story. Yet, though he does not attempt to modify the state structure, Pareja demonstrates once more the thesis that the Ecuadorian novel succeeds through sincerity, violent realism, and social sense, and in the picture of the struggles of the three "rats," he of necessity has had to show the good and bad of their society.

The story concerns the adventures of three sisters, Carmelina, Eugenia, and Luisa, who go to Guayaquil where Eugenia steals some jewels from a family friend who had robbed them of their inheritance. Shamed because of her subsequent imprisonment, she takes poison, is saved by a young doctor Ramírez, and finally becomes the mistress of Carlos Alvarez who later abandons her. Eugenia returns to a former lover and shoots him when he abandons her. Carlos learns of the incident and forces her to help him in some smuggling activities, but she denounces him and he is imprisoned. Ramírez asks her to marry him but she refuses and to support her future child by her first lover, eventually returns to the country to become the mistress of an hacendado. Luisa, converted to the Socialist viewpoint of her boyfriend, Francisco, marries him and they go off to the country to work for the party. Carmelina, alone and disillusioned, decides to live with Doña Tarjella, the dress shop owner for whom all the girls had worked.

Alejandro Carrión finds the characters "personajes de carne y hueso" and continues: "Y todos los días en nuestra vida hemos encontrado a alguna de las tres, o a las tres juntas, y hemos participado en fugaces capítulos de sus picardías, sus ilusiones humildes, sus maldades, sus accesos de infinita bondad." [25] Pareja adds to his gallery of excellent women characters in the person of Eugenia. She stole to revenge herself on society, but in the final analysis is willing to sacrifice herself in order to secure a good future for her child. Carmelina, the oldest sister, sees youth escaping her, and she longs for a home of her own. Conservative and proper, she is shocked at and resentful of Eugenia, whom she feels has stolen the only man who offered her a chance for happiness. Embittered by the lack of love she needed, she finally dedicated herself to religion in irate frustration. The third sister is little more than a shadow and serves only as a foil for the other two and to bring Francisco, the Socialist, into the plot. Shocked by the terrible punishments inflicted on hacienda Indians, he believes that the only hope for Ecuador lies in left wing movements and not with the nineteenth century liberals who continue to be landowners and Indian beaters. His status as a friend of the poor is not completely convincing, and Pareja strains too much at idealizing him. Pareja cannot refrain from attacking the privileges which the law allows those with money and speaks of "el indio y el montuvio . . . bestias productoras, sin capacidad de consumo. Aun heredan las deudas y se venden como objetos." [26]

The novel, because of its colorful scenes, smugglers, sex, and fighting, was well adapted for the films and was made into an Argentinian movie. Among the contemporary Ecuadorian novels, only *El cojo Navarrete* of Enrique Terán has more color.

Pareja gave up writing fiction for a time, aside from sporadic stories such as *Los Gorgojos* (*Letras del Ecuador*, no. 100, 1954), but he worked intermittently on a long novel tentatively called *Don Errante*, the struggles, lives, and loves of the Ecuadorian people from 1925 to the present. This finally was published in 1956 as *La Advertencia*, the first novel in a series to be called *Los Nuevos Años*. Pareja hoped that the second volume of the

cycle, *El aire y los recuerdos,* would appear sometime in 1957. "Espero
que la segunda, ya terminada, aparecerá a fines de 1956 o a mediados de
1957." [27]

In the preface to *La Advertencia* Pareja says, "Espero ser justo con la
época y los hombres de mi generación." [28] He reveals a change in emphasis and has attempted an interesting fusion of the historical and the imaginary, both in plot and characters, as the real and imaginary walk
hand in hand. Social emphasis here is indirect but all pervasive nevertheless, as it would be in any work which attempted to portray the human
emotions and political events of the late 1920s. Pareja uses a series of
plots within plots which find meaning in the character of Clara, the
woman who could not find or understand herself. Pablo finds his manhood. Luis Salgado discovers death. A host of characters are in constant
movement throughout the book: Comandante Canelos and his vain dreams
of personal glory, Salgado, the painter, who could never possess completely
the thing he most wanted, and Teresa and her sisters in whose house one
could dance and discuss social revolution. The wealthy Froilán no longer
represents the completely stereotyped rich business man, for though he is
vain and selfish, he offers an occasional glimpse of human feeling. The
others, the little people, the impotent ones, the frustrated poets, the would-
be revolutionaries, the good and simple folk, and the petty and mean ones,
make up the background with which Pareja unites his historical analysis.
No longer does Pareja preach his message, but there is much discussion of
the meaning of Ecuadorian socialism. As Ordóñez says: "Nuestro socialismo no es romántico: es científico y aspira a la fraternidad universal. No
nos gustaría defender una patria de especuladores y capitalistas que solo
piensan en salvar sus riquezas. A ellos sí que no les importa la Patria, por
que no tienen otra que la del dinero." [29] Pareja reiterates the thesis of his
generation in Ordóñez' summation. "Así también a partir de 1920, y avanzada ya la conquista ideológica liberal, su acción, muchas veces a su pesar,
por los hombres más que por las ideas, deja libre paso a las ideas socialistas,
de las que la revolución juliana es una expresión imperfecta, débil y sin
fundamentos prácticos o científicos, pero de todos modos clarificadora.
Estos son los nuevos años, compañeros. A nosotros nos toca vivirlos. . . .
Hemos de sufrir, ésa es nuestra tarea, aunque nuestra generación no alcance
la victoria. Es la misión de nuestra época. Nuestra tristeza y nuestra
algería." [30]

All of the elements of Pareja's past works are here: sex, both idealized and brutal (Berta and Canelos, Ramiro and Lola, Lucia and Héctor); socialism in its various ramifications (Ordónez, Jarrín, Ruiz). Pareja uses these elements because they belong to the historical and cultural framework he is discussing, and he lets the novel flow naturally as the character and the theme lead him. He does not attempt to twist the background to fit any preconceived notions of a group or theory, and in this first volume of the story of the birth of a nation, Pareja has shown that he is a mature novelist.

Aside from his early unpublished poetry, Pareja dedicated himself briefly to the Montuvian in *El Entenao, cantar montuvio* and wrote a series of essays: *La dialéctica en el arte, El sentido de la pintura, Actualidad y presencia de la Montaña Mágica, Consideraciones sobre el hecho literario,* and *Defensa del trópico.* In April of 1956 the Casa de la Cultura Ecuatoriana published a further essay on *Thomas Mann y el Nuevo Humanismo.* His three major nonfictional works are *La hoguera bárbara, Historia del Ecuador,* and a biography, *Vida y leyenda de Miguel de Santiago.*

Eloy Alfaro, according to Pareja, one of the truly great men of Ecuador, might have succeeded in putting out the constant flame of civil war in which Ecuador indulged, "la hoguera bárbara." He strove to create a modern country and improve the lot of the Indian and the other unfortunates of his country, for he was the only Ecuadorian president with a social conscience.

In 1951 Pareja published *Vida y Leyenda de Miguel de Santiago,* which deals with the youth, maturity, and death of the great seventeenth century painter. The first of the so-called Quito School, Santiago had fascinated Pareja who wanted to do more than give "el solo recuento de los hechos exteriores y cuotidianos." [31] Pareja treats of the legends about and the interpretation and meaning of his personality and his art.

In his history of Ecuador, published in four volumes in 1955, Pareja admits to a Spanish background and tries to adapt a position which emphasizes the injustices but also credits the positive virtues of the conquest. The two most interesting volumes are those dealing with colonial administration and politics and what the author terms the "luchas sociales desde 1925 hasta 1944." "Todas las luchas populares de los últimos tiempos se han caracterizado por su profundo contenido social, por un anhelo ya incontenible de pan, de tierra, de libertad." [32] The Indians of his country were striving for national integration in a trial and error manner, and Ecuadorian progress was further hindered by the geographical problem, the rivalry and economic clash between the burgeois coastal region which controls the export trade and the highland region in which huge estates still enslave the Indians. Though nonfiction, his history is full of poetic language, "páramos hinchados de vientos, peñas bruscas, gargantas profundas, la nieve trepada dulcemente en los montes, etc."

Pareja has undergone shifts in his position, but he has been associated always with the left wing in Ecuadorian literature. In *La dialéctica en el arte,* 1933, he insisted that art and social conflict could not be separated in Ecuador and to deny one was to deny the other. In *Defensa del trópico,* one of his early essays, he pointed out: "Our voice does not want golden garments to hide its poverty. Naked, our voice seeks the truth, not pretty things. Our blood is the blood of free men and courses through our veins with a velocity impelled by violent colors." [33] In *Consideraciones sobre el hecho literario,* 1948, he does not repent the improvisations of the early writing, but he traces new paths for the development of the Ecuadorian novel and comments on the presentation of human characters and the insistence on the anonymous hero by some of the novelists as the greatest weakness of the early Ecuadorian novel.

Of his early work one might say that a revolutionary literature by its very nature deals with wretchedness and must be full of bitterness and brutality. Pareja expressed his horror at the cruelty of man towards man, but he also affirmed the power of love as a redeeming force. His very belief in the righteousness of his cause imbues his work with a force which overcomes the occasional lack of aesthetic niceties.

Many Ecuadorian writers give the impression by a vicious selection of substantiating material that sexual perversion is a national pastime. Pareja recognizes and portrays national defects, but he does not accept these as the whole truth. He deals with sorrow and disaster, with the pathetic, disgusting, and mean, but he also deals with the noble and heroic. Like Demetrio Aguilera Malta, Pareja makes use of short and choppy sentences, but he avoids the brutal and filthy language of certain members of the contemporary Ecuadorian group. His works have color and his dialogue has an almost dramatic intensity. He has used in his writing all the twentieth-century techniques: the flashback, the stream-of-consciousness, the dialogue carrying action forward, and the interior monologue. In his last works he has tried to construct his novels according to a preconceived overall plan before setting down a single word, but however carefully he may diagram his novels, one can still see that he is not interested in making sacrifices to form. Like Pío Baroja he finds in the "novela cerrada" a frame too small for the bitter reality of the Ecuadorian canvas. Life then is a jungle where ideals, freedom, and love are waiting to be set free. Underneath all of the many struggles in his works we see, in the final analysis, the struggle against evil by the lonely and the weak, and we know where the author stands. Benjamin Carrión has labeled him "El Buscador incansable de caminos," [34] and implies that Pareja has finally found himself, but to the reader of his total work, Pareja stands forth, not as a man who found himself, but as one who was never really lost.

[From *Hispania,* vol. XLII, no. 2, May, 1959]

Animal Symbolism in the Fiction of Ramón Sender

ANIMALS and their relationships to man have preoccupied human beings since the beginning of time. Some ancient peoples felt animals to be their brothers in a physiological sense; others believed in metempsychosis. Aesop and Aristotle used animals to reflect human character and to portray individuals or groups. Actual or imagined resemblances between men and animals were used in the Greek drama and epic, in the works of Virgil, Shakespeare, the Bible, and in medieval moralizing and allegorical treatises. In France and elsewhere in the sixteenth and seventeenth centuries, although much of the religious significance of the medieval treatment had been lost, animal life and its importance concerned a great number of writers and philosophers, including Montaigne, Charon, and Descartes, and acrimonious debate ensued about the human attributes or defects of animals in their relationships to men. Animal metaphor and imagery have been used throughout literature for derogatory, satirical, or sympathetic purposes, to make characterization more vivid, and to pose generalizations about human beings.

Although Ramón Sender makes great use of animal imagery and has hundreds of metaphors and similes involving animals, only broader animal-human relationships will be treated here.[1] In many of his novels, in addition to these relationships, an animal serves as a central theme or leitmotiv for the work. In *Imán* the recurring symbol is the crow. "Las manadas de cuervos . . . denuncian los lugares donde fue aniquilado el convoy," [2] "brincan tomando aire . . . olor de carne descompuesta" (p. 117), "los graznidos de los cuervos son la expresión . . . de la llanura. . . . Más cuervos arriba" (p. 132), "los cuervos hartos—siempre los cuervos" (p. 171),

"Los cuervos hallarían en sus entrañas más condumio . . ." (p. 268),
"Cuervos, lo mismo que allá" (p. 266). When Viance returns home, his
village has disappeared along with the graves of his parents, but overhead
he sees the same crows.

In *Siete domingos rojos* the principal totem figure is a nameless rooster
owned by the young girl, Star. For her the rooster symbolizes loyalty,
friendship, and love, although he is "un gallo provocador al que temían
los perros y los niños de la calle, porque . . . se lanzaba lo mismo sobre las
piernas desnudas de los chicos que sobre los hocicos de los perros." [3] The
rooster accompanies Star everywhere and is "para ella . . . antes que todo"
(p. 256). During a labor strike Star worries largely about feeding her
rooster. After her father's death the rooster is her one consolation, and she
takes her meals with him and talks to him constantly. The rooster is finally
killed by a passing train, but in death, as in life, he is inextricably involved
with the fate of the characters (pp. 141, 446).

In *Los cinco libros de Ariadna* bees and an owl are used with symbolic
overtones and for identification of the protagonist. The owl appears in the
first chapter and throughout the work. "Desde la cornisa ha levantado el
vuelo un buho. Vuela pesadamente bajo la bóveda. . . . El fru-fru de las alas
. . . nos da una sensación de bienestar" (pp. 34-35). "Cada uno de los
hombres . . . recuerda que la lechuza era el ave de los presagios en tiempos
de los griegos . . . y en la Edad Media española" (p. 34). At various times
the owl breaks the silence of the assembly. "Hay otro largo silencio durante
el cual se oye al buho dar las dos notas de su canto: guh, guh" (p. 37).
"El buho . . . canta tres veces . . ." (p. 40). "El buho vuelve a cruzar la
sala dejando un rumor . . ." (p. 46). The owl makes a greater and greater
effort to reach the heights. At one point he becomes frightened and strives
to fly to "una moldura más alta, en el domo" (p. 144). He reappears at
significant moments. "Ha vuelto a parecer el buho . . . Recuerdo que de
chicos nos decían que los buhos bebían el aceite de las lámparas. Este buho
vuelve a decir en el silencio de la asamblea: guh, guh" (p. 508). Finally
the owl comes to rest on the arms of a cross and "esta vez guarda silencio"
(p. 514). At times he seems to represent the absurdity of human folly
striving for an ideal in imperfection of attainment, and his "guh, guh"
reflects the lack of communication among human beings.[4]

The bees almost cost Ariadna her life, as she tells Javier, "Tus notas sobre las abejas casi me costaron la vida. . . . Nadie podía creer que fueron inocentes" (p. 270). There are long discussions of bees, their habits, number systems, and life spans. Javier feels that "un enjambre no es una multitud de pequeños seres independientes sino un solo ser con células diseminadas alrededor pero ligadas a una sola voluntad y una sola idea. Es como si nuestras células humanas echaran de pronto a volar pero conservaran . . . la misma relación con nosotros que tenían antes" (p. 257). He later postulates an even closer human relationship. "Cada enjambre ha sido antes un ser humano. En una antigüedad de algunos millones de años el hombre aprendió a usar fuerzas desintegradoras de las cuales fue víctima" (p. 460). He insists that bees have a language and that they "pueden decir muchas cosas más que nosotros" (p. 209). Ariadna rejects his claim that entomologists had already deciphered bee messages, but she accepts the probability of bee communication. For a time Javier carries a bee in a tiny cage (p. 460), helps paint bee wings, and in general relates to bees throughout the novel.[5]

The bear and the stork in *El lugar del hombre* [6] and the rats in *El rey y la reina* [7] serve similar roles, while in *El verdugo afable,* although Ramiro's dream states are peopled with various animal visions including Gibraltar monkeys, a white rat, and sleeping bats, it is the fictitious monster, Tarascio, "un dragón mitad tortuga mitad lagarto, que habla como las personas . . .," [8] who reflects the hidden nature of man as it reappears throughout the novel.

In general, aside from thematic implications, Sender uses animals to indicate a variety of human relationships, both direct and indirect, among which are death, danger, sex, hunger, politics, religion, and friendship. He stresses constantly the totem or identification aspects of animals and humans, gives us information about customs involving animals, has curious interludes and animal descriptions, and peoples his work with a great variety of animal metaphor.

Animals play a prominent part in human death and danger. As Viance falls beside a dead horse which has been partially devoured by crows and jackals and takes refuge inside the horse's body to escape death himself, he reflects: "Nosotros, como los mulos, sólo tenemos deberes cívicos, no derechos: el deber cívico de morir" (*Imán,* p. 150). Mules bear a cargo of dead on their backs. "Pasan los mulos cabeceando, indiferentes, con su carga fresca" (p. 15). On the field of battle a hog flees "gruñendo con medio antebrazo humano en la boca" (p. 171). The Moors fatten the pigs on human flesh and sell them afterwards to the army.

In *Orden público,* which concerns the death of liberty as well as the death of prisoners, birds, both live and dead, presage danger or death. "El tedio de la cárcel era negro, pesado, agorero. Tedio de las alas del buho, en las noches que presagian tormenta." [9] In *El lugar del hombre* Pepe is intrigued by Ana Launer, the village witch, and decides to wait for her at midnight. An owl in the church tower hoots, a frog croaks, and finally the boy, frozen with terror, hears someone. It turns out to be "una cabeza de mulo, negra, de grandes ojos inmóviles" (p. 22). Pepe mounts the mule and gallops through the night until he falls off and fractures his arm.

Saila, in *Proverbio de la muerte,* thinks of a ghostly boat with a dead crew "en cuya cubierta había siempre pájaros carniceros que iban devorando los cadáveres." [10] As he thinks on life and death, he sees in the desert "un cadáver con la cabeza rota, con un ojo vacío porque se lo acababa de llevar un cuervo en el pico" (p. 128).

Fau (*Siete domingos rojos,* p. 253), in death, is accompanied by a lizard. "Una lagartija ha quedado aprisionada bajo su bota y asoma el hocico asfixiándose. Los tres compañeros se acercan más. Disparan cuatro, seis, diez veces . . . el monstruo da con la nariz en el suelo. . . . La lagartija, con el rabo partido, anda trabajosamente por el pantalón de Fau."

Rómulo (*El rey y la reina,* p. 223), in playing with the puppets, reenacts the scene which led to the captain's death. The latter had not believed that planes had dropped flares to attack his headquarters, but rather that somebody had turned on the tower reflector. One puppet says that he saw "luz de plata en el hocico de una rata," and the other that "yo la vi de oro en los cuernos de un toro."

In *El verdugo afable,* Lucía, who assumes responsibility for her brother-in-law's death, recalls the "hija moscarda" which had intrigued her since her youth. To her it suggested a woman "con patas de moscardón, con un pico elástico que se contraía o se alargaba para chupar el néctar de las flores" (p. 368). In her mind she relates her betrayal to the song about the "hija moscarda." Supposedly after thirteen executions the executioner's instruments come alive and meow like a cat.

In *Los cinco libros de Ariadna,* dead prisoners are placed on top of the freight cars. Their blood drips through the cracks and "antes del amanecer llevaba el tren una escolta de cuervos y buitres carniceros en el aire" (p. 205). Often the relationship between animals and human death is an indirect one. One of the prisoners, Casilda, was to be shot the next day. "Estuvo veinticuatro horas en capilla—y el hombre tuvo tiempo para todo. Me decía que quitó un gato muerto . . . y quitó también algunas suciedades de perros" (p. 243).

In *Réquiem por un campesino español,* a moving work of human wickedness, man's attempts at dignity and his betrayal, the three rich men who come to the requiem mass chase Paco's unsaddled mule which is running loose through the church, as he had been running wild and uncared for since Paco's death. "Anda como siempre, suelto por el pueblo . . . era una alusión constante a Paco y al recuerdo de su desdicha." [11] Just as the colt is trapped "un saltamontes atrapado entre las ramitas de un arbusto trataba de escapar" (p. 50). When the city bullies kill six peasants, their bodies are guarded by the Duke's men to keep the dogs from licking up their blood. Jerónima with her guilty conscience feels she deserves to be killed "a pedradas, como a una culebra" (p. 120).

Among the many incidents in *Mexicayotl,* Tototl causes Teicu's death by replacing her tame jaguar with a man-eating one; an old buzzard hovers over a corpse in great doubt as to his demise but finally devours him; and a rabbit crosses the street, which is "un augurio terrible." [12] Mister Witt, in *Mister Witt en el cantón,* takes a horse ride and disturbs a bird in the bush as he awaits word of Froilán's possible pardon. He suspects the latter of being his wife's lover and holds back the horse enough to cause Froilán's death. "Bastaba con que yo no hubiera tirado de las riendas al caballo." [13]

In *Epitalamio del prieto Trinidad,* the festivities occurring after Trinidad's death parallel primitive animal totem feasts.[14] The convicts put Trinidad's corpse on the chair, holding him from behind to make him preside. While el Careto discourses at length about the gelded father and the wolf, the others shout "murió el lobo, murió" (*Epitalamio,* p. 137). "The dancing and singing are given the slain enemy. At specified solemn occasions, like religious ceremonies, the skins of certain animals were donned" (*The Basic Writings,* p. 885). One of the convicts walks around in the skin of Trinidad, obviously wishing to take the place of the father, Trinidad, and find Niña Lucha, the female. According to Freud in *Totem and Taboo,* originally there were men who lived in small bands dominated by a single father image who had access to all the women and power over the men. The jealous sons finally united to devour the father, their enemy and yet their ideal, but they were unable to take over his heritage because they stood in each other's way. An almost identical situation prevails in the death in *Epitalamio*.

Fire and carrion birds, both classic death symbols, play a part in this novel. El Careto discovers Trinidad's remains in the forests where dogs and especially birds are gnawing on the body. The thought comes to el Careto's mind that the sire of the clan is being eaten. "Al macho, al padre del clan, al lobo padre fornicador, se lo comían" (p. 218). Darío discovers the body and forces Careto to bury it, while on the tree trunks the "pájaros de alas desnudas, impacientes . . . parecían más que pájaros, frutos podridos . . ." (p. 224). The birds serve as a death omen, and throughout the novel the night bird sings its ominous song. For el Seisdedos "alguno lleva ya el zopilote detrás" (p. 80), and he is constantly talking about the buzzard which may be after them.[15]

The death involved is not always that of the human. It may be the animal that suffers or is in danger. "Curro escupió de medio lado y atrapó con la saliva una mosca" (*Orden público*, p. 75); "los codornices, para los sacrificios a Paina, los quetzales por su carácter sagrado, los loros para proveer de plumas amarillas a la nobleza" (*Mexicayotl*, p. 14). Elsewhere in the same collection, a bird twice as large as Xocoyotl carries her to the priest of Culua who kills the bird to keep the girl. An old puma discusses the attributes of various animals. A young puma can't believe that man, the weakest animal of all, is dangerous, until he chases one and is shot. El Buen Leñador, on dying, descends into the water to sleep the long sleep, and watches Picos de Pato trap and eat the beautiful butterfly fish. In *Crónica del alba*[16] Pepe sacrifices a pigeon and feeds it to the dog. In *The Sphere* Saila recalls how Christel used to sit under the bridge on a rock where they used to "kill new-born pups with a sharp blow against a corner" (p. 239). In *El rey y la reina* Elena finally manages to kill the giant rat, la Pascuala. In *El verdugo afable* Ramiro brings Paquita, the prostitute, to live with him in his native village. During a charivari Ramiro fires at the villagers, but later he finds only a dead dog on the porch. In *Emén Hetán*[17] participants buy roosters for their sacrifices. They sacrifice, also, dozens of bats, three or four owls, and toads, dressed in black and scarlet. Paco's cat in *Réquiem por un campesino español* is chased away by his dog. Paco's father informs him that a predatory animal, probably an owl, has killed it, for owls resent other animals who can see in the dark. Paco had always been indignant since then "contra los buhos que mataban por la noche a los gatos extraviados" (p. 99).

Another typical animal human relationship concerns sex and love. Ramiro makes love to the two novices, as a nightingale sings outside in the small cemetery. Ramiro realizes that the bird is love and "se reconocía enamorado lo mismo de la una que de la otra" (*El verdugo afable,* p. 87). He also loves the circus girl who acted the part of a mermaid, and they exchange "largos besos de pez" (p. 110). Later Ramiro recalls his past loves and reflects that all he has left is "el ruiseñor del convento y el sabor de los besos de pez unido al de la carne humana" (p. 149).

In *El rey y la reina,* as Rómulo embraces the Duchess, she sees in his eyes yellow lights "como en los de los gatos" (p. 174). Rómulo spends hours watching a bank of calla lilies. Occasionally a big velvety bumblebee goes slowly into the flowers' womb "como un rey en su cámara," and Rómulo observes how a stamen moves downward to stain the bumblebee yellow.

> Nada se podía imaginar en la vida humana superior. . . . Aquel penetrar con la delicia del tacto, la vista, el olfato y el sabor mezclados en una sola impresión era algo que el hombre no conocía, que el hombre sólo podía imaginar. . . . Si los milicianos no regresaran nunca y él se quedara allí con todo aquello y con la duquesa también él se sentiría como aquellos moscardones que entraban despacio en la entraña de una magnolia (pp. 121–122).

In *Los cinco libros de Ariadna* Javier notes that in times of peril man's sexual desires increase. Animals react identically. "Tenían miedo los animales y su reacción era la misma. La especie les hablaba: 'Es probable que mueras esta noche, pero no te vayas sin haber dejado fecundada a tu hembra' " (p. 267).

Steep inclines, ladders, and stairs going up or down are symbolic representations of the sexual act. Animals most utilized as genital symbols in folklore and mythology play this role also in dreams: the fish, the snail, the cat, the mouse, but above all the snake (*The Basic Writings,* p. 373). In *Epitalamio* el Careto, who is constantly concerned with castration, wanted to carry his snake with him everywhere, coiled on his shoulder. When Darío seeks refuge in the lighthouse, he discovers a dead cat in the heart of the beacon. In the cave Niña Lucha sees a giant crab with greenish claws. It waves its claws in the air as its pincers seek something to fasten on, just as the impotent Rengo seeks something to hold on to in life. La Niña couldn't look at the crab because it wasn't an animal but a thing, as Rengo was a thing. She says, "Las cosas que se mueven como animales o los animales que se están quietos como las cosas le producían hormigueo en la espina dorsal" (p. 143). El Careto urges the men on in their attempts to violate Lucha. He feels frustrated and sees in the young widow the heritage of the father wolf. "El lobo no existía sin ella, ni ella sin el lobo." He seeks power on the same path as that of the "macho castrón de mi clan" (p. 149).

Darío the school teacher, loves nature and animals. "Le hizo gracia . . . oir a los pájaros, e incluso en la noche el rugido de las bestias. También de esos hechos nacían otros no menos milagrosos. Y pensaba en la Niña" (p. 180). He feels that life is an ideal in flux, fused into the image of beauty which is the girl. Rengo, when Niña scratches her finger, won't use spider webs. The only medicine good enough for her would have been star dust and butterfly spittle, and he looks at her "a través de las sombras, como los gatos" (p. 133). One of the convicts dreams his wife has betrayed him with Trinidad. In his dream a turkey sits beside some meat. His wife is selling it and crying out, "El guajolote vale veinte pesos y la carne sesenta centavos." Trinidad earned twenty pesos, and the prisoner, sixty centavos. The convict "quería ser un pavo y valer veinte pesos" (pp. 196–197).

In *The Sphere* Saila warns himself that "I must not give her the impression of stroking a cat" (p. 158) as he makes love to Eva. In *Emén Hetán* during the saturnalia the lascivious couples kept "imitando a los animales en actitudes grotescas" (p. 118), and we learn about the "toro blanco de las riberas del Guadalquivir . . . fecundó a la reina Pasifae de Creta y dio vida al minotauro" (p. 82).[18]

Food and hunger play a part in the relationship. In *Orden público* Curro feeds the birds with bread crumbs from his scanty meal. He is later distressed when the bread is unfit even for sparrows. The *periodista* shares his food "con las grandes ratas hambrientas" (p. 72), and the Englishman tells his friends he made the sandwiches from an animal which eats orangoutangs, "Gato hermoso negro. Era el gato de un oficial. . . . Contó como lo habia atrapado. . . . Lo guisó en trozos en el infiernillo. Pero los gatos comen orangutanes? El inglés afirmaba. El alemán rectificó:—ratones"

(p. 142). In *El lugar de hombre* dogs eat better than the peasants. Don Manuel takes ham from a platter and feeds it to his dog. "El perro lo tragaba sin masticar. El pastor lo contemplaba con un asomo de envidia porque el jamón no lo probaba durante años enteros" (p. 159). There are many references to hunting for food, among them impaling a lizard and preparing it, and the killing and preparing of a rabbit. In *Siete domingos rojos* Fau, feeling a need for steak, cuts one from a living cow. "Trazó una curva con el cuchillo encima del brazuelo. Cerró la curva por abajo y dio un tirón. El mugido, largo y profundo, parecía salir de las entrañas de la tierra. El animal dobló el brazuelo y quedó con la cabeza en alto, los ojos muy abiertos, sin comprender" (p. 196).[19]

Political relationships are also quite common. In *Los cinco libros de Ariadna* Javier recalls that during years and years "la democracia para mí era una colección de hombres dando brincos como los carneros" (p. 42). One of the recurring references reflects the political rivalry between East and West. A plane landed in Russia without a crew. When the Russians opened the plane, they found a dog seated calmly in the pilot's seat, and they think he must have landed the plane. Immediately the Russians decide they must find similar dogs in Russia to train. In *Siete domingos rojos,* Star says that her father "nunca dijo que el gato fuera anarquista y si lo puso a éste Makno fue cuando era muy pequeño y no sabía aún sus mañas. Yo creo que el gato es comunista autoritario" (pp. 58–59).[20]

Animals and men also exist in friendly relationships. In *Hipogrifo violento,* the lay brother's cat is a beautiful and friendly animal. The lay brother says it is his "buen amigo. . . . Creo que sabe más de lo que parece natural en un gato." [21] The lay brother loves him greatly, and the cat returns his affection. "El hermano lego se lo quedó mirando con ternura. . . . Sabiéndose el gato acariciado por aquella mirada, rosnaba, feliz" (p. 116). "Mientras hablaba el fraile el gato escuchaba bondadoso, y rosnaba lleno de amistad" (pp. 186–187). In *Crónica del alba* nobody likes the light red cat except Pepe. The cat used to wait for him on the roof, pick his way down the tiles, and often "ponía sus patas húmedas en mis libros abiertos señalando una declinación latina . . . y pasando y volviendo a pasar para frotar su lomo contra mi barbilla y su rabo contra mi nariz" (p. 14). Whenever Pepe's father scolded him, the light red cat would jump on Pepe's shoulder, purr, and pass from one shoulder to the other "frotándose contra mi barba y mi occipucio" (p. 20). In *Epitalamio del prieto Trinidad*

Barbitas, the doctor's mongrel dog, follows him everywhere. The doctor, embarrassed by his presence and tempted by his physical desire for Niña, tries to drown the dog. The dog avoids him for a while, but the doctor repents and welcomes the dog back. As he says, "Al fin y al cabo . . . no tengo otro verdadero compañero en la vida" (p. 122).

Religion plays a part in the human-animal relationship. In *Orden público* Sender refers to the fable of the black dog which came to Calvin's deathbed and killed him "ahogándolo bajo sus lanas sucias" (pp. 40–41). In *Hipogrifo violento* the lay brother's cat is always seated on the crosspiece of a crucifix, and Pepe wonders what it thinks of the religious images around it. The lay brother hastens to "advertir que aquella imagen no estaba bendecida ni consagrada y por eso el gato sentado encima no representaba irreverencia alguna" (p. 112). The cat and crucifix are always related. "Estaba el gato, como siempre sentado sobre el pecho del crucifijo de madera" (p. 142). "Desde el pecho del crucifijo el gato me miraba y miraba al lego" (p. 158).

Sender's short story, *The Black Cat*,[22] shows the most obvious relationship. An old priest decides to keep a cat he hears meowing in the portico of the abbey. His servant, Deogracias, doesn't like cats and schemes to make Father Baltasar get rid of it. Whenever the priest is out of the house, she hits the cat with a broom and says, "Jesus, Mary, and Joseph." After a while, upon hearing the words, the cat runs off. Deogracias almost convinces the skeptical priest to try and exorcise the Devil which she claims is in the cat. The Devil is upset because he doesn't want people to believe in his existence, so he may ruin them more easily. He appears and insists that Deogracias tell the priest the truth. She feels it is all right not to obey the Devil and refuses at first to confess. She finally confesses to the priest and he pardons her, but she goes off to live with her relatives. A few days later a man of indefinite age visits the priest, accompanied by a very pretty girl. He says the girl is his daughter, who will act as the priest's housekeeper. The cat follows the man.

Animals reflect the process of growing up. Pepe in *El mancebo y los héroes* remembers his relationship with Valentina which recalls "la voz de la gata llamando a sus gatitos—que era parecida al arrullo de las palomas." [23] The cats constantly remind him of his youth and his protected familiar childhood. He regrets that the cats of former years have disappeared as has his childhood. As he says: "Don Joaquín, el caballo, los gatos. Todos morían a mi alrededor" (p. 188). The boar hunt is also his initiation into manhood. A similar bridging of the gap between youth and adulthood occurs in *El lugar del hombre* as he recalls that "Cuando era niño (lo recordaba con emoción) en mis soledades hablaba con . . . los esparveres y con aquellas oquedades negras en donde localizaba todo lo irreal de mi infancia" (p. 18).[24]

Other animal-human relationships reflect the many facets of that bond: lethargy (*Los cinco libros de Ariadna*, p. 87) ; moral, idealistic, and psychological comparisons (*Los cinco libros,* pp. 69, 190, 229, 448–449) ; music (*Los cinco libros,* p. 37) ; communication (*Crónica del alba,* pp. 39, 48); jealousy (*Epitalamio del prieto Trinidad,* p. 29); intelligence (*Los cinco libros,* pp. 284, 492; *El mancebo y los héroes,* p. 61; *Hipogrifo violento,* pp. 116, 205, 207; *Emén Hetán,* p. 122) ; and a variety of miscellaneous relationships (*Emén Hetán,* pp. 19, 23; *Epitalamio,* pp. 31, 103; *Imán,* pp. 34, 49–50, 165; *El verdugo afable,* pp. 47, 129, 296).[25]

Throughout Sender's novels a physical identification occurs between animal and man. In *Los cinco libros de Ariadna,* Javier is wounded. A drop of his blood dries on a stone, and an ant carries it off. "La hormiga debía pensar que yo la pertenecía a ella. Con mi gota de sangre en alto . . . la hormiga marchaba a su casa contenta. Una parte de mí—pensé—quedará enterrada en el hormiguero y servirá de alimento a las hormigas" (p. 323).

In *The Sphere* Saila is pleased to discover his ganglionic consciousness with which "the lower animals and especially the insects organized their elemental geometries" (p. 33). In *Proverbio de la muerte,* an earlier version of *The Sphere,* he says that "Miles de años de lucha animal por la vida salen a flor de nuestros ganglios en la manifestación de la mayor parte de nuestros afectos" (p. 57).

In *Mexicayotl* Ecatl feels "los pequeños animales graciosos, las grandes bestias de la noche, todos son mis hermanos" (p. 184). In *La quinta Julieta* Felipe's cousin Juan identifies with the sufferings of a fish pulled from the water. He asks: "Qué te parecería a ti si alguien te agarrara con un gancho de acero por la garganta . . . y te arrastrara adentro del agua hasta que murieras allí ahogado. Porque eso es lo que hacemos a los peces. Es decir . . . los sacamos . . . a la tierra donde se mueren asfixiados" (p. 58). In *Siete domingos rojos* the men see a kind of seal or walrus who does a dance to earn its fish. Samar says: "Estamos en la vida como ese animal en el cajón. Para agarrar el pez tenemos que bailar y llenar los bolsillos del patrón" (p. 366).

In *El lugar del hombre,* a story of man's injustice to man combined with the struggles in Spain between conservatives and liberals, Sabino, a villager, disappears for sixteen years. Juan and Vicente, two other villagers, are accused of his murder and sent to prison for fifteen years. Sabino reappears, and necessary adjustments must be made all around. As the villagers argue over the reintegration of Sabino into society, a young stork, unable to fly, is trapped in the Ayuntamiento. His parents fly back and forth outside the window waiting for him. "Pero la impaciencia y la angustia tenían esa serenidad que hay en los movimientos y en las líneas de las grandes aves y que es en las cigüeñas uno de los elementos que las hacen venerables para los campesinos" (p. 76). The young stork agitates its wings in the corner as he "seguía fiel a su destino soñando con los lejanos horizontes y las altas nubes' (pp. 78–79). Just as the village assumes responsibility for Sabino, the municipality pays the children of the village to bring frogs and other animals to keep the stork alive until they can return him to his parents, or to keep him alive until he can return to his society.

Sabino himself sees at various times an old gypsy and a dancing bear with which Sabino becomes obsessed. "Terminó hallándole un parecido incluso físico, con su padre, capaz también de hacer cosas terribles pero que no hizo nunca más que despertar la risa en los demás" (p. 197). Later he insists that "entre aquel oso y su padre había una cierta relación y se consideraba él tan lejos de su padre socialmente como del oso. Pero sin embargo, sabía que podía ser el hijo del uno o del otro" (p. 213).

Vicente and Juan are tortured to make them reveal the hiding place of their supposed victim's corpse. They finally hit on the stratagem of saying they have fed Sabino to the pigs. A man who supposedly eats the flesh of the pigs grows ill, and another peasant claims he had to kill the pigs after the Sabino affair because his wife "los oía hablar con voz humana . . . y vio a uno de los cerdos avanzar hacia ella de pie, como un hombre" (p. 159).

In *Epitalamio del prieto Trinidad,* Ojos de Rata, Huerito Calzón's uncle, used to take some goats to pasture, but he would always bury the newborn kids. He had to kill them "porque parían animales con cara de persona" (p. 231). Bocahula insists that "los perros parecen lobos y los lobos parecen hombres, y entre perros, lobos y hombres, no es fácil distinguir" (p. 101). At school the teacher keeps a dead King spider in a glass cage. El Careto exclaims, "Se parece a Trinidad" (p. 71). He repeats again, "El araño King se parece a Trinidad. . . . La boca ancha y abultada, los pelos, hasta los movimientos que tenían el uno y el otro en vida" (p. 72). El Careto feeds birds to his snake, Ruana, every day. He reflects that it is cruel to defeather the live birds, especially since "era más fácil identificarse con el pájaro, porque tenía patas y las usaba para andar como nosotros" (p. 95).[26]

Several times in each novel Sender inserts short interludes involving animals, and the action seems to stop momentarily. As Rómulo muses on the Duchess and future possibilities of adventure with her, a lizard climbs the stones in the wall. It crawls a little, stops, begins crawling again. "Parecía escuchar también los cañones antes de volver a avanzar" (*El rey y la reina*, p. 120). Mister Witt, tired of investigating human matters, turns his glasses on the sea birds flying in white legions over Escombreras. "Las gaviotas, palomas encanalladas, tenían una pureza aparente, magnífica. Volaban en grupos que de pronto se deshacían, hacia abajo, en racimos alborotados" (*Mister Witt en el cantón*, p. 52). In *Imán*, "Cuando una rata, enorme, con patas de liebre, calvas a trechos—asoma entre los sacos, Viance le da la novedad. La rata no huye" (p. 16).

Among other interludes are: "Un ratoncillo gris mide el ángulo en silencio con los dos abalorios fijos en el recluso" (*Orden público*, p. 25); "Un gorrión cruza el espacio descubierto por la falta de techo . . . la avecica parece bañada en oro" (*Los cinco libros de Ariadna*, p. 30); "Un gato apareció en el cuarto, nos miró, volvio la espalda y se marchó lentamente con un silencioso desdén" (*Los cinco libros*, p. 216).[27]

Sender's work is filled with information about the customs and habits of animals and the customs and habits of people involving animals. "Cuando el gato ha herido al ratón de manera que éste ya no puede escapar, se pone a jugar con él. No es justo culpar al gato, sin embargo, de crueldad. El miedo sostenido del ratón ante la ferocidad fría del gato produce en el pequeño roedor una cantidad de albúminas que lo hacen más sabroso y apetecible" (*El verdugo afable*, p. 231); "Los labradores tratan a sus perros con indiferencia y crueldad—y es, sin duda, la razón por la que esos animales les adoran" (*Réquiem por un campesino español*, p. 65).[28]

[From *Hispania*, vol. XLVI, no. 3, September, 1963]

4 | Theater

Benavente and Shakespearean Drama

BENAVENTE'S lectures and essays contain many constantly recurring ideas about various facets of Shakespearean drama, though his findings often appear somewhat contradictory.

In raising the question as to whether Shakespeare should be read or performed, he quotes Charles Lamb's well-known statement that the figure of Lear is of too gigantic proportions to be represented on the stage. Indeed many admirers of Shakespeare, even in England, feel that *King Lear, The Tempest,* and *A Midsummer Night's Dream* lose much of their greatness and beauty by being performed (*Obras completas,* IX, 751).* Benavente agrees that even with the most modern theatrical techniques, it would be impossible to present with absolute reality Shakespearean battle fields or supernatural creations (VI, 615). Yet, says Benavente, even though in certain plays like *The Tempest* it is difficult to portray what must exist only in one's imagination, Shakespeare's works were meant to be performed.

The Spanish authors of the sixteenth and seventeenth centuries accepted the fact that they wrote for a public, national and popular, and none really elevated himself over the nation and the times. "Shakespeare, por eso, es el más grande autor dramático; entre los horrores, brutalidades, groserías y bufonadas de su teatro (idéntico en asuntos, forma y procedimientos al de todos los autores de su época), deja libre vagar a su espíritu

* All citations from Benavente here are to *Obras Completas,* 11 vols. (Madrid: Aguilar, 1950–58).

de poeta, ideal Ariel, que a su vuelo todo lo concierta y todo lo esclarece, como espíritu superior a su tiempo y a su obra misma" (VI, 599).

Benavente wonders whether one reads in Shakespeare the author and actor's works, composed of bits and pieces of previous works intended to please the London masses who attended the Globe Theatre, "aquel teatro en donde se apreciaba el número de espectadores por el olor más o menos fuerte a la ginebra, que se quemaba para disipar el producido por una gran cubeta, en donde los espectadores vertían sin miramiento, lo que Molière llamó 'lo superfluo de la bebida' " (VII, 55). Benavente assumes that we read in Shakespeare the great overlay of critical works on him which have helped create his powerful image, but he insists that from time to time it is necessary to bathe oneself in sincerity and confront one's judgment, satiated by such literature, with the spontaneous sentiment of a virgin spirit. Only before a popular audience can Shakespearean theatre truly be given, for the popular audience makes up with its perceptiveness what it may lack in intelligence.

For the Shakespearean lovers, among whom he includes himself, "a los que llevamos en el corazón y sobre nuestra cabeza el nombre de Shakespeare, es difícil que una representación de cualquier obra suya pueda satisfacernos nunca" (IX, 751). However, certain precepts will make the play more palatable. Since the impact on an audience, for Benavente, should be primarily an emotional one, the actors should not try to read too much into the roles, but should act them simply as the plays were written. Shakespearean characters, he contends, are of a simple psychology. "Pero ¿hay nada más sencillo que la psicología de Otelo? ¿Nada más infantil que su credulidad ante las burdas maquinaciones de Yago? ¿Hay nada más infantil que la conducta de Yago? Un malvado que nos avisa él mismo de que es un malvado. ¿Hay nada más infantil que Romeo y Julieta? Ni sería bien que fuera de otro modo. El mismo Hamlet, considerado como prototipo de la complejidad psicológica, ¿hay nada más ondulantemente rectilíneo, valga el contrasentido?" (VII, 815). The best Shakespearean actors follow the text, and those who receive the constant applause of the audience for their effects may have performed very well indeed, but they will not have been faithful to their role (*ABC*, April 24, 1949).

Benavente mentions the various actors he has seen and comments that they all tried to add to the dimensions of various scenes, either in a search for something new or because of the tradition of their national interpretations. The Italian actors sought inspiration from Modena y Salvini, the French from Talma, the English from Garrick, and the Americans from Booth. Most of the actors lacked the lyric force to portray tragedy, but they did the comedies creditably. However, "si en la representación no parece el poeta sobre todo, puede decirse que la obra gana poco representada y es preferible su lectura" (IX, 702).

The Germans were the best critical interpreters of Shakespeare, and the Italians the best actors, though he takes Garavaglia to task for his theatrical attempts. Benavente considered the greatest single Shakespearean actor to be Ernesto Rossi, even though he saw the latter at an advanced age when he was ill. In his interpretation of Lear and Hamlet, he was unmatched. "Fué el gran intérprete de Shakespeare; la representación de sus obras por Rossi era un curso explicativo que siempre descubría algo nuevo al más conocedor del teatro de Shakespeare" (VI, 658). Even in his performance of Romeo, in spite of his figure, more like that of Falstaff than of Romeo, if one closed one's eyes, one found his interpretation superb in spite of his physique. "Y es difícil que actor alguno pueda superarle en sentimiento y comprensión del apasionado amante veronés" (VI, 637). Benavente's two favorite women actors were Eleonora Duse and Sarah Bernhardt, both of whom he liked in the role of Cleopatra. He laments the fact that Eleonora Duse acted primarily in *Antony and Cleopatra,* but explains that in most of Shakespeare's plays the women had a comparatively inferior role, and it would have defrauded the public to have a star of her magnitude perform them (*ABC,* May 16, 1948).

In several essays Benavente discusses Hamlet's age. He must have been young, otherwise he would have been elected king on the death of his father. Furthermore, we know that he intends to return to the University of Wittenberg to study. Benavente insists that the first Hamlet was younger, but that Shakespeare's actor friend Burbage, an associate in the Globe Theatre and according to the testimony of his contemporaries an older and plump man, prevailed upon Shakespeare to create an older and stouter Hamlet. Today, of course, no one imagines a fat Hamlet. In some of his essays Benavente seems to prefer the age span of fifteen to eighteen years for Hamlet; in others, sixteen to twenty years of age.

Benavente commented on the anachronisms to be found in so many of Shakespeare's plays. For the most part, he feels that the human quality of the characters transcends their time and that Shakespeare offered his spectators through the ear what he well knew was impossible through the eye. He disagrees with Oscar Wilde, who insisted that Shakespearean tragedy demanded great historical and geographical fidelity. Speaking of a performance of *Antony and Cleopatra,* the latter interpreted by the professional beauty Miss Langtry, he points out that the production paid the greatest attention to archeological details in clothes and accessories, but that in view of the anachronisms in Shakespeare, such care was excessive. In discussing the movie version of *Hamlet,* he criticizes Olivier, who, in his judgment, went to violent extremes both of repulsion and affection, especially in the third act where he tells Ophelia, "Get thee to a nunnery." Benavente criticizes, too, the lack of tragical decorum and the poor acting of Ophelia, but what bothers him most is the lack of accuracy in geographical background and dress. Here Benavente admits that though anachronisms are inevitable, they should be similar ones and not from different historical periods in the same play.

In view of Benavente's obvious admiration for Shakespeare, one wonders how the latter fares in a comparison with Spanish writers. Benavente deems his countrymen superior. He says: "Nadie duda de mi admiración, conocido es mi culto por sus obras: pero al compararlo con nuestros autores dramáticos del Siglo de Oro: Lope de Vega, Calderón, Tirso y otros también, bien sé que pudiera enfrentárselos a Shakespeare y decirle, como los nobles de Aragón ante su rey: 'Nos, que cada uno somos tanto como vos, y todos juntos más que vos' " (XI, 424). He insists that in the Spanish theater, the vigor and tragic breadth equals that of Shakespeare, and that the comedies are superior to those of Shakespeare in force, richness of invention, and elegance. "Nuestros autores del Siglo de Oro pueden muy bien enfrentarse con Shakespeare" (XI, 608). He claims throughout that Lope de Vega is superior to Shakespeare: "Para mí, Lope de Vega es superior a Shakespeare" (XI, 471). "Yo por mi parte, a nuestro Lope de Vega lo considero muy superior a Shakespeare" (XI, 608). "¿No nos atreveremos, por fin, a decir que es superior a Shakespeare, y que cualquier nación que contara con Lope de Vega no sabría donde colocarlo?" (IX, 1031). In comparing the themes of *Hamlet* and *La vida es sueño,* he feels that "por la concepción y el desempeño del asunto, es Calderón el que más puede presumir de originalidad" (XI, 174). Benavente considers Calderón's masterpiece, in concept and thought, "muy superior a todas las de Shake-speare" (XI, 608).

Benavente has written on almost every aspect of Shakespeare, has trans-lated two of his plays and a soliloquy, has adapted part or all of six Shake-spearean works in his own plays, and has written some poetry on Shake-speare. Benavente refers constantly to Shakespeare's characters. He quotes incessantly in every volume of his *Obras completas* his favorite Shake-spearean lines, among which are: "The rest is silence," " 'Tis meat and drink to me to see a clown," "There are more things in heaven and earth, Horatio, than are dreamt of in your philosophy."

In summing up Benavente's findings, we might do well to use his own statement: "Todos los críticos detractores de Shakespeare, desde Voltaire y Moratín con el conde Tolstoi y Bernard Shaw y el autor francés . . . — no recuerdo su nombre. ¿Lo ven ustedes? No recuerdo su nombre—que escri-bió un libro titulado *La superstición shakespiriana,* todos tienen razón. Contra lo razonable no hay objeción posible; pero ninguna de sus críticas razonables ha podido restar un solo creyente a Shakespeare; porque, como decía el misántropo de Molière: Cela mène, la raison me le dit chaque jour, mais la raison n'est pas ce qui règle l'amour" (XI, 716).

[From *Romance Notes,* vol. I, no. 2, Spring, 1960]

Benavente on
Shakespearean Characters

BENAVENTE, influenced by Shakespeare in many of his dramas,[1] has also written extensively on various Shakespearean problems such as acting, staging, and the like.[2] Benavente fancied himself an expert on all matters pertaining to Shakespeare. He quotes constantly and often dogmatically from Shakespearean texts: "The rest is silence. This does not signify the remainder as many translators of Shakespeare have understood it; the rest means . . . repose which meaning it still has in English and it was so used almost exclusively in the time of Shakespeare." [3] Even numerology interested him. He commented that Shakespeare's birth date, 1564, has digits totaling 16. Twice sixteen equals 1616, the date of Shakespeare's death, which fact impressed Benavente greatly to judge by the number of times he refers to it (*O.C.,* XI, 174; *O.C.,* XI, 70; *O.C.,* XI, 297; *O.C.,* IX, 697).

When Benavente visited Stratford on Avon, he found the general atmosphere congenial and full of "the spirit of sweet Shakespeare" (*O.C.,* IX, 700), but he was shocked to discover that most Englishmen knew Shakespeare only superficially and then only the most popular works. He distrusted English admiration for Shakespeare as dogmatic, cold, and insincere and felt that the Shakespearean spirit was neither very English nor very Protestant (*O.C.,* IX, 1028).

As a playwright, much of Benavente's interest focused on Shakespearean characters, who, he felt, given their point of view, behaved acceptably and were properly motivated. In *The Merchant of Venice* the only one right was Shylock. All deceived him, stole from him, or mistreated him. Shylock had to be a villain, but Shakespeare gave him life and so must have pitied him. His works are full of traitors and human perfidy, but even Iago's conduct Shakespeare seems at times to justify. Indeed, the most cogent expressions of free will are made by his villains (*O.C.,* XI, 259).

King Lear, the work Benavente's father was reading when he died (*O.C.,* XI, 566–567), was Benavente's favorite play. He was impressed by Lear's great spiritual implications. Dispossessed of his kingdom, deserted by his courtiers and servants, and punished by the ingratitude of his older daughters, Lear pays for his inability to appreciate the rectitude of the youngest, Cordelia, who is truth and kindness personified. We all pity the kind and unfortunate father and do not forgive the daughters when they cast him out. Yet, it is not Shakespeare who is the avenger. Shakespearean justice is impartial. Death and tragedy are the same for all. His characters, good and bad, fall victims to the same brutal destiny, leaving to the spectator the duty of moralizing their position. In the spectator's role, Benavente finds the ingratitude of the older daughters just, because the king unjustly divided his kingdom (*O.C.,* VII, 68).

Benavente read *Hamlet* countless times in the original, in a Moratín Spanish translation, and in a French translation by Victor Hugo's son. In addition to stressing constantly the necessity for a young Hamlet and the twisting of dates and facts by Shakespeare to accommodate his friend, Burbage, Benavente attempts to refute the possible homosexuality of Hamlet. It would be easy to maintain that Hamlet was homosexual in his love for his father, hatred of his mother, and in his discussions with his friend Horatio and others, but Benavente denies it as well as any potentiality on Hamlet's part of Oedipal love for his mother (*O.C.,* XI, 338).

Hamlet's attempt to decipher the meaning of life and reality intrigues Benavente. To test the king, Hamlet will put on the play, for "The play's the thing," and he analyzes the various motivations which cause Hamlet to recast the story. Hamlet, insofar as his speeches are concerned, has a passive role and is a spectator rather than an actor. He was not born as was Oedipus to fulfill his destiny and never had to confront it or defy it. He was curious about life, but he was not eager to take part in it. Benavente also takes exception to Moratín's translation of the phrase in Hamlet's soliloquy, "to be or not to be," as "to exist or not to exist." For Benavente the phrase means to create or not to create one's essence (*O.C.,* XI, 328).

Benavente has written much on Shakespeare's feminine characters. Ophelia was the victim of Hamlet's filial relationship, as his mother's fragility caused him to doubt the virtue of all women. Ophelia's madness was caused not by her father's death but because it was the man she loved, Hamlet, who had killed him. Unable to keep from loving, she sought escape, first in an innocent childhood and later in the more permanent form of death. Juliet, unlike Ophelia, ran to meet love. Curious, almost childlike, she lost her soul to love and, at last, willingly drank the potion. When Romeo died she too accepted death, a more faithful ally of love than life itself, for it is through death that love triumphs over hate.

Desdemona loved enthusiastically and emotionally. Had Othello been vain instead of noble, he might not have doubted her great love which became the very proof of her treachery. Calumny triumphed over simple innocence when her own nobility and heroism caused her destruction. Portia, happy and lucky, also aroused her husband's jealousy, but she dissipated it with her laughter. Had Desdemona known laughter she, too, might have averted tragedy. Beatrice challenged dangerous love to frighten it away. Her intelligence made it difficult for her to realize that a woman in love should be a bit deceived and should reject irony and anticipate attack.

Lady Macbeth, in her wifely ambition, dreamed of a throne for her husband. She was both Eve and the serpent at the same time, both temptation and seduction. She died before she could see the fall of the throne in which her ambition and her love were fused. Cleopatra, however, the eternal woman, wanted to rule the world to show what her womanly charms might accomplish. To lose or win—and many lost and won for her: Pompey, Caesar, Marc Antony—was a game of chance, and the outcome not of great import as long as she was set at more value than anything else which might be lost. Her glory lay in the certainty of her dominion over man, for this was the empire she craved. Tears and laughter, caresses and cruelties, carried Marc Antony to his doom, and when she failed with Octavius, there remained for her only the final seduction of death (*O.C.*, VII, 108). Benavente believed Shakespeare's women characters complemented the men and created what he called, "force and repose; turbulence and serenity; rough and smooth . . . masculine and feminine" (*O.C.*, VII, 116).

In the final analysis, Benavente says, various attempts to prove that Shakespeare's works were written by Lord Bacon, Lord Rutland, the Counts of Southampton, of Stanley, of Pembroke, or of Oxford are unimportant. All the critics fail in not recognizing that Shakespeare, more than any other author, left the secret of his soul. Critics are men of books and not of souls and so have succeeded merely in obscuring the Shakespeare, who, as Wordsworth claimed, opened his heart for us (*O.C.*, XI, 716).

[From *Modern Drama*, vol. 4, no. 1, May, 1961]

Shakespeare's Influence on Benavente's Plays

ALFONSO PAR has examined briefly certain aspects of the relationship of Benavente's plays to those of Shakespeare, but a study of Benavente's *Obras Completas*[1] reveals greater influence than Par had imagined. Par feels that "quizás la obra de Benavente de mayor influjo shakespeariano es *La noche iluminada* en la que amalgama los personajes fantásticos del *Sueño de una noche de San Juan* con otros reales de su invención, pertenecientes a la época actual." [2] In the play, first performed at the Fontalba theatre in Madrid on December 22, 1927, one of the characters, Mr. Plum, recalls Horatio's dictum in Hamlet, Billy feels that Titania is representing a motion picture version of Shakespeare's *A Midsummer Night's Dream,* and Titania, the fairy, mentions that "lucharemos como en aquella *Noche de Verbena,* eternizada por nuestro poeta, nuestro Shakespeare" (*O.C.,* V, 144). Puck comments that it is a good thing that few Englishmen have read Shakespeare. "Pobre Shakespeare . . . Acaso no fuese tan admirado porque nada gana un poeta con ser leído" (*O.C.,* V, 154). Oberon and Titania quarrel over the use of the love juice against her, and she threatens to leave him if he uses it again. In addition to Puck, Oberon, and Titania, Pease-Blossom (Flor de Guindo) and Mustard-seed (Mostacilla) are the only characters who also appear in Shakespeare's play.

The plot concerns a group of young men and women on a picnic outing. Roland, one of the young men, sees Titania, queen of the fairies, but he attempts to dispel her illusions through reason, and the others believe she is part of a movie company on location. Titania, angered at a world where cowboy stories have replaced fairy tales and where humans communicate more easily with telegrams than fairies can with magic, changes Roland into a bear whose enchantment will be broken only if a woman falls in love with him. Oberon, in turn, causes Titania to believe she is a woman and disguises himself and the fairies as actors on location. All ends well as Roland regains his normal shape. Benavente stresses here one of his favorite themes, the redemptive power of love: "lo que es alma del mundo, el espíritu eterno que crea y redime" (*O.C.*, V, 158).

Cuento de amor, based on *Twelfth Night or What You Will,* is much closer to Shakespeare's work, but Par insists that "aparte de la trama y de los nombres y situación de los personajes, la comedia española tiene mucho menos de la obra inglesa de lo que da a entender su refundidor." [3] Benavente's drama is in three acts. The Condesa Olivia is Olivia of Shakespeare's play; Florisel (Elena) is Cesaria (Viola) ; Dorotea corresponds to Olivia's gentlewoman, María; Duque Leonardo is Orsino, Duke of Ilyria; Tobias is Sir Toby Belch; Malvolio remains Malvolio, Olivia's steward; El Bufón is the clown, Feste; Lauro and Leoncio are Curio and Valentine, gentlemen attending the Duke; Sir Andrew Aguescheek, Olivia's suitor, has no counterpart in the Benavente play, and Antonio, a sea captain, does not appear; however, Sebastián is the sea captain in the Benavente play who is both a friend to Florisel and her brother. The theme of Viola's brother, Sebastián, is almost completely subordinated and we learn of him at the end through the speech of the other characters. Belch is a drunkard in both plays; Malvolio loves the countess and is considered mad in both; Dorotea plays the same trick and Olivia mourns the death of her brother in both. Benavente's humor is somewhat different because of the nature of the untranslatable English puns.

Benavente admits his debt to Shakespeare and stresses his own inferiority. Shakespeare is "un semidiós . . . Amparado del poeta divino, temeroso como profanador al presentaros en una redomilla, gotas de agua del mar y deciros: 'Éste es el Océano,' un poeta humilde de estos tiempos pide admiración para Shakespeare en lo admirable, y para sí toda censura" (*O.C.*, I, 383).

Los favoritos, a one act comedy first performed in 1892, is based on an episode from *Much Ado About Nothing.* An Italian duke and his wife each have their confidants, the Duchess, Beatriz, and the Duke, Benedicto. Beatriz and Benedicto dislike each other and insult each other until the Duchess manages a bit of successful matchmaking. Benedicto, Benedick in Shakespeare's play, and Beatriz, Beatrice in the English play, are not well developed as characters. The Duquesa, Celia, and the Duque, Octavio, do not correspond to Leonato, Governor of Messina and his wife, Innogen of Shakespeare's work. Beatriz is the dear friend of Celia rather than the Governor's niece, but Benedicto is the duke's favorite, much as the young Lord of Padua in the Shakespearean version was favored by Don Pedro, Prince of Aragon. In the Benavente play the change from hate to love occurs abruptly; in the Shakespearean play the uncle, the prince and Benedick's friend convince him of Beatrice's love while Margaret, Beatrice's cousin, and Ursula convince Beatrice of Benedick's love.

Titania, a three act comedy first performed in 1945, refers constantly to *A Midsummer Night's Dream.* Evaristo says: "Sí, mujer, sí lo sabes; es que no te acuerdas. Hemos leído a Shakespeare. En una obra suya, el *Sueño de una noche de verano,* en *La noche de San Juan,* o en *Noche de verbena,* que de los tres modos puede traducirse, Titania es la reina de las hadas . . . (*O.C.,* VIII, 864). Evaristo discusses various incidents from the play and Matilde, the heroine, assumes the role of Titania. Matilde, the queen, falls in love with Benigno, the donkey. The latter wants to be certain that Matilde loves him sincerely. He wants to deserve his Titania's love and not because "había perdido la razón al querer a su Botton" (*O.C.,* VIII, 896).

Many other works of Benavente contain briefer references to Shakespeare. *La Infanzona* (vol. VIII, 941–995), quotes Hamlet as does *Cualquiera lo sabe,* (*O.C.,* VI, 243–317). *La Historia de Otelo,* a one act play, refers several times to Othello. The Viajero says: "Otelo, llorará usted la triste suerte de Desdémona" (*O.C.,* III, 122). The other characters discuss Shakespeare's play, and in the final scene the daughter who has been reading it comments on its beauty and quotes: "Ella me amó por las desdichas que he padecido, y yo la amé porque supo compadecerlas" (*O.C.,* III, 128). In *La ciudad alegre y confiada,* a continuation of *Los intereses creados,* Colombina says, "tener unos amantes inmortales como los de Verona," and Leandro exclaims: "Ten en cuenta que Romeo y Julieta murieron muy jóvenes, que de su despedida en el florido balcón de Verona a su muerte en la tumba de los Capuletos solo mediaron unos días de ausencia; si hubieran vivido muchos años de plácido matrimonio . . ." (*O.C.,* III, 1135). *El susto de la Condesa,* often suggested as Shakespeare-inspired, lacks any resemblance to Richard's attempts at power through Anne to which its scenes have been compared.

Shakespeare's most penetrating influence occurs in *El bufón de Hamlet,*

Benavente's last comedy which was not performed. The characters are those found in *Hamlet*, but the action takes place much earlier when Hamlet is only fourteen and Ophelia ten years of age. As the children are playing at Elsinore, Yorick, a beggar, approaches and discourses on his own hunger and that of the poor. Hamlet feels sorry for him, and since the king's jester has died, he offers Yorick the position. Hamlet, thoughtful and kind-hearted, is tormented by a variety of doubts, as he bemoans the unhappy lot of the Danish subjects and comments that man is a player who plays his part on the stage of life. He discusses many things with his father, among them Fortinbras, the hostage, and Yorick, the fool. Hamlet constantly reveals his dislike of war and of his uncle, Claudius. Ophelia shows her great love of flowers and almost drowns as the children go rowing. Yorick overhears Gertrude and Claudius in an intimate conversation. He informs Hamlet that his uncle is spreading discontent among the nobles because Hamlet's father has avoided war. As Polonius and Laertes talk of his future education, Laertes insists that he is a better swordsman than Hamlet. Hamlet informs his father of Claudius' impending treachery and of his love for Gertrude. Yorick sleeps on King Hamlet's bed in the garden and Claudius poisons him by mistake. The king is going to send Hamlet to Wittenberg to study and Laertes is to go to France. As the play closes Hamlet's father falls asleep in the garden as Claudius, Hamlet, and Gertrude watch and pledge to guard his sleep.

Benavente tried direct translation of some of Shakespeare, and he made a partial translation of *Hamlet*. A good part of the first scene is omitted and parts of the speeches by Marcellus and Horatio are combined. Several passages are very loosely translated, scene divisions are not given, and several other speeches are combined. The entire first scene of Act II between Polonius and Reynaldo is omitted. Part of the conversation between Guildenstern, Rosencrantz, and Hamlet and the Comedians' play are left out, and many of the speeches are rearranged. In Act III the third scene between the king and Rosencrantz and Guildenstern is missing, and Benavente's translation ends with Hamlet's final speech to his mother as he tugs Polonius off.

Hamlet continued to interest Benavente. One of his poems, called "El monólogo de Hamlet," reflects on the problem of being: "Ser o no ser! El soliloquio eterno—que hace apurar un mundo de amargura por temor a las penas de un infierno . . . Triste quien, como Hamlet, duda y vive"

(*O.C.*, VI, 1048). Aside from his translation of the famous soliloquy in his version of *Hamlet*, Benavente attempted it at least one other time. The translations differ in many lines, reflecting, perhaps, the difficulty Benavente had in coming to grips with his self-imposed task.

Translation in Hamlet	*Independent translation* (*O.C.*, XI, 50).
Si es un tropiezo	Ya es un tropiezo.
Los ultrajes y escarnios del siglo,	Los estragos del tiempo,
la injusticia de un tirano opresor.	el despotismo de un tirano
	opresor, el orgullo insolente de
	los poderosos, las tristezas del
	amor que se ve menosopreciado.
Las vejaciones que el verdadero	La vejación que el verdadero
mérito ha de sufrir.	mérito ha de sufrir.
El camino abrumado por la carga	camino abrumado por la
de una penosa existencia.	carga abrumadora de una
	penosa existencia.
Si ante el más alto de la muerte	Si ante el más allá de
	la muerte.
La región ignorada de donde no ha	La región inexplorada de
regresado nunca ningún viajero.	donde ningún viajero ha
	regresado nunca.
Sus impulsos más decisivos des-	Sus impulsos más decisivos
fallecen a la pálida luz del pensa-	desfallecen enfermizos a
miento.	la pálida luz de nuestro
	pensamiento.
Y lo que había de ser acción en	Y la que había de ser
nuestra vida.	acción en nuestra vida.

Benavente's translation in volume 11 was based on a series of rough notes not intended, originally, for publication.

King Lear was the only Shakespearean play which Benavente translated completely, and he had a special motive for so doing. In 1944, in a speech he gave to a medical association meeting in Cádiz, he explained in part his love for this play. When Benavente was a youth his father sat down to read the first volume of the Biblioteca Clásica, the first volume of which was the works of Shakespeare and the first book of which was *King Lear.* This was a somewhat unusual event as his father regularly attended the Café del Siglo. As soon as his father let the book drop, young Benavente pounced on it because he was so anxious to read it, for he had read almost all the other works of Shakespeare except Lear. He sat down "dispuesto a no acostarme hasta haber leído mi Rey Lear" (*O.C.,* XI, 228). Suddenly his older brother entered to tell him that his father had just died. Many years later, when Benavente undertook a translation of a Shakespearean work for a publishing house, he chose without any hesitation whatsoever, *King Lear,* the last book which his father had read.

[From *The South Central Bulletin,* vol. 21, Spring, 1961]

Some Recent Works of
Joaquín Calvo-Sotelo

JOAQUÍN CALVO-SOTELO, one of the good playwrights of contemporary Spain, often speaks for the conscience of his country, especially in matters of politics and religion with which his best works are replete. Born in 1905 and a lawyer by profession, he has occupied a variety of positions either directly or peripherally concerned with literature. Since his first of some thirty dramas, *A la tierra, 500.000 kilómetros*, 1932, he has won a variety of prizes including the National Prize for Theater, and in 1956 he became a member of the Royal Academy.

Calvo-Sotelo has written comedy, farce, and thesis plays, many of them refreshing and original, but he seems overly sensitive about the antecedents of his works, perhaps because on various occasions he has been accused of borrowing themes and plots. His most successful play, *La muralla*, took its title from a work by Federico Oliver—which Calvo-Sotelo acknowledges. Joaquín Dicenta's daughter, however, claimed that he had taken the play from one by her father, *La confesión*.

In his dramas, especially the thesis ones, the prevalent themes concern Catholicism, the redeeming possibility of love, and the current political situation of the world and Spain. Even in dramas such as *La visita que no tocó el timbre*, 1950, and *Una muchachita de Valladolid*, 1957, ostensibly pure farces, political or religious implications can be found. In the former a character ironically alludes to "La salvación está en la República" [1] and in the latter to "leyenda negra, la España fascista." [2]

Good Catholicism consists of living up to the spirit of that religion, both in faith and works, and performing the latter regardless of possible practical or worldly discomfort. Representatives of that philosophy are persons who repent at the last moment either through confession or intent (Lorenzo Monteverde in *Historia de un resentido* and Jorge Hontanar in *La muralla*) and a variety of good and devout women. At times Calvo-Sotelo criticizes the less spiritual Catholic clergy, but most of his priests are good and kind (the Dominican father, Daniel O'Conner, in *Criminal de Guerra;* the sympathetic and humble priest, Ángel Bernárdez, in *La muralla;* and el Párroco, Daniel Martínez, in *Historia de un resentido*). They are all normal human beings who drink liquor in moderation and understand human foibles.

In stressing his Catholic position the author adopts orthodox views, although at times, as in *La ciudad sin Dios,* 1957, he approaches his theme in a startling fashion. Suicide is against the laws of God, for "el hombre no tiene derecho a robar a la Divinidad la libre disposición de este último segundo que, acaso, reservaba la Divinidad para el milagro" (*Criminal de guerra*).[3] A man may be forgiven if he becomes a good Catholic at the end of his life, as do Monteverde and Jorge Hontanar, regardless of previous shortcomings. On the other hand, a true Catholic is not one who pulls shady deals and then devoutly goes to church. As Jorge says, "Así hay millones que se llaman católicos y no lo son sino de nombre . . . Yo soy un español que se ha convertido al catolicismo" (*La muralla*).[4] Jorge's mother-in-law reveals her own lack of faith and Christianity as she claims, "Esos curitas están bien para lo que hacen, en sus aldeas con sus beatas y sus niños pequeños . . . pero en cuanto vienen a la ciudad, arman siempre la de Dios es Cristo" (*La muralla*).[5] Good works are important, for as Claudio says in *Milagro en la Plaza del Progreso,* "el hacer el bien nos convierte en reyes."[6] Calvo-Sotelo's religious treatment recalls, at times, Linares Rivas' works, and one is often reminded, also, of the nineteenth-century novel of Pereda, Valera, and Pardo Bazán.

In politics Calvo-Sotelo stresses the concept of forgiveness. One should not live by the sins of the past. El Párroco in *Historia de un resentido* asks for pardon and understanding for the Republicans, for "hubo también almas limpias, equivocadas, pero limpias."[7] The author stresses the need for authority, however, for in speaking of Primo de Rivera he says: "Hay que coger el toro por los cuernos. Que vean que con la autoridad no se juega" (*Historia de un resentido*).[8] In *La herencia* the implicit question is whether the sins of fathers should be visited upon the children. Calvo-Sotelo, who himself suffered loss through the civil war, strives artistically and at times successfully for an objective position, as he stresses love and pardon. As the son says, "Hay en España millones y millones de hombres y de mujeres que pisamos fuerte, y que llevamos la cabeza sobre los hombros y que no vivimos en el 36 o éramos unos niños entonces. Tengo derecho a pensar y a sentir por mi cuenta." [9]

Nevertheless, we ourselves are to blame for our anguished world. We must be responsible to future generations for what we have done and what we do, but our only salvation lies in the power of love and true religious and spiritual feeling which may redeem man from the current problems of the twentieth century.

Among lesser plays performed in the last decade we find: *Nuestros ángeles,* 1950; *María Antonieta,* 1952; *Cuando llegue el día,* 1952, a one act play; *La mariposa y el ingeniero,* 1953, about fidelity and a jealous husband; *La ciudad sin Dios,* 1959, about possible preoccupation with God; *No,* 1958; *Garrote vil para un director de banco;* and *La República de Mónaco,* 1959.

La visita que no tocó el timbre, 1950, is a comedy about two brothers over forty years of age at whose doorstep a woman leaves her child. They try to give the child away but finally obtain a nurse, Emma, who convinces them they should adopt the infant. The mother, who had contemplated suicide because the child was the result of an illicit affair with a married man, repents and claims him. Emma captures the heart of one of the brothers, both men are rejuvenated, and more happiness seems in store for them in the future.

Criminal de guerra, 1951, concerns the North American occupation of Germany after the Second World War. An American colonel, William Kennerlein, in charge of local forces, comes to live with his German relatives. He discovers that Elizabeth's father, General Hoffman, has been arrested and accused of having executed twenty American flyers who were prisoners of war. Kennerlein seeks to prove the general's innocence, and proof is finally obtained, but meanwhile, the general commits suicide. It turns out that Kennerlein had given him the poison capsule, asking him to wait until the last possible moment, but the general, wishing an honorable death, took it just as his innocence was being verified. Kennerlein admits his crime, praises the potential sacrifice of his German kinsman, Frederic, who wished to assume the blame, and receives Elizabeth's forgiveness and love, as they discover that their feeling is mutual. Frederic bitterly claims that Germany's only crime was that she lost the war. Kennerlein blames both America and Germany. Calvo-Sotelo's objectivity slips a bit here, as elsewhere, as he seeks to equate Nuremberg and Buchenwald. In other dramas his feelings about America are revealed from time to time. "El todopoderoso americano dispone de un aparato eléctrico para preparar el café, de otro para tostar el pan, de otro para untarlo de mantequilla" (*La vista que no tocó el timbre*).[10] The American says of the Germans, "La obediencia tiene un límite, y la rebelión puede ser tan sagrada como la obediencia" (*Criminal de guerra*).[11] Calvo-Sotelo, however, feels that we all can be judged only by history and by God at the Last Judgment.

In *El Jefe,* 1953, some prisoners escape and flee to an island. They have broken society's laws and refused to obey established order, but for self-preservation they decide to elect a chief. Ironically they choose Anatol, a former anarchist who had been condemned to death for having assassinated the head of a government. Anatol falls in love with Esther, one of the island women, but is killed by Tommy, one of the prisoners, who also kills Esther for refusing his advances.

Milagro en la Plaza del Progreso, 1953, offers no great psychological penetration or theme, but the farcical and comic effects do not shroud the positive philosophy of "hacer bien." Don Claudio steals a million pesetas from his company to distribute them, at the suggestion of an angel, he says, to various people. His pre-Christmas largess evokes various human responses from the recipients when he is later charged with the theft, but all ends happily with the idea that good Christians always share what they have with those less fortunate than they.

La muralla, 1954, which had over two thousand performances, resembles the case of conscience presented by Echegaray's *O locura o santidad,* with an equally tragic resistance on the part of ordinary human beings to performing their Christian duties. Jorge Hontanar y Villamil, by falsifying a will which fell into his hands during the civil war fighting, inherited an estate which rightly belonged to Gervasio Quiroga. Jorge is now a pillar of society while Quiroga, a man of doubtful reputation, has been in jail for smuggling. One day, after suffering a heart attack, Jorge sees the light, decides to repent, becomes a good Catholic, and wishes to make restitution. When he attempts to turn over the hacienda, his friends, servants, wife, and daughter turn against him. They feel it is foolish, indeed wicked, to confess his shame and dishonor, return the money, and create a scandal.

They build a wall of interest, of prejudice and socially "normal" reactions to his attempts, and lie and cheat to keep him from his Christian action. Jorge dies before he can give back the property, the scandal is avoided, and the family will continue to be "good" Catholics who go to church and arrange for masses. For so many, unfortunately, says Calvo-Sotelo, conventions of society and family name are more important than spiritual goals.

Historia de un resentido, 1956, is one of Calvo-Sotelo's best attempts at psychological characterization. Dalmiro Quintana is a failure in a world of failures. He fancies himself a playwright and author with talent, but he has none. He becomes terribly frustrated and embittered, for as he says, "lo normal es que quienes sufren ese desengaño se hagan resentidos." [12] Dalmiro's ambition far outstrips his talent. His wife, Pilar, a good and religious woman, is prepared to forgive him all his deficiencies, even a repeated affair with an old girl friend, Cristina. Dalmiro submits a play to a literary contest and is awarded the prize by Lorenzo Monteverde, a famous writer whom Dalmiro admires. He awarded him the prize, not because the play had merit, but because he had designs on Pilar. The play is a resounding failure. When the civil war starts, Dalmiro fights for the Republic and kills Lorenzo Monteverde when he finds the latter in a café. Monteverde, a wayward son of the Church, repents before he dies and is absolved by the conveniently present priest. Dalmiro is tried and executed.

The play covers a period of eighteen years, the first act from 1921 to 1924, the second from 1927 to 1931, and the third from 1932 to 1939. An extra character, called El Cronista, Pilar's brother, keeps up a running commentary on Dalmiro's life and on time transitions. The conclusion of the work is that the world is full of Quintanas, and in spite of the author's protests that no political motive was intended, it is obvious that he equates Dalmiro's wickedness with his Republican sympathies.

Una muchachita de Valladolid, 1957, treats Mercedes and her husband Patricio. The latter is a diplomat to a South American country and wishes to obtain an important petroleum concession for Spain. His wife is jealous of his Don Juan activities and threatens to employ her own charms to obtain the same oil concession. A local revolt ends their potential problems, and the double standard of marital behavior is obviously though comically condemned.

La herencia, 1957, relates the story of Laura Romero, the widow of a naval hero of Franco's forces. She lives only in the past, worships her husband's memory, and mourns his loss. Her son meets a young girl and falls in love with her. To the mother's horror it is discovered that the girl's father was the Republican who had condemned her husband to death. She wants her son to give up his plans of marriage, but he refuses. The mother's brother feels it is necessary to pardon the children, even though he hates Republicans. The mother is inconsolable, but the implication is that she may find it possible to pardon the children some day. The older generation, says Calvo-Sotelo, cannot forget the horror of the civil war, but the younger one, consisting of those who did not experience it directly, may, through love, forget the past and look to the future.

In viewing the drama of Calvo-Sotelo as compared with that of the more artistic and younger Buero Vallejo, striking similarities and significant differences emerge. Both dramatists moralize about the misery of their contemporary world and the anguish of real people, view life as essentially tragic, and avoid over-emphasis of sentiment. Calvo-Sotelo, although his themes may be more naturalistic and his stage action more violent, is not as consistently tragic in tone. Calvo paints somber canvases (along with many light and pleasing ones), but he allows for redemption through love, religion, or both. Buero also consistently sees modern life as tragic with a final hope of betterment. Calvo-Sotelo stresses a thesis; Buero concentrates more on ideas. Calvo-Sotelo insists on the Catholic and political implications of Spanish life; Buero largely ignores them, although they may be read into some of his plays. Buero, on the other hand, understands reality in a broader form and his human values have more universal application. Fantasy, consistently present in Buero's works, is largely missing in Calvo-Sotelo's, but the latter writes amusing comedies which the former has not attempted.

Calvo-Sotelo offers nothing startlingly new, for although his moralizing deals with contemporary themes, it echoes a tendency almost as old as Spanish literature itself. His popularity stems from an ability to express not only what many Spaniards say but also what many of them believe. He appeals to the dream image they have of themselves as good and successful men, but he touches, also, the subconscious of those who carry an inevitable burden of guilt in a cruel world which some of them helped to create and which some of them unwillingly inherited.

[From *Hispania,* vol. XLVI, no. 1, March, 1963]

Jacinto Grau and the
Meaning of Existence

ANGUISH and despair have marked the Spanish literature of twentieth century man. One can trace the existential anguish in the works of Ortega y Gasset, Unamuno, Sender, Laforet, Cela, and in the *tremendista* writings in general. Pedro Laín Entralgo in *La espera y la esperanza* opposes to this trend his analysis, claiming that Machado and others exhibit in their resistance to despair, a philosophy of hope.

Pérez de Ayala emphasizes man's free will and the importance of living one's life. Baroja insists on a constant battle with the world to create one's own environment. Unamuno, in addition to his themes of immortality, anguish, and search for God, in discovering life's absurdity, finds life as he becomes life. He stresses the idea of the final boundary, and his heroes, like Alejandro in *Nada menos que todo un hombre,* although they fight with passion and with a will to dominate life, must in the end succumb to unconquerable death. All share the concept of man as a builder of his own moment, the maker of his own future.

Sartre claims that man, unlike objects, through present action to construct a future creates a future which permits understanding and changing the present. Ortega, much earlier, expressed the same idea more clearly in his essay, "En torno a Galileo":

> Porque esto es lo que verdaderamente diferencia al hombre de la piedra: no que el hombre tenga entendimiento y la piedra carezca de él. Podemos imaginar una piedra muy inteligente, pero como el ser piedra le es dado ya hecho de una vez para siempre y no tiene que decidirlo ella, no necesita para ser piedra plantearse en cada momento el problema de sí misma preguntándose: '¿qué tengo yo que hacer

ahora?, o lo que es igual, ¿qué tengo yo que ser?'...El hombre, cada
hombre, tiene que decidir en cada instante lo que va a hacer, lo que
va a ser en el siguiente. Esta decisión es intransferible; nadie puede
sustituirme en la faena de decidirme, de decidir mi vida.[1]

Thus, the true difference between man and stone is that the stone's nature
is fixed whereas man must decide it at each moment.

Jerónimo Mallo (*Hispania*, XXXIX (1956), 49–55) and Gerald E.
Wade (*Tennessee Studies in Literature*, I, 51–58) have mentioned some of
the existential trends in contemporary Spanish novels such as *Nada, El verdugo afable,* and *La familia de Pascual Duarte,* which exhibit both a philosophy of despair and yet one of choice. As Wade points out, Pascual
Duarte has "been thrown into the world" and is inextricably involved with
life. In Sartre's *L'Être et le Néant,* a young man has to choose between
staying with his mother or fighting in England and choosing his own values. He has been flung into a world that involves his relationship with his
mother and hers with him. Camus' Meursault, too, resembles Pascual in
many ways.

The existentialism of Ortega, Unamuno, Sartre, and others is a personal
drama, as it is in Grau, but he gives it a broader base, and shows both existential anguish and optimism through human love. He stresses individual
problems, but he sees more than the individual alone, thrown into a world
he never made; he sees a humanity which cannot escape itself as he presents various aspects of the individual's struggle with the forces which hem
him in and impel him to his fate. Among the many themes we find: (1)
the wish to love and be loved, (2) the creation of one's environment
through will, (3) the need for action in living one's life, (4) freedom as
an absolute value and man's choice of values, (5) man's attempt to realize
existence in spite of the absurdity of Death, and (6) religion as something
to be lived rather than discussed.

1. Love according to Sartre is the wish to be loved and lies in the absorp-
tion of the Other and becoming the Other's source of values and the meaning of his freedom, an impossibility which brings frustration. The intru-
sion of another person into one's world brings fear and shame as reactions.
Grau's works present this annihilating quality of sexual desire. In *El Conde
Alarcos* (1907) the Infanta and the Count ensnare each "Other's" freedom in the flesh. One character reduces itself to nothing but an object

before the other's freedom. Grau accepts Sartre's contention that the inability to express oneself or be a part of another being causes anguish, but he rejects Heidegger's conclusion that the ordinary mode of being with others is impersonal, debased, and unauthentic. Mariano (*El mismo daño,* 1919) desires to possess Isabel in every respect. "Sabe que mi amor por ti, en vez de amenguar y transformarse, crece, crece y como si todo yo fuera carne encendida, alma entre llamas, me retuerzo ebrio de ti, y hasta en la médula de mis huesos, siento la angustia de que tu pensamiento, tu deseo, toda tú! no seas mía, mía sola . . . y ante la impotencia de mi voluntad fuerte para conseguirlo, una locura de iras contenidas, parece destrozarme dentro, una a una, todas las entrañas." [2] The father suffers in his lack of possession of the loved one and the rivalry of his son Albert, married to a woman he cannot comprehend or love. Nor does Albert's wife, Elisa, love him, although they finally escape their anguish through love. *El burlador que no se burla* (1927) is full of the theme of possession of and identification with the loved object. Don Juan expresses it thus to Adelia: "Como dejarte, si me abrasa el deseo insaciable de ser tú misma. . . . Quisiera fundirme en ti. Ser tú. Ante ti me siento incompleto. Ansío confundir mi vida con la tuya. No ser yo, para ser tú, sin dejar de ser yo. Vivir contigo tu vida y la mía a un mismo tiempo." [3] At times this feeling of possession becomes a hate of all others in one Other, as Sartre expressed it in *L'Être et le Néant.* One conserves one's existence by pursuing the death of a particular Other. Florencio's hate for Veneranda (*Entre llamas,* 1907) stems from her beauty which humiliates him, and he feels subconsciously that he must destroy her in order to be free. Nevertheless, he makes the final desperate attempt to appropriate and possess her in order to appropriate the world symbolically. The Infanta hates and loves Count Alarcos at the same time, and he must resolve his anguish by obtaining the loved object. Don Juan de Carillana's tragedy (*Don Juan de Carillana,* 1913) is that he cannot possess his daughter. Other characters fitting Sartre's definition of the sadistic and the masochistic would be Alejandra of *El caballero Varona* (1925), Gabriela in *El tercer demonio* (1908), Carillana's daughter and "la señora guapa" of *La señora guapa* (1932).

2. More important than the love or hate identification is the creation of man's essence through freedom and the assertion of his will through action, even though he must live dangerously at times in the expression of that will. Dilia (*En Ildaria,* 1913), Sonia's younger sister, insists on her inde-

pendence and an overpowering compulsion to follow her will in order to
determine her own future through that will, for only those who live their
lives are important. Delmas, who is in love with Dilia, evidences the same
existentialist independence. He insists that the world is will or nothing.
"Yo soy Delmas! Yo deseo, quiero las cosas de veras. Yo soy lo que son
pocos: una voluntad! Ella me ha hecho hombre. Ella me ha hecho Delmas
en fin. Es tan grande esa voluntad que vería al destino frente a frente sin
pestañear, y sabría dejarse aplastar por él impasible; porque yo soy más
fuerte que el destino, y sé sonreír indiferente . . . Mi vida depende de mí.
El mundo es voluntad, o no es nada." [4] El caballero Varona insists that
the only friend he has in the world is himself and his will power, and the
only person indispensable to one's self is that self. He feels he is in absolute
control of his environment but shows bad faith in refusing to battle with
personalities which he fears are too strong. He declares that he prizes his
freedom and will so much that he is willing to use them to destroy himself
"antes que ser vencido por otra voluntad más fuerte que la suya . . . Yo
quiero ser el solo dueño de mis horas, el único señor de todo yo, el amo
de mi fuerza y hasta de mi abyección. Todo mío, hasta mis miserias de
mortal." [5] For Varona to be free to act out his own life is as indispensable
as life itself. Alejandra, too, wants to be free to arrange her life through
her own will and action. "Yo soy una mujer para toda una vida o para nada
. . . Yo soy una mujer independiente, sin más autoridad sobre mí que mi
voluntad, ni más deberes que los que yo me impongo" (p. 139).

In *Los tres locos del mundo* (1925) the doctor feels that only we are
important to ourselves in acting out our lives. The señora says to Ilusión,
"Esta humanidad viene a ser un hormiguero más sobre la tierra, con algunas hormigas rebeldes como yo, que hacen lo que les parece." [6] She
plays with men to satisfy her "amor propio" and insists on carving out her
own destiny. Antonio (*La señora guapa*) also asserts that "la vida es lo
que quieren que sea los que la viven." [7] In *El burlador que no se burla*
Juan refuses to follow the Devil's suggestion that he rebel against God
before he dies. Juan states that he is the ruler of his own destiny and has
no master. "No necesito rebelarme contra nadie para hacer lo que se me
antoja . . . La rebeldía supone tener un amo contra quien rebelarse, y yo
no tengo ninguno. Soy el amo de mí mismo" (p. 126). He tells Destiny
that he is and will continue to be his own destiny. "Mi destino soy yo."
Telesforo (*Las gafas de don Telesforo*, 1954) creates for himself a new

world and finally teaches his wife to do the same. He maintains that each person determines his own life: "elegir la ilusión que más les plazca y vivir con arreglo a ella en la seguridad de que la ilusión escogida no es menos real que lo que llamamos realidad." [8] He creates for himself as does Criserea (*El dominio del mundo,* 1944), who says that she still has her will which is stronger than things, and that until death she will always seek out the answer to its own enigma.

3. Part of the expression of one's will and freedom lies in action. For Grau, most men aspire to a resigned and moderate life of a grayish tone, but some men forge for themselves a rich and wonderful world which it would be a tragedy to abandon. The most important thing is "crearse a sí mismo y a su obra." [9] Sartre, too, states there is no reality except in action. In this action of Sartre and Grau only the present, separating the past from the future, is important. The past is gone, and the future is a nonexistent now not yet present. The Gerente in *La casa del diablo* (1933) emphasizes this point. "Lo que fué y lo que será me tienen sin cuidado. Me importa sólo el presente." [10] Don Juan (*El burlador que no se burla*) insists: "De lo pasado sólo vive la vida pobre que se va muriendo. Yo vivo de lo presente, como todo" (p. 74). The three old ladies of *Los tres locos del mundo* must die, for they live in the past and refuse to act in the present. Mariano (*El mismo daño*) thinks: "El mundo está lleno de criaturas tibias : sólo viven y duran en él las almas ardientes" (pp. 237–238). The Novio (*La casa del diablo*) calms the Esposa and shows her where her future lies by saying: "No es cuestión de decir sino de hacer" (p. 26). Reality can be found through action and not by dreams. Ilusión (*Los tres locos del mundo*) believes that one should fight always to act out one's desires. Tamara (*El dominio del mundo*) admits that "no venimos a la vida para ser dichosos, sino para vivirla," but Criserea rebels against her destiny and gives up a throne for "quise el camino tortuoso de mi voluntad, que me llevó a encontrarlo forjándolo de nuevo. Mi vida ha sido siempre únicamente mía, y nadie puede juzgarla más que yo." [11] The Devil in *Los tres locos del mundo* revolts against Destiny, for he will fight for eternity even though defeated, "el único rebelde que, derrotado, sigue luchando eternamente" (p. 155). The Gerente (*La casa del diablo*) claims that philosophy has no answer any more than does religion, the hope of the weak. One's destiny lies in one's will power to live his life, and if one gives up, one dies. "Cuando se vive no se filosofa; se vive" (p. 52).

4. Though man moves in an absurd world without guidance except his own will to action, he is responsible for what he will make of his life and the values he chooses to create. Grau dislikes orthodox moral codes and emphasizes one's responsibility to humanity. Camus, too, in *Caligula* and *Le Malentendu* seems to insist that even in an absurd human existence human beings are responsible. The individual in Grau's plays realizes his complete freedom; yet he is responsible, too. Don Telesforo says to the Devil: "Debiera usted advertir que yo prefiero la ilusión del deber cumplido, por la fuerza que me da saber que poseo una voluntad que satisface mi orgullo. Usted con todo su poder diabólico no puede comprender a hombres cual yo necesitados de trazarse normas supremas para autogobernarse. . . . No debemos aceptar como verdades más que las que son útiles a la vida humana" (p. 155). Portales, Alejandra's husband, preaches harmony through which men together can give inspiration to one another and without which one's existence would be unbearable. The doctor of *Los tres locos del mundo* agrees that only humanity is important.

In Sartre's *Huis Clos* Garcin remains in hell, and in *Les jeux son faits* the characters, after a violent death, are given a brief second chance for happiness but cannot take advantage of it. In *La casa del diablo* the characters return to attempt to change their essence. Only those who have learned the meaning of love have a chance for eternal life. La Viajera and the Esposo refuse to remain enslaved to their pasts and exercise their liberty of action. Pablo states man's responsibility for his action, and fear, even in a fearful world, is no excuse. No matter what the values, man struggles constantly to create them, and in their responsibility the Novia goes to her death, the Director to his betrayal, the Señora to the imposition of her will, and the Devil to his revolt.

Freedom, the use of one's will power to act out one's life and create one's essence, the need for humanity and good faith, form but one aspect of Grau's existentialism. The constant interplay of the will to dominate and the will to be dominated leads to antagonisms, for two human individuals can never completely agree. There is always some force of domination, and one cannot escape the sense of guilt or of being superfluous or of not belonging. The sense of guilt and anguish in Grau takes three general forms, although at times they fuse into one multifaceted form. These are: the lack of ability to communicate, lack of will and clash of personalities; the realization of death's inevitability; and the search for and conflict with God and Love.

5. Jaspers and others have analyzed the various aspects of chance and suffering which limit one's existence or the existence of others. Jaspers talks in terms of "boundary situations." [12] Man feels himself oppressed and hemmed in by a strange and hostile environment, limited by physical and psychological factors. He is a prisoner of his world and of himself, and in his efforts to gain mastery he meets new boundary or limit situations. He soon becomes conscious of the abysses which cannot be bridged over, and at times is overwhelmed by a feeling of anguish in his conflicts with these boundaries. One of these boundary situations is man's feeling of not belonging or communicating in a clashing and often meaningless world. Doña María (*El burlador que no se burla*) expresses it as: "Desde que nacemos estamos en guerra con todo y con todos, empezando por nosotros mismos" (pp. 32–33). Telesforo agrees with the doctor who implies that the whole world is one big contradiction. He believes that "cada cual se crea su realidad. La mía tan ilusoria como la de usted, no es la de usted. Por eso no podemos ponernos de acuerdo" (p. 145). The Esposo (*El burlador que no se burla*) says that one feels futility in trying to evaluate life and things. "Cómo se desespera. . . y para qué. Tan inútil es vivir como morir" (p. 26). This feeling of futility and aloneness in the world is most concisely expressed in *La casa del diablo*. The Esposo admits that "todo lo que se hace de fuerte y grande en el mundo . . . a la postre, un día se enfriará . . . y todo este grotesco fenómeno de la humanidad, será en el infinito algo tan inútil, con su saber, sus religiones, sus ideas, sus ambiciones, sus dolores, tan inútil, como algo que no ha existido nunca. Un hecho insignificante en el tiempo, nada, absolutamente nada, en ese eterno juego de los universos pavorosamente inmensos" (p. 61).

Alejandra suffers what Varona calls "hastío de la vida que es el . . . infierno del vivir" (p. 227), and her husband agrees that the world with the limitations it imposes is an enemy of the individual. In *Destino* (1945), Laura, abandoned in the world, can resolve her impossible love for Edmundo only through her death. She scorns existence which has been gray and sterile for her and thinks only in terms of "librarme de mi angustia." [13] The Hermano (*Horas de vida*, 1902) asserts: "Estamos condenados en una cárcel infranqueable." [14] In *Entre llamas*, a play of clashing personalities, lover and lover, mother and son, reveal the challenge of love and hate which man must meet. Veneranda says, "Me parece que estoy siempre sola, estando acompañada. Ni yo misma me lo sé explicar. Estoy a tu lado, y no estoy a tu lado. Estoy aquí y no estoy aquí." [15] She tells Daniel that man cannot comprehend what he is, and the decision as to what path to take is an agonizing one. Miguel feels what Sartre and others have termed "nausea," and Florencio cannot escape his feeling of not belonging.

In escaping from one situation we fall into another from which we cannot escape, but while insignificant happenings may ruin any existence, the only boundary situation we cannot overcome is death. Even Juan (*El burlador que no se burla*), the man who fears nothing, finds it a profound secret which he cannot fathom, "un secreto inacabable . . . incogible" (p. 131). Grau in his work on Unamuno says: "La muerte es la coacción suprema que nos tiene cogidos en sus garras . . . y he ahí todo el nudo gordiano del hecho de vivir, para morir como el único fin claro . . . La muerte . . . sigue tan desconocida para nosotros como todo" (pp. 53–54). Grau sees that life is less than a dream whose end is the inconceivable and absolute "nothingness." One's agony is frightful in the persistent fight of one's reason to try to fathom the mystery. Life is devalued tragically by being confined in the temporal, which he terms "agonía." Man's anxiety to know what his fate will be in order to know if he can live, cannot be calmed with vague abstractions, scientific or philosophical, which say nothing. As with Unamuno, Grau's characters face the boundary of death as a personal and irreplacable affair. Tamara (*El dominio del mundo*) informs Criserea that they are not in life to be happy but to live it while they can because "todo lo que vive va conducido por un camino fatal a la muerte y va obligado a seguir ese camino . . . El mundo es y será siempre . . . una gran cárcel de esperanzas y una tumba inllenable de vidas" (p. 14). Laura recognizes the necessity of adapting her existence to the prospect of death and also that there can be no life without death. Carillana, a man of what Grau calls "el dolorido sentir," realizes in anguish that life passes and death waits for all mankind. In *La señora guapa* Adivina's contention that mankind suffers from "una enfermedad mortal," a death which it cannot avoid, implies the Kierkegaard and Heidegger "dread" of a potentiality denied and unmaterialized. She fears the loss of her ego and being. The Novio of *La casa del diablo* knows that everything may have a remedy in life except death, something to dread. He continues: "No podrás comprender nunca qué pena más insondable y terrible tuve, . . . cercano ya de la asfixia, ya casi en plena agonía, sólo podía pensar en el horror de que estuviera irremediablemente para siempre en la nada" (p. 109). The caminante in *Horas de vida* tells the sister she cannot know or understand the lives of others since all are condemned to a march whose only boundary is the mysterious one of death. Florencio expresses anguish and despair at the forlornness of human existence in a universe where the only justice which awaits man is death, a part of what Grau means when he talks of "la íntima tragedia que toda criatura humana más o menos consciente lleva dentro." [16]

6. The idea of death leads us to the next existential relationship in Grau. Grau's religious sentiments partake of both Christian and non-Christian existentialism. Whoever has no God has no self, and who has no self is in despair. Yet faith in humanity may be more important than faith in God. Kierkegaard dealt with states of anguish in terms of man's relationship to God, the constant awareness of death, and the realization of the gap between him and God. Grau believes the only real change God can bring about is to get man to understand himself—to the degree that we understand our existence, it is authentic or unauthentic. In other works the characters deny God, and each person must manufacture for himself his own essence from existence without the help of God. For some of the characters He exists, but they suffer for they cannot find Him, as man's anguish is solved to the extent that he has faith. For others man must rebel against God. "La señora guapa" insists, "Yo no tengo más Dios que yo misma" (p. 170). Whether God prevails or not, the greatest power of salvation in the universe is the power of love.

Grau's humanity ofter suffers from an insatiable appetite for the continuous resurrection of the flesh. This thirst for divinity separates the superior man from those limited ones closer to the animal, but life for man will continue to be what God wants, and Christian agony will continue as man suffers before the impossibility of possessing faith. The Hermana (*Horas de vida*) insists that God lives outside our souls, too, and may be sought there as well as within us. Yet she is anguished at being cast into a world she never made. "Dios quiere que lloremos. Mi ansiedad es tan grande . . . tan grande mi sed, tan infinita, que tú no podrás apagarla, hermano" (p. 119). In *El hijo pródigo* (1917) Elda's anguish is part of her guilt-ridden complex in the sight of God, for she has lost Him through her love for her own stepson and suffers a martyrdom, as she says, without end nor hope until death. Lotan will continue to determine his destiny, but disillusioned with the various stages of human existence, he hopes to discover his destiny, "anhelando verlo un día más allá de mí, eterno en Jehová." [17] Pigmalión (*El señor de Pigmalión,* 1921) does not agree that God is an answer to the anguish man feels in a senseless life and death, but he feels guilty in the sight of God whose function he has tried to assume. "Dios me castiga por haber querido meterme en su oficio." [18] Count Alarcos suffers, anguished and guilty, in the presence of God at the thought of his crime, though the Infanta is willing to suffer the consequences of her desires. Carillana entertains the idea of seeking the eternal through a renewal of his faith as the only escape from the suffering "en hastío el mañana angustioso." [19] Tamara (*El dominio del mundo*) carries this a step further and contends that it is useless to hesitate or try to change one's path, for everything about us "no tiene más libertad ni voluntad que las que le han dado dioses que tenemos y no conocemos ni conoceremos nunca probablemente" (p. 14), and Criserea, blind and miserable after having once possessed the world, insists that "sólo a unos dioses que no conozco podré dar un día mis razones" (p. 4).

Many are not willing to give in to a superior being. Pigmalión's puppets revolt against their creator, renounce his authority, and cause his death. They hate him and want their liberty. Pigmalión brings to his creations not happiness, but an awareness of their existence, and like Jupiter in Sartre's *Les Mouches,* he cannot command his puppets when they realize their existence. Pigmalión has to die, for "yo los inventé entre anhelos y fiebres, y ahora que viven y asombran cual un prodigio desconocido hasta el presente, ellos me poseen a mí, a su creador, y en lugar del amo, he pasado a ser el esclavo de mis juguetes" (pp. 45–46). Urdemalas determines his own future by revolting against his creator. Even Juan refuses sympathy to a creator who gave him nothing to work with, and his "cu cu" reflects the absurdity of all human existence. The Devil in *Los tres locos del mundo,* summoned by Destiny, refuses to acknowledge God's jurisdiction, renounces Him, insists he alone will determine his life, and exclaims: "Acabo de presentar mi renuncia irrevocable a Dios" (p. 102).

Human love and love of humanity may supplant faith in God, and man saves himself through love rather than through faith. Guilt and fear of the unknown may be tempered by love. Pablo (*La casa del diablo*) gives the characters two alternatives, life on earth or entrance into Heaven. The Esposo, Novio, and Viajera achieve eternity, but the others must return to earth once again to learn about life and love. The conclusion of salvation through love resembles superficially that of Sartre in *Les jeux sont faits*. Eve and Pierre are allowed to return to earth through love, whereas in *La casa del diablo* those saved achieve eternal knowledge of God, the reverse of Sartre's position. Idealism, pity, love, and charity, especially love of humanity, appear more obvious in Grau's work, although in both cases the love of humanity or the love of the Other must be true love. The Gerente, who never had time for love and did not understand the meaning of anguish, returns to earth. The Viajera, who found love before death, goes to Heaven, and the Novio, lacking faith in God, will find Him through true love. The Esposo saves himself since he feels compassion for the world's suffering and stresses charity as the greatest of all virtues.

Heidegger stresses the "debasement of others to mere tools by the rare men of character who had risen to the level of a richer genuine existence," [20] but Grau can envisage a relation of togetherness in which two human beings stand as free and equal, can know each other, and achieve salvation through the power of love.

[From *Hispania,* vol. XLIV, no. 1, March 1961]

Reality in The Works
of Alejandro Casona

PEDRO SALINAS has examined the poetry of Garcilaso, Góngora, Espronceda, and others and has shown how each poet attempts to reproduce, accept, idealize, and exalt reality or escape from and revolt against it.[1] A theme of conflict between reality and idealism or the interplay of the material and the visionary has been a characteristic of many Spanish authors, of whom Cervantes and Calderón are outstanding examples.

Alejandro Casona continues this tradition in his acceptance of the theme. He combines fantasy and reality in a special manner, insisting on the human quality of his fantastic reactions in their relationships with worldly beings. His devils in *Otra vez el Diablo* and in *La barca sin pescador* are more human than supernatural in their portrayal, as is the frustrated Peregrina in *La dama del alba*. Casona, however, adds further vigor to the tradition in keeping with twentieth-century psychological and philosophical concepts. His addition might be termed not so much acceptance of as adjustment to reality, as he insists that man's happiness lies in facing the truth instead of seeking to escape into a variety of fantasy worlds.

In schizophrenia, interest in adjusting to reality has become secondary to other interests. Casona has examined the lives of individuals whose experiences with other people have been painful or dangerous, so that avoiding them became a measure to preserve comfort or safety. His concern is with having these individuals adjust to reality, for his conclusion is that only in such adjustment, even when it entails giving up privileges, lies the enjoyment of a full and meaningful life.

Casona's characters, in their desire for flight from the world, exhibit essentially a negative attitude and only in their adaptation, complete or partial, do they convert to positive aspirations. Very often a return to a struggle for a positive end implies conversion, not only to reality but to an ethical life, for the sense of duty and ethics is very strong in Casona, and very often ethical living and reality are synonymous for him.

Casona had to face difficulties in his own life in his partisanship of the Republican cause and in devoting himself, in his play *Nuestra Natacha,* to a truth he felt it was his duty to portray. As Don Florín says in *La sirena varada*: "Mentirlo no; por dura que sea la verdad, hay que mirarla de frente. De nada sirve vendarse los ojos." [2]

Casona's characters attempt to escape through illusion which will disguise the unhappiness or the sordidness they have known. In general, they make their temporary "escape" from reality through fantasy, evil, desertion or rejection of the world, and sacrifice.

The Infantina in *Otra vez el diablo,* Sirena and Don Joaquín in *La sirena varada,* and the Amante in *Prohibido suicidarse en primavera* all weave their lives into a fantasy world to defend themselves from the cruelty of the real one. The Infantina thinks of life as a fairy tale and seeks her romantic ideal in the young and handsome bandit captain. "Y yo que estaba dispuesta a creer que todo era cuento." [3] She is awakened from her dream world by the real advances of the Estudiante and realizes that life has many complications which she must accept in order to know true love. She stops seeking imaginary dangers and faces the real ones which confront her.

Sirena, in order to forget the sordidness of her circus life, creates for herself the fantasy that she is a mermaid. She tries to believe she had lived at the bottom of the sea and only recently has become a land prisoner. Through the help of Don Florín she forgets the false universe and adjusts to the real one. Her unborn child becomes the symbol of the future to her, and for its sake she will not return to the formerly attractive sea. "No, ya estuve una vez. . . . Es un abismo amargo" (p. 96). Though reality is not a perfect state, she recognizes it as the only way to a happy future. She rejects her beautiful fantasy and helps her husband reach a livable compromise.

The Amante Imaginario pretends to be the lover of a famous opera star and, even though at times he sees the falseness of his pretense, he insists: "Necesito que la crean todos. Necesito creerla yo también." [4] When he finally meets her, he realizes that she is not the solution to his problems and that illusion cannot offer permanent escape. "La quiero, me gustaría verla siempre. Pero un poco desde lejos" (p. 188). He denies the fantasy that he has created and adapts to reality by becoming a travel writer.

Don Joaquín, the hired ghost, is not sure whether he has really died or not, but he finally realizes that he cannot be happy in his make-believe and decides to become a gardener. As he says: "Esto es vivir, y no aquello de antes. . . . Aquella vida era un disparate." [5]

Both Ricardo Jordan in *La barca sin pescador* and the Estudiante in *Otra vez el diablo* thought that they could rise above their reality through evil. Ricardo, betrayed by his friends, accepts the Devil's aid in order to escape the problems which face him. He wishes the death of an innocent man and rationalizes that since he doesn't know his victim, he will not be affected. He soon realizes that "en la vida de un hombre está la vida de todos los hombres." [6] Good triumphs over evil, reality over illusion, and through his love for the wife of the victim, he can begin to try to atone for the damage he has done. The final solution is not perfect, as Ricardo renounces the Devil and the evil Ricardo Jordan and makes an adjustment to a new life. In spite of the hardships involved, through his new found love he will find the way to happiness.

Ricardo in *La sirena varada* and Doctor Roda in *Prohibido suicidarse en primavera* remove themselves physically and spiritually from the everyday world. Ricardo has had material wealth but has missed much of childhood's pleasures, having been an unhappy and unloved child. He seeks to escape the sorrows of the world, which he finds boring and stupid, and establishes a refuge for others who seek escape. "Encuentro que la vida es aburrida y estúpida por falta de imaginación. A inventar una vida nueva, a soñar imposibles . . . un asilo para huérfanos de sentido común." [7] He achieves temporary satisfaction in his love for Sirena but soon wants something more substantial in their relations than her mermaid story. "Pero hoy no me bastan. Esta vida arbitraria que nos hemos creado empieza a marearme" (p. 53). His new happiness is not without its bitterness and an occasional relapse. "Y es esta la verdad? Siempre? Ah, no. No será!" (p. 94). But Sirena convinces him that even ugliness is better than illusion and Ricardo finally agrees, saved through love.

Doctor Roda rationalizes his *Hogar de Suicidas,* making much of the stages of readjustment of those seeking to flee their responsibilities, until he realizes that by giving the victims a refuge from the world with other unfortunates, he is not helping their recovery. "Han ideado un refugio para almas vacilantes pero no han sospechado lo que un ambiente así puede contagiar a los otros." [8] By withdrawing from society he failed to accomplish his noble purpose, and so he takes the advice to return to the real world and its problems. "Cierre esta casa, amigo Roda. Emplee su talento allí donde los hombres viven y trabajan." His decision to close the *Hogar* is his first step in dealing with the problem of suicide in a realistic manner.

Some of Casona's characters refuse to accept reality. The Madre in *La dama del alba,* Daniel in *La sirena varada,* and Hans in *Prohibido suicidarse en primavera* escape in this manner. The Madre grieves for the supposedly dead Angélica and refuses to live a normal life. She will not allow changes in her daughter's room. "Ni el sol tiene derecho a entrar en su cuarto. Ese polvo es lo único que me queda de aquel día." [9] She cannot agree with Abuelo's contention that what has happened has happened and that life must go on in positive rather than negative fashion. When Adela enters her life she begins to realize that life has meaning and she finds happiness again in reality. As she says: "Ya había comprendido la gran lección" (p. 126).

Daniel, the blind painter, is one of the few characters who never adjusts to reality and therefore can find no happiness. He is bitter about what he terms the "dirty world" and pretends he is trying to invent new colors. When Ricardo rips the blindfold from his eyes and accuses him of being a coward, Daniel demands his bandage back. He cannot allow himself to admit his blindness, even though Sirena encourages him to adjust, "Hay tantas cosas hermosas en el mundo. ¿Por qué no te quitas la venda un momento?" [10]

Hans, too, is unable to face normal life. Ruined by the war, he has become obsessed with the thought of death and seeks pleasure only through the sufferings of others. He is doomed to a perpetual search for a contentment he will never find.

Martín of *La dama del alba* escapes by concealing the truth temporarily. He knew that Angélica was not the image of purity all thought her to be. By refusing to tell the truth he had been contributing to the world of fantasy, but when he fell in love with Adela he felt that real escape lay in building a life for himself elsewhere. He had been living one lie and wanted to escape now into a more involved one. He was spared the decision of a choice between the real and the unreal by finally telling the truth about Angélica, so his return to the real world is through truth. Even La Peregrina of *La dama del alba* dreams of escape. She wants to "adornarme de rosas como las campesinas, vivir entre niños felices y tener un hombre hermoso a quien amar" (p. 51), but as Death she realizes the impossibility of her fantasy and makes the best of her destiny, for she knows that through suffering may come peace.

Sacrifice and duty are key aspects of Casona's philosophy. Adela of *La dama del alba* sought escape in suicide, but later she found meaning in life in her love for Martín. "No quiero recordar ese mal momento" (p. 93), she says, and though she weakens momentarily when Martín reveals the truth to her, she resolves, with Peregrina's help, to continue to face life. Chloe, in *Prohibido suicidarse en primavera,* attempts to kill herself in order to bring two brothers together, and then tries to sacrifice her love by marrying Juan instead of Fernando, whom she really loves. She wants to create for Juan the illusion of being loved for once in his lonely life. "Yo seré a su lado la madre . . . la hermana que no tuvo" (p. 196). She discovers that her choice is false and one more illusory attempt at happiness. True happiness can come only from the real love she feels for Fernando and sacrificing that reality for an illusion would have brought unhappiness to all three. Her final philosophy, like Casona's, is: "La vida no es solamente un derecho. Es sobre todo un deber" (p. 138). Juan has attempted suicide to keep from murdering his brother. Full of guilt feelings, he maintains a paranoid obsession that his brother has robbed his life of love. He finally makes the adjustment in spite of his anguish and refuses Chloe's sacrifice, although he will need continuing help to maintain his adjustment. Alicia is another who sees temporary refuge in Roda's retreat. She is tired of struggling against solitude and hunger, but basically she is not a neurotic type and she is willing to help Dr. Roda adjust others to life and thus find happiness through service.

Isabel of *Los árboles mueren de pie,* like Adela, unhappy, friendless, and unable to recall any past happiness, seeks escape through suicide. When offered a chance for friendship and, more important, for service to fellow sufferers, she recovers her sense of belonging and becomes a useful member of society. Love saves her from a return to her cold room and dusty geraniums. Balboa in the same play, with noble motivation, has lied to his wife about her worthless grandson, seeking to create a false illusion to protect her, but when La Abuela learns the truth, she is willing to give up her fantasy, for, as she says, "Muerta por dentro pero de pie, como un árbol." [11] Her sacrifice, like that of Natacha and others, is a positive one to further the happiness of those who have helped her.

In *Nuestra Natacha* the idea of adjustment to reality is not the central theme, but even here there prevails the idea that each person must find his own place in life and that moral responsibility must be met before personal happiness can be achieved. It is not only Natacha who sacrifices herself for the reform-school youths. Most of them go from rebellion and frustration to adjusted lives. Juan channels his animal energy into constructive channels for Marga. She ceases to rebel and seeks redemption, as did Sirena, through motherhood. Lalo, pictured in earlier scenes as an unmotivated, continual, intentional failure at the university, through his love for Natacha, becomes the man who works hard and faces honestly the problems of life.

Angélica of *La dama del alba* has been living a life of illusion. She returns to the family thinking that the sordid reality of her past life can be forgotten. Peregrina points out that in her case this is not realistic thinking: "Una vez destrozaste tu casa al irte; quieres destrozarla otra vez al volver? . . . A salvar valientemente lo único que te queda: el recuerdo." [12] Casona appears to argue that sometimes sacrifice for the happiness of the many and society may justify suicide. Angélica's sacrifice to avoid ruining the lives of all around her is a bitter duty she must face.

Most of Casona's characters forsake their worlds of fantasy and find happiness by adjusting to the world they wanted to leave. Some compromise with reality as the best solution possible. Very few continue to live in their world of illusion, as do Daniel and Hans, and their dissatisfaction and continuing unhappiness show how fruitless is the attempt to escape.

For Casona the idea of duty to society is all important. Don Florín, when asked whether he thinks he is doing good by returning reason to Sirena and opening her eyes again to the dirty world which surrounds her, can say only that it is his duty and that the truth, no matter how bitter, must be faced. Natacha is willing to work for others and give up her own rights, for as she tells Don Santiago, each person must seek his place in life: "Con lágrimas y sin gloria, pero estoy en mi puesto." [13] Don Florín brings reason to Ricardo and shows him that his previous life was not good. The Abuelo in *Lo dama del alba* tries to convince the Madre that she should not live in the past but try to make a new life from the present. Cascabel, of *Otra vez el Diablo,* is the realistic gracioso opposed to the idealistic escapists.

Casona doesn't claim that all illusion is bad. The Abuela in *Los árboles mueren de pie* lets those who tried to help her believe they have succeeded, but, on the whole, Casona's conclusion is that the worlds of reality and happiness are synonymous.

[From *Hispania,* vol. XL, no. 1, March, 1957]

Buero Vallejo and the Concept of Tragedy

BUERO VALLEJO not only composes tragedies, but in his essays, articles, commentaries, and self-criticism he has continued to discuss his ideas on tragedy, particularly the dramatist's moral and social responsibility and the meaning of tragic hope. He has refocused some of his earlier comments on "esperanza" through the years, but his position has remained consistent.

In 1950, Leopoldo Panero, the great Catholic poet, asked Buero about himself and his work. Buero wrote that he dared think his work promoted a positive tragic feeling, "una concepción trágica que, aspirando a ser como la velazqueña de los bufones o la barojiana de los parias, quiere ocultar en su fondo una delicada piedad y fortalecer nuestra moral, sin necesidad de discursos y moralejas, por su solo impulso conmovedor o suspensivo. En una palabra: de acuerdo con las más viejas tradiciones del teatro, mi comedia intentaba poseer una virtud catártica." [1]

From Aristotle on, catharsis, through its engendered emotions of compassion and terror, has served as a special functional effect of tragedy. Formerly, the function of tragedy was to purge these emotions and lead to a kind of balance and moderation. Later, Aristotle added anger and other passions which might be purified or modified but not extinguished. In the process a spectator might acquire new human and ethical qualities. Catharsis, as Buero views it in almost all his works, is a sublimation, an improvement rather than a relief. Compassion, terror, and anger, once sublimated, must clearly approximate the human condition which tragedy attempts to define for us, but every spectator will react differently to the pathetic, moral, or religious ingredients of the tragedy. The theater's function, whether it leaves us passive or calls us to social action, is to elevate. Even a comedy should reflect life positively. Concerning itself with pseudo-conflicts of an ideological nature and productive of cathartic tendencies, comedy, too, may do more than arouse one emotionally. The lack of solutions in a theatrical piece does not imply their nonexistence. For Buero, it is precisely "su amargura entera y sin aparente salida la que puede y debe provocar, más allá de lo que la letra exprese o se abstenga de decir, la purificación catártica del espectador." [2]

Even in his published critique of *Historia de una escalera* (1950), a work he has since somewhat rejected because of its naturalistic emphasis as not typical of his tragic theory, he finds, in the face of the bitterness, the depressing touches, and the lack of rational solution, that "el teatro trágico se hizo siempre para aumentar el valor de los valerosos y la piedad de los piadosos. Incluso a los deprimidos puede consolar si éstos se le acercan sin prejuicios." [3] He rejects the tragic conflict between characters as implying their inevitable destruction. "Tampoco necesita . . . una concepción del Destino a la manera clásica, externo en sus irrevocables decisiones a la voluntad de los personajes; el libre arbitrio de éstos es de por sí bastante fatídico. Nuestra percepción de la realidad se ha afinado, y la chispa trágica puede saltar hoy en la escena y hasta incendiarla utilizando figuras, situaciones o lugares que los clásicos nunca emplearon más que para las acciones secundarias." [4] The failure of the children of *Historia de una escalera* is not implicit. They may or may not fail as their parents did. Jean Paul Borel views this play as open tragedy, granting the possibility of another chance born from the very heart of the impossible situation. "La tragédie est toujours sous un certain aspect, tragédie de l'espoir. Notre condition d'humains, seul ressort en definitive de toute l'oeuvre que nous abordons, n'est pas autre chose que cette espérance pathétique." [5]

Buero disputes that the happy ending of *La señal que se espera* (1952) or its classification as "comedia dramática" detracts from its tragic classification.

> Así terminaban algunos de los ciclos trágicos de la antigüedad; . . .
> En el perdido ciclo de "Prometeo," su adjudicada desventura le era finalmente levantada al reconciliarse con Zeus. En el ciclo conservado de "La Orestíada," la agonía de Orestes termina al convertirse las sanguinarias y vengadoras Erinnias en providenciales y serenas

Euménides. El sino de los héroes trágicos puede ser inmodificable, pero su infortunio no tiene por que serlo siempre. El encadenamiento de causa a efecto; de exceso o delito a castigo; el mantenimiento de la adversidad, pueden ser rotos en un ciclo trágico por la gracia del cielo. Pero esta gracia no es caprichosa, aunque puede ser infinitamente misericordiosa. Le sobreviene al protagonista cuando éste la desea en lo hondo; cuando, a través de su experiencia dolorida, comprende de verdad la necesidad de remedio y la busca por un acto de libertad interior o de confianza ... Tragedia no es necesariamente catástrofe final, sino una especial manera de entender el final, sea feliz o amarga.[6]

Having outlined the moral and ethical implications inherent in his concept of tragedy, Buero elaborated his theories more fully between 1952 and 1956,[7] arriving at the fullest expression of his ideas on tragic hope from 1957 to the present. Buero states that he writes theater of a tragic nature about the problems of man and their doubtful final outcome, factors inherent in all tragedy, whether it be labeled realistic, symbolic, or imaginative. Considering tragedy a flexible phenomenon which may include disparate elements foreign to the dictionary definition of the hero conquered by fate, elevated action, noble language, and fatal denouement, he uses a variety of labels for his dramatic works such as *tragedia, fantasía, drama, tragicomedia, parábola,* and *fábula.* In these works he proposes that man is not necessarily a victim of fate—a tragic affirmation which stresses human capacity for overcoming obstacles and reverses, as tragedy itself enables us to see. "Esa fe última late tras las dudas y los fracasos que en la escena se muestran; esa esperanza mueve a las plumas que describen las situaciones más desesperadas. Se escribe porque se espera, pese a toda duda. Pese a toda duda, creo y espero en el hombre, como espero y creo en otras cosas: en la verdad, en la belleza, en la rectitud, en la libertad. Y por eso escribo de las pobres y grandes cosas del hombre; hombre yo también de un tiempo oscuro, sujeto a las más graves, pero esperanzadas interrogantes."[8]

In his discussion of *Hoy es fiesta* Borel agrees with Buero that if man had no possibility of free will he would resemble an animal in an abattoir, an absurd thought. The chance for a better world creates a tragic possibility for man based on a future hope which may not provide a solution. Man lives in a world where he must fail, triumph, and live. Thus, "Il y a espoir;

il doit y avoir espoir; et cet espoir est tragique parce que le monde ne nous laisse pas vivre." [9] Pilar's death does not deny the ultimate truths which will help her husband and the other characters, whatever their future, to maintain their hope as consolation. As Buero Vallejo exclaims through Doña Nieves at the curtain: "Hay que esperar. . . . Esperar siempre. . . . La esperanza nunca termina. . . . La esperanza es infinita." [10] Buero intended to write a tragedy of hope and in his own criticism of the play gives us the premise on which he bases his theory.

At the heart of all tragedy Buero finds the problem of hope. When we despair or feel anguish, it is as though we were projecting the reverse side of the coin of hope, which insists on maintaining its force within our heart. Without light there can be no darkness; without good, no evil; thus, without hope there can be no despair or existential anguish. Man may deny life, but his rebellion occurs within the framework of unfulfilled and existing hope, at the very least, for change. One always hopes: "Se espera incluso sin creer en la realidad de lo que esperamos. Se espera porque la esperanza es una tensión del hombre, un modo—no moda—de ser humano, independiente de la probabilidad racional de realizarla. Presentar esta tensión como tal, con su probabilidad de realización, pero también con su improbabilidad, parece objetivo básico de la tragedia. . . . Cuando alcanzamos a entrever . . . que desesperación y esperanza son sólo grados, o caras falaces, de algo grandioso e inmutable que está más allá de todas las tragedias, pero a lo que sólo por ellas podemos arribar." [11] Whatever their ability to communicate, the existential characters within a given work are not inevitably doomed to death and destruction as victims of an adverse fatality which, at the whim of the gods, may destroy them.

In the twentieth century, tragedy, implying the need for an heroic and loving response to the fear of a meaningless world which causes our anguish, may result not only in catastrophe but in victory. Fate need not be blind or arbitrary, for its consequences as well as its creation stem from the errors or excesses of man, as hybris begets Nemesis, punishment, vengeance, and expiation. Humans were always free to choose, and the oracle instead of determining the choice simply indicated its consequences. In our world of complex and mysterious moral order, fate may seem unjust, but we must maintain faith. "El último y mayor efecto moral de la tragedia es un acto de fe." [12] Even when a catastrophe occurs, as in the Greek theater, moral order remains. Protagonists, learning through sorrow, may come to doubt the inexorability of fate and with new confidence in the help of Heaven will try to transform the Furies into Eumenides. Spiritual struggle, as it promotes nobility of soul in the tragic conflict, will lead to a kind of affirmation.

Buero accepts the Greeks' moral transcendence as well as a duality of negative and positive poles where arousal leads to assuagement, destruction to renewal, and suffering to expiation. This kind of tragedy in its metaphysical or human aspect is part of a great vital affirmation whose eternally positive quality "confirma la función positiva de la tragedia. Puede ésta postular verdades de orden religioso, moral o social, como en el caso ya comentado de 'La Orestiada,' y entonces se encontrará muy cerca del polo extremo adonde la esperanza conduce: el de la fe sin sombra de duda, que es tanto como decir el de la esperanza cumplida." [13]

Sorrow in tragedy is no more pessimistic than laughter in comedy is optimistic. The Greeks had no concept for pessimism or optimism, although they realized that tragedy might contain both euphoria and melancholy, nor can today's author write pessimistic tragedy, even when it is his intention to do so, for behind his philosophy,

> siguen obrando, aunque sea bajo nombres muy distintos Dionisos y su posible—o cierta—resurrección. El auténtico pesimismo es, aproximadamente, lo contrario de la tragedia. El pesimismo es negador, mientras la tragedia propugna toda clase de valores. La identificación del terror, la lástima y el dolor trágicos con el pesimismo es propia de personas o colectividades que huyen de sus propios problemas o deciden negar su existencia por no querer o no poder afrontarlos; propia en una palabra, de personas o colectividades pesimistas. Interesa aclararlo, pues tal actitud se disfraza a veces con las más enfáticas afirmaciones.[14]

To reestablish the truth of tragedy's positive values matters in a society whose members refuse to face the anguish of belonging to the twentieth century, and they, rather than the tragedies they reject, are pessimistic and destructive. Tragedy helps man understand life's sorrows, face his situation positively, and attempt to overcome it as he seeks meaning in a world whose reality may be sombre and pessimistic in appearance. While one cannot define tragedy as optimistic in the accepted definition of that word, one must hold an optimistic position while fully aware of life's negative aspects. Tragedy's positive projection may appear as conciliation and harmony and lead to catharsis for the protagonist as well as for the spectator.

Buero accepts ideas held by Brecht [15] and parallels thoughts on tragedy held by Arthur Miller. "Pathos truly is the mode for the pessimist. But tragedy requires a nicer balance between what is possible and what is impossible. And it is curious, although edifying, that the plays we revere, century after century, are the tragedies. In them, and in them alone, lies the belief—optimistic, if you will—in the perfectibility of man." [16] For Buero, even in the closed or desperate situations of Sartre or Beckett, hope must exist, if not in the context of the drama, then in the possibility of a posterior hope. Through its philosophical denial, concern for or belief in the absence of hope motivates the creation of the work itself. By definition, all who write tragedy of despair and anguish do so from the indestructible background of a threatened but existing hope. Otherwise there could be no anguish.

In the eternal struggle between faith and doubt, the essence of all' tragedy, hope helps revitalize faith and aids spiritual development, as part of the living conflict in man's soul. The blackest tragedy ending in catastrophe without apparent hope reveals the dangers which beset man and invites us to create conditions to obviate future problems. Modern tragedy may create new myths, but it must deal with both the struggle of man to realize himself and with his conflict with the Absolute, which leads to hope in the metaphysical justification of the world and to a possible earthly solution to human sorrows. Since both doubt and faith are integral parts of man's fate, and neither is capable of perfect realization, doubt can never lead to absolute despair nor faith be so certain that it leaves no room for tragedy. Buero constantly reiterates, "Debo repetir algo que a menudo defiendo: tragedia no significa negatividad o desesperación." [17]

The collective tragedy of the Greeks, "a flexible literary tendency determined more by feeling than by form," [18] often had conciliatory or even happy endings. In their refutation of the inexorable character of a fatal destiny, even in the description of desperate situations, the Greeks revealed they could create tragedy only when they could doubt their own reality. For them tragedy implied empathic identification of the spectator with the play together with critical reflection, and both reflection and emotion are needed in the twentieth-century theater. Paul Claudel—concerned with problems of grace, penitence, and atonement—and others have recognized the Greek message of hope and its application to the modern world: "Ou déjà l'on reconnaît les ombres de la Verité future, la Resurrection, la Verbe, l'eternelle Genération." [19] Many Greek authors found that their gods were not "immuables, mais semblent prises dans le mouvement d'une humanité en marche, et capable de tirer des leçons de l'erreuret de la souffrance." [20] Eugene O'Neill as early as 1922 accepted the exalting and ennobling happiness of Greek tragedy: "It's mere present-day judgment to think of tragedy as unhappy! The Greeks and the Elizabethans knew better. They felt the tremendous lift to it. It roused them spiritually to a deeper understanding of life. . . ." [21]

But Buero, as we have seen, states more forcefully and repetitiously that tragedy in its raison d'être cannot stem from a belief in an infallible destiny. We have tragedy when, consciously or unconsciously, we begin to question destiny.

> La tragedia intenta explorar de qué modo las torpezas humanas se disfrazan de destino. 'Durch Leiden Freude,' dijo Beethoven. 'Por el dolor, a la alegría.' Este es el sentido último de lo trágico. Tal es el sentido final de las Euménides de Esquilo. Toda tragedia postula unas Euménides liberadoras, aunque termine como Agamenón.[22]
>
> Porque me parece que . . . en contra de opiniones muy extendidas, de lugares comunes muy difundidos—el auténtico meollo de lo trágico es la esperanza. No habría tragedia sin esperanza . . . la constante de la esperanza que en fin de cuentas es la constante humana de la futurización, de ir hacia una mejora.[23]

Ricardo Domenech feels that the only problem in Buero's dramas is that of man in his limitations facing his possibilities. Carlos survives, and "ha quedado abierta la puerta de la esperanza y de la angustia que es la única que nos puede conducir a la verdad" (*En la ardiente oscuridad*). "Y sin embargo hay que esperar, porque la vida empieza—recomienza—cuando cae el telón y el espectador, que ya no es el mismo que entró en el teatro, sino otro mejor, sale a la calle" (*Hoy es fiesta*). "Y hay que soñar . . . esta vida que palpita en torno nuestro. Y de este sueño hemos de hacer vida, vida palpable, vida total" (*Un soñador para un pueblo*).[24]

In *Aventura en lo gris* hope lies in the sacrifice of adults willing to die so that the world and future generations may continue to live and hope.

Carlos Muñiz claims that in *El concierto de San Ovidio* "la esperanza nos alienta al abandonar el teatro. . . . No se ha equivocado Buero al calificar esta parábola suya como una tragedia optimista. Lo es. Tragedia de hoy, comprometida." [25] Domingo Pérez Minik, like Borel and Domenech, states that "con rigor nos atrevemos a afirmar que el teatro de Buero Vallejo es un teatro lleno de esperanza. . . . Esto se percibe en todas sus obras." [26]

Buero's ardent defense of his theory of tragic hope stems from his desire for a better world of peace and brotherhood for which he feels all men are responsible. As early as 1951 he stated that he had made no deliberate effort to write social drama, but that one could find in his works "los problemas del hombre de nuestros días, los cuales, incluso cuando son de carácter metafísico, poseen una social trascendencia. La misma que posee siempre el verdadero teatro que es por escencia el arte representativo de las sociedades humanas." [27] In later years Buero has preached that the duty of the theater is to pose conflicts of man and the society in which he lives and "despertar las conciencias frente a ellos, enfocarlos con autenticidad y verdad; combatir los errores y los males; abrir los ojos; denunciar las injusticias; mostrar lo que el hombre tiene de humano y de inhumano; y lo que tiene de ser histórico; y, siempre, lograr arte auténtico." [28]

Buero claims his tragedy reveals his preoccupation with man's fate, both metaphysical and social, as reflected in the repeated conflicts one finds in his theater between individuality and collectivity, between necessity and liberty. All drama, including social drama, is a kind of theater of evasion, for no matter how polemical a work may be, it carries within it always "un impulso armónico, un consentimiento parcial del mundo que critica, una pretensión de ennoblecimiento inmediato, una satisfacción estética, en suma, sin la cual nada puede ser." [29] Ricardo Salvat, active in Spanish theatrical circles, praised Buero's social, metaphysical, and moral commitment, his hatred of despotism, his condemnation of injustice, and his hope for a better future.[30] Carlos Muñiz, himself a playwright of some reputation, insisted that Buero writes for the society of our time: "De todos nuestros autores ha sido él quien más a la española ha abordado nuestros problemas españoles," [31] Being a realist, Buero realizes that true Christian love is difficult to promote in a world of established material values, but each individual, he feels, must strive to overcome his own shortcomings as a human being and in the process aid his society.

Given the injustices and the social evils which confront modern man in the twentieth century, some writers think that through a theater of social agitation they can create tragedy as well as social transformation. Buero, on the contrary, claims that only social drama which aids one to feel more deeply the problem of man and his destiny deserves the name of tragedy. This problem may involve the elevation as well as the destruction of the hero, and the spectator may be as much moved by the former as by the latter. Buero rejects strictly social works which neither promote catharsis nor possess unique tragic importance, but he cannot, as some do, accept the idea that "where the conflict can be resolved through social means we may have serious drama but not tragedy." [32] He rejects also those doctrinaire critics who accuse as reactionary those works which fail forcefully and openly to advance social causes. Through an exclusively didactic treatment of social problems, unless they involve individual conflicts and concrete situations, one may produce sociology instead of social theater. One must maintain a balance between the lyrical and poetic on the one hand and the didactic on the other, while achieving artistic integrity; for esthetic and ethical considerations, which are far from being mutually exclusive in the modern drama, serve to reinforce one another.[33]

While reality is the greatest task confronting the dramatist, he may interject personal intuitions, avoiding fixed formulas or a simple repetition of reality as well as exclusive reliance on intuitive forms. Good theater must involve active contemplation and may suggest much more than it explicitly expresses. Often implicit social truths prove more vigorous than explicit ones.[34]

Buero's social message has not been more explicit, not because he denies esthetic liberty and responsibility, but because he realizes the inefficacy of direct action against the resistance of the spectator to change his established ideas. In order to produce works of some originality, Buero had to invent special filters for his message, which attempted to overcome these prejudices and to communicate with a spectator who never had any interest in "comprometerse en nada, que quería olvidar o que sólo ansiaba divertirse . . ."; "Su máscara no ha sido una careta sino una imperiosa necesidad de su existencia. No creemos que sin estas máscaras nuestro público lo hubiera soportado, dada la índole de nuestra realidad, de sus narraciones dramáticas, y del problematismo de su pensamiento dolorido . . ."; "el dramaturgo que supo encontrar la máscara idónea para sacar al público de sus casillas. Este hecho es una victoria incalculable." [35] Other critics have also observed his somewhat subtle efforts to use the theater as an instrument for the transformation of society. Jean Paul Borel feels that Buero has inherited a long theatrical tradition of what he calls the "theater of the impossible," "dont l'aspect essentiel est de denoncer l'impossible de la vie, pour ensuite en tirer certaines affirmations de caractère éthique." [36]

Buero, understanding the problems of conveying social thought and having it accepted, offers spectacles for the myopic who wish to see. Not all viewers have the same degree of optical difficulty; some may have sharper vision than the author himself, creating obstacles to an effective theater for a given audience at a given moment. One of the most positive ways to engage in social action, then, is to "adelantarse. Ver más lejos que los demás es una de las más hondas maneras de actuar a favor no sólo del futuro, sino de la sociedad contemporánea, aunque desde sus diversos estamentos se puede ello considerar como un acto antisocial o como una evasión de lo real." [37]

Buero stresses the impossibility of absolute freedom in writing, not only in Spain, but also in countries considered politically free. All writers are conditioned, even though they are not always aware of it and may not realize their compromise until some years have passed: "Sin embargo, lo hicimos con auténtica buena fe, sin creer que lo hacíamos. . . ." In any event, no playwright should have too many illusions that his activity "sea resolutiva y directa." [38] Although the problem of presenting social theater is complex, Buero sees the Spanish public as increasingly capable of accepting at least in principle a somewhat severe criticism of the status quo, including ideas which may differ radically from theirs because they may have "mala conciencia, acaso porque le gana un oscuro movimiento psicológico de autojustificación, o de desahogo o de catarsis. Creo que el público es receptivo, aunque sea burgués." [39]

In his own way Buero has fought for ethical and moral beliefs, hopeful that in the not too distant future the public, not only in principle, but in fact, will be receptive to openly social drama. "In fact, the most common circumstances of our time—doubt and distress—already form, although in a subterranean and inorganic way, an enormous public, inwardly united before the literary manifestation of tragic order; it is a collectivity without name which perhaps tomorrow, if we arrive at fuller and more harmonious forms of social life, will transform itself into that organic collectivity which will fervently support a socially representative tragic stage." [40]

Pedro Laín Entralgo, in discussing the anguish felt by Miguel de Unamuno, believed that his resistance to complete despair came from his Spanish condition which could not deny the possibility of hope, a vital part of his existence: "Es que el problema de la esperanza fue centro vital de su existencia de hombre y de su obra. . . . En la esperanza vio la esencia de la vida humana, sobre la esperanza pretendió fundar su religión, con esperanzas quiso hacer lo mejor y más cimero de su espíritu." [41] One might easily apply this assessment to the less anguished Buero Vallejo, who encourages the hope which lies in the human soul, postulating the possibility that one has of gaining victory over himself, because as long as man fights for faith and against his own evil, humanity and the world will survive.

[From *Hispania,* vol. LI, no. 4, December, 1968]

Tragedy and the Criticism
of Alfonso Sastre

SASTRE has written two collections of articles on his concept of tragedy, but in spite of the apparent contradictions therein, one may understand his message and appreciate his constant concern with social, realistic, and closed existential factors.

Throughout his theatrical career Sastre has complained that the Spanish theater is in the hands of special interests, controlled by the state and by censorship. Because of the profit motive, producers are unwilling to take a chance on theater of real concern.

> La situación es ésta: el teatro español es un negocio de carácter privado, dirigido por los empresarios. Pero no sólo eso: es un mal negocio, y de él se empeñan en vivir y obtener beneficios dos o más empresas en cada caso... En este panorama, el minúsculo sector "oficial"—los teatros nacionales—no se ha movilizado nunca en un sentido que compensara las limitaciones que impone a nuestro teatro interior de lo que hemos llamado, al referirnos a los privados, el "contexto", de modo que lo que para éstos es una limitación más desde fuera—la censura—, para los nacionales es una determinación interior mucho más compleja y que los incapacita para ese trabajo profundo y arriesgado de la revitalización, y más teniendo en cuenta el carácter inconformista del nuevo teatro.[1]

Sastre constantly held this position over the years, perhaps because of public resistance to his theater, in spite of his obvious talents.[2]

Buero Vallejo, with whom Sastre has carried on a theatrical polemic for more than fifteen years, criticized those Spanish dramatists who deliberately presented impossible theater, knowing full well that it would be rejected and that resulting publicity would help them stage their productions in foreign countries. Sastre, seeking to affirm the dialectical sense of his position as that of applying social pressure necessary for freedom from control, and to achieve interior or ironic liberty, admits that a theater may be impossible for the moment, but reiterates that all theater is possible until clearly revealed as impossible. Progress is never made through accommodation but through contradiction and opposition.[3] Sastre keeps returning to this theme, citing the fact that some of his supposedly impossible dramas were later performed, and concludes that while "possibilism" or "impossibilism" may have a meaning "en lo social-político, no lo tiene en lo estético-poético. A este puede reducirse mi posición desde un principio . . ." [4]

Sastre created the Grupo del Teatro Realista with José María de Quinto in 1961 and belonged to the Arte Nuevo group along with José María de Quinto, José María Castellet, and Ignacio Aldecoa. With Quinto he planned the formation of a Teatro de Agitación Social, and they issued an inefficacious manifesto during the 1948–49 theatrical season to reinforce the concepts they were trying to promote on stage. In that manifesto and elsewhere, Sastre insisted that "Lo social, en nuestro tiempo . . . es una categoría superior a lo artístico." [5] The social intention of the dramatist may take different forms: "formas de 'agitación' (ante pueblos dormidos y embrutecidos por el sueño), formas de 'propaganda' (según la confesionalidad religiosa o política del dramaturgo), formas de puro 'testimonio apolítico', formas de 'denuncia' más o menos cargada de intención política. . . ." [6] The esthetic and technical aspects are of lesser importance to Sastre, who views social art as doing more than provoking esthetic emotions. Functioning socially in the struggle of our time, the theater, he claims, has to understand and denounce social anguish but avoid the pitfalls of destructive proletarian propaganda. The dramatist's duty is to write good theater, not for professional pleasure, but to serve more effectively the social, ethical, or political intention it conveys. This, says Sastre, "es una de mis más fundamentales convicciones, aunque no se me oculta que hay que hacer desde luego obras teatralmente buenas." [7] Since only work of great esthetic quality is capable of social transformation, bad works of art should be rejected, not only for their lack of esthetic formulation but for their uselessness as social documents. "Arte de urgencia," as he calls

this life-related art, takes up the great themes of liberty, responsibility, cul-
pability, repentance, and salvation. Since the principal mission of an artistic operation should be the transformation of the unjust world in which
we live, the artist will feel justified, not through the perfection of his
work of art in itself, but at the thought of social purification which his work
serves.[8] Sastre would prefer to live in a world organized justly, without
art, than in an unjust world full of artistic works. In painting as well as in
literature an artist views the world as something to organize; ". . . diríamos, extremando las cosas, que el mundo está mal hecho, plásticamente,
y que se pinta, en parte, para corregirlo en la medida de lo posible." [9] This
rectification, as he calls it, is part of the mechanics of all art. We all belong
to society and we all need purification and punishment through tragedy.
"La tragedia nos ha purificado; esa purificación es revolucionaria." [10]

Sastre believes in the application of Aristotelian definitions of tragedy
but feels that the above-mentioned tragic purification, and ethical, social,
and political considerations are modern contributions as opposed to former debate on moral justification and the nature of real passion. Modern
social polemics may involve class and political struggle, socialist agitation
against capitalism or existentialism versus Marxism, but the dramatist himself should profess no personal ideology, allowing his characters to convey
their feelings and his situations to develop freely. Any resulting ideology
stems from the dialectical interaction between the author and the immediate social and historical reality he faces. The artist need not lose his auton-
omy or feel inhibited, but his social action is of more moment than artistic
considerations, and the reality of the moment and freedom of action out-
weigh metaphysical considerations which cannot, however sound they may
be spiritually, relieve us of our material compromises.[11] Sastre defines
tragedy as a kind of current criminal investigation of great social crimes
and collective sufferings, and seeks those responsible, stating, "trataré
de llegar sin miedo a las últimas consecuencias de esta interrogación." [12]
Since the function of theater is social revolution in both its moral and metaphysical aspects, Sastre presents his revolutionary tragedy to torture the
spectator who, through his sense of guilt which allows him to understand
the necessity for change, may communicate his anguish to others. The tragic
exaltation of the stage performance provokes tragic tension in the spectator
and enables him to learn about human existence.[13]

Sastre, who cherishes the rights of the individual in a tragic modern world, avoids espousing a special political ideology. He uses characters skillfully to project his attitudes, being especially effective in his portrayal of women to help set off the emotions which motivate the hero as he faces his particular social problem. Sastre seeks to balance man's rights with his obligations and define human dignity. In his preface to *Cuatro dramas de la revolución* (1963), repeating statements made in the first issue of *Primer Acto* in 1957, he states: "Me refiero . . . a la revolución social de nuestro tiempo . . . Concibo en estos dramas, y desde ellos . . . la Revolución como una realidad trágica . . . si toda revolución es un hecho trágico, todo orden social injusto es una tragedia sorda inaceptable. . . . Parece evidente, en efecto, que la tragedia sorda del orden injusto sólo puede ser destruida por la tragedia revolucionaria." [14] By 1965, however, Sastre changed his position slightly, commenting that he had been mistaken in viewing revolution as the only possible solution. He had acted as a "moralista social . . . con mi, a la sazón, casi absoluta ceguera para la estructura profunda de los desarrollos reales: para la Dialéctica." [15] He reiterates, nevertheless, that "hacer literatura . . . *no es bastante.*" [16] He feels his ideas "han cambiado fundamentalmente. Lo que permanece—y ha facilitado el cambio—es un sustrato moral." [17]

Francisco García Pavón, adjudging Sastre's message obscure and demanding of great insight on the part of the spectator, denies that he is really a social or revolutionary playwright. Sastre himself said he was as horrified by ambiguity as by didactic simplifications, but ambiguity occurs, and the concerned author will either hold up production or risk the ambiguity, hoping that the true nature of his message will be visible.[18] García Pavón finds Sastre overly intellectual and a writer of treatises on revolutionary philosophy rather than a revolutionary playwright. "De donde resulta que este drama [*El pan de todos*], en su intención última, como otros de Sastre, es casi un artístico y metafórico tratado de filosofía revolucionaria." [19]

His social awareness of the need of utilizing an "arte de urgencia" leads Sastre to demand a special kind of theater sustained by the postulates of a "realismo de urgencia." [20] which he defines somewhat existentially. He states: "Je m'efforce d'observer un réalisme non naturaliste, un réalisme soucieux de l'actualité et du probléme de l'homme en géneral. . . . Je cherche toujours à provoquer une double prise de conscience: celle du moment historique que nous vivons, et celle de notre situation en tant qu'hommes

Telle est ma métaphysique, telle est ma politique actuelle." [21]

In *Drama y sociedad* (1956), Sastre contended that modern drama leads spectators to a truth which may not be that of the dramatist, because the theater can present reality more clearly than life can. "El dramaturgo intenta que el drama—extraído de la realidad—repercuta en la realidad. . . . El drama es la forma de la denuncia por la que el dramaturgo hace patente algo, dando testimonio de la realidad." Thus in modern tragedy the artist serves largely as a witness for a kind of social realism. We live in a world of anguish, misery, and hunger, in which human existence is a tragic exaltation which rejects the concept "que haya felicidad en los 'finales felices' de la comedia rosa." Of the two categories of modern drama, that of magic and that of anguish, only the latter truly represents modern tragedy, "sustentada en los postulados del realismo. Es el teatro que recoge la existencia como un tremendo desgarrarse temporal sin magias ni fantásticas evasiones." [22] Theater, nevertheless, succeeds only to the extent that it destroys real space and time, substituting another space-time of dramatic action. Sastre rejects the epic theater of Bertolt Brecht as primarily concerned with real space-time which implies the irreality of dramatic space-time.[23] Sastre deliberately avoids, through the geographical dispersion of his dramas, an identification with current space-time, in spite of his social preoccupations. Although some of his plays are set in Spain, even here he deals largely with eternal themes of life and death.

In *Anatomía del realismo* (1965) he reexamines many aspects of reality. He reconsiders his ideas on the impossibility of political theater and the impartiality of the author as a kind of medium or invisible man whose function is not to think but to reject ideological theater. The artist should always present reality as a revelation that man has experienced throughout history, viewing it dialectically rather than scholastically. Of the various forms of reality, that of social injustice is the most urgent. The theater, in reflecting reality, offers a socially progressive possibility which each artist projects in accordance with his particular esthetic and moral conscience. While social realism implies a certain independence on the part of the author to choose, he may not avoid his social preoccupation. In revealing the structure of reality and fulfilling a function of justice, the artist, even when rejected by society, is useful to it.

Until recent times naturalism seemed adequate for achieving social goals, but a new form of realism is needed for the modern world. Also, the concept of art for art's sake was a false one, for modern reality asks of the artist that he be more than a decorator and that he work to the best of his ability for the future of all. An artist's position in and concept of the world will of necessity determine his view of reality, but as long as the artist takes part in the social struggle in some manner, uniformity of style and technique are not needed. One may view reality as an esthetic entity without the detailed description of the naturalists and conceive of a world "que no es una descripción pero que está cargado de significaciones reales." [24]

Sastre admits that Bertolt Brecht was one of the first to deny naturalism, but he states that modern theater must be based on a "negación dialéctica de la negación brechtiana, tanto a través de la crítica como de la praxis teatral." [25] Brecht shows, not an inevitable evolution, but rather a series of possibilities, leaving to the spectator the task of forming a judgment. Although Brecht believed man can act on the world, for the most part his heroes live in a naturalistic environment as matter to be shaped by exterior forces. Sastre, however, appreciates the value of narrative theater in the development of drama, its revolutionary character, and Brecht's help in "averiguar que pasa en el teatro de hoy y que ha de pasar, seguramente, en el futuro." [26]

Sastre criticizes objectivism, another form of realism which he situates somewhere between naturalism and vanguardism. Spanish authors run the grave risk of showing a trivial and insignificant reality in the histories which they pretend to view objectively. They are playing a kind of game, for they feign ignorance of the very facts they present. "Se imagina una situación y se afecta ignorar su estructura." [27]

For him the theater is in the final analysis "un modo lúcido de investigación e intervención en la realidad." [28] As his friend and companion José María de Quinto phrased it, "Alfonso Sastre parece desenvolverse dentro de lo que él ha bautizado con el nombre de 'realismo profundizado' y que los franceses llaman 'evasión del realismo' en el inequívoco sentido de una mayor profundización dentro de él. Toda profundización dentro del realismo presupone, sin duda, un proceso de intelectualización." [29]

Sastre sees modern tragedy as involving a closed existential situation in which the hero, in reality innocent, feels guilty, and suffers one more self-inflicted torture in an attempt to find a solution where none exists. Tragedy is not nihilistic, but it is basically without hope. "Seguiremos esperando,

pero nuestra espera será ya una espera sin esperanza; una espera desespe-
rada." [30] In a drama in which apparently nothing happens, we may see
the reflection of our daily existence and recognize ourselves with horror.
The essence of tragedy, its metaphysical substance, lies in authentic human
existence. Tragedy involves concrete existential situations or episodes of
human existence. "Esta situación general, que nos es revelada a través de
una concreta situación trágica, es la sustancia metafísica de la tragedia." [31]
Moral beings are impelled by fate to torture or are tortured by an entity
superior to themselves. In representing zones of authentic human existence
which other types of drama, even those with a cathartic effect, may only
approximate, tragedy may use Aristotelian elements of artistic form, rede-
fined in modern terms. Sastre bases Aristotle's horror and pity on those
authentic human limiting situations where man, faced with nothingness,
feels anguish. Under certain conditions where a solution exists but is unavailable to the individual, tragedy may still prevail. The tragic situation
may disappear, but what will not disappear is the "tragicidad de la existencia humana en general." [32]

In spite of his reiteration of the necessity for a closed situation, he admits that at times tragedy may have a happy ending.[33] Elsewhere he states:
"Si se cree, como yo lo creo, que la tragedia significa, en sus formas más
perfectas, una superación dialéctica del pesimismo . . . y del optimismo . . .
en este sentido propongo como fundamental determinación de lo trágico
la esperanza—, es claro que la disolución de uno u otro de los términos
acarrea la decadencia y la defunción de la tragedia." [34] "La tragedia . . .
cuando se cumple como tragedia—, es una unidad dialéctica superior que
quizás podamos llamar la esperanza." [35] Absolute pessimism leads to de-
formity and anarchy, while absolute optimism leads to conformity. True
tragedy, rare in occidental culture, poses a difficult tension between the
existential and the historical situation, between the anguish of living for
death and the collective attitude of living for progress, between a private
anguish and public action, in which the spectator may find hope or be destroyed with the hero. The spectator realizes he is an existential creature
born for death but also acts as a kind of agent in the social and historical
situation, his task or "praxis" and his agony.[36]

Sastre, in spite of his ambiguities, apparently favors a closed situation
of existential anguish but one which encourages social action. Therefore
he again rejects Brecht's theater as showing us senseless tragedy "porque

él encuentra y presenta las razones de un optimismo fundamental y fundamentante." [37] Brecht fears to present tragedy as without remedy and thus treats it as the past, when in reality it is here and now and should be the object of our struggle. The danger is that historical optimism may inhibit the spectator from practical action, for if the pain is presented as past, it implies that the present will also change. Just as the spectator shown all tragedy as without remedy refuses to act because it is impossible to change things, so will the one shown a happy ending decide not to act, for history will act for him. "A la conformidad del otro correspondería el conformismo de éste. El otro riesgo . . . es el esteticismo: la descarga de lo trágico a que procede Brecht se parece mucho a la catarsis aristotélica entendida como aliviadero estético de lo que en realidad es insoportable." [38]

As we have seen, Sastre finds that tragedy, in addition to its artistic formality and metaphysical substance, functions as a part of social dynamics. Revolutionary tragedy, which is, "o debe ser, aguda y abierta, frente a la otra (tragedia sorda del orden social injusto) sorda, crónica, cerrada," [39] may contribute toward a better future for all. This tragedy will enable some spectators who attend the performance to recognize themselves as subjects and objects of the catastrophe. "Y ese doble impacto—extrañeza y reconocimiento—es el motor purificador, catártico, de las acciones humanas a la salida del teatro." [40] Afterwards, in coming days when the play fades to a vague memory, other events which we may not even directly associate with the drama will act in our existence. The epic, dramatic and vanguard manifestations, represented by Bertolt Brecht, Sartre, and Samuel Beckett respectively, will, in their interaction, provide the theater of the future. In the present, although dramatic tragedy runs afoul of bureaucratic optimism and vanguard nihilism, it attempts to propose to the spectator the double theme which Sastre feels is fundamental, that of an existing concrete condition in which man is surrounded by anguish, pain, and death, and that of historical reality, where man participates in the development of humanity towards more just conditions.[41] Dramatic tragedy involves theater which aims neither at the individual (bourgeois theater) nor the collective mass (political theater), and its task is to "dirigirse a cada uno sin perder de vista la generalidad y a todos sin perder de vista al hombre de carne y hueso." [42]

The task of the dramatist then is the noble one of presenting art, which may not seem to bear immediate fruit but which takes on immediate utility

in the form of "una progresiva toma de conciencia; un inútil actual fu-
turamente útil." [48] Sastre, seeking to agitate society through direct action,
has undertaken this task sincerely and seriously. As one critic has said: "No
cabe duda que su escenario muestra bien ajustado gran parte de las formas
de la obra comprometida o existencialista, con su pensamiento que se dis-
cute a sí mismo, con su discurso que equivale al silencio y con esas razones
que no son sino la máscara de la sinrazón." [44] In spite of their emphasis
on a social conscience and action, transcending cathartic effect, Sastre's
dramas are in no way sociological. He incarnates his social problems and
investigation of reality through the individual conflicts of his lonely and
isolated heroes who live in an absurd world of false values. He maintains
a delicate balance among the sometimes difficult and obscure social message, the metaphysical, and the lyrical poetic note which permeate his dramas, preserving artistic integrity by writing tragedies of great esthetic
quality without sacrificing his authentic social commitment to fight for a
better future. As a realist he sees man's anguished problems, but he keeps
hoping that, within the limitations of our existential world, his dramas
will have direct social consequences for good.

[From *Symposium,* vol. 21, no. 4. Winter, 1967]

5 | Essay

Ortega y Gasset and Goethe

ORTEGA Y GASSET, whose interest in Germany and things German is well known, went to that country in 1905 to escape what he called the cultural decadence of his native land and to find what he termed the romantic and fair Germany. He studied at the universities of Berlin, Leipzig, and Marburg, where neo-Kantian philosophy influenced him considerably. As Curtius says: "findem wir ihn in Marburg als Schüler des grossen Neo-kantianers Hermann Cohen . . . Auf der Terrasse vor der ungeheuren Fassade pflegte Ortega mit achtzehn Jahren auf und ab zu gehen und seinen Kant zu studieren." [1]

Ortega urged an intensive study of Kant but emphasized that he himself had lived in a kind of philosophical prison as a result thereof. "Con gran esfuerzo me he evadido de la prisión kantiana y he escapado a su influjo atmosférico." [2] Although he recalls the unforgettable nights when he visited his teacher's home to discuss esthetics, neo-Kantian narrowness stifled his spirit. "Toda mi devoción y gratitud a Marburg están inexorablemente compensadas por los esfuerzos que he tenido que hacer para . . . salir de su estrechez hacia alta mar" (*O.C.,* III, 433).

Juan Ramón Jiménez recalls that Ortega was not in agreement with his love of French symbolist poetry . . . "porque era tan germanista, tan goethiano." [3] Curtius acknowledges that Ortega understood Germany better than any other European critic. "Ein weiterer Zug seiner Originalität liegt in der Art wie er deutsche. . . . Kultur verarbeitet und zusammenführt. Ich wüsste keinen Kritiker in Europa der mit derselben Sympathie und demselben Verständnis über . . . zu schreiben vermöchte. . . . Er kennt und übersieht die ganze bedeutsame Entfaltung der deutschen Geisteswissenschaften. Mommsen und Eduard Meyer, Max Weber und Dilthey, Cohen und Rickert . . . alle diese Namen sind ihm ebenso vertraut wie uns. Es dürfte wenige Ausländer geben, welche die Erkenntnisarbeit unserer Historiker und Philosophen so genau kennen und so sorgsam verfolgen wie Ortega." [4] Curtius recalls, too, that Ortega had a goodly number of enthusiastic readers in Germany in the 1920's. "Sie fandem bei ihm die Analyse unseres Massenzeitalters, die Diagnose unserer geistigen Situation. Die Philosophie berührte sich bei diesem Denker mit der Wirklichkeit unseres Daseins." [5]

Several generations earlier Sanz del Río had emphasized the ethical and educational implications of krausismo, and its concomitant influences have been well documented, but one of Ortega's motivations in founding the *Revista de Occidente* was to discuss new philosophical and scientific findings, especially German ones. He discussed all fields of German endeavor: music, painting, poetry, drama, foreign affairs, politics, history, and philosophy. From 1920 to 1935 he familiarized his students and readers with the great German names, and he was the first to introduce Franz Brentano and Edmund Husserl to Spain.[6]

But Ortega did more than introduce Germans to Spain or discuss specific authors. He undertook to analyze the entire range of German culture and its relationships to Spain and other Romance countries. Niedermayer claims: "Se tacha a Ortega de ser el mayor germanizante de España. A nosotros nos parece que Ortega . . . sólo ha tomado de los alemanes aquello que convenía bien a su temperamento y a su estilo de pensar." [7] But what appealed to Ortega is full of contradictions, and the contention that he owes four-fifths of his intellectual discipline and richness to Germany is open to question. Even though he proclaimed his intellectual dependence and gratitude to Germany on various occasions, Ortega feels his debt may have been exaggerated for him. "Debo enormemente a la filosofía alemana y espero que nadie me escatimará el reconocimiento de haber dado a mi labor, como una de sus facciones principales, la de aumentar la mente española con el torrente del tesoro intelectual germánico. Pero tal vez he exagerado este gesto y he ocultado demasiado mis propios y radicales hallazgos" (*O.C.,* IV, 404).

Ortega liked German culture, but he was constantly torn by his need to affirm his own country's values. Although he constantly admonished the

Spaniard to reorganize his thought along the German scientific and objective lines, he wanted Spain not to copy but rather to form a civilization which while continuing to be Spanish would at the same time be European. At first he claimed that if Spain wished to advance culturally, it was vital to concentrate on German science, language, and culture, for "la cultura germánica es la única introducción a la vida esencial" (*O.C.*, I, 210). Elsewhere he repeats the essential German base for Spanish culture. "¿Por qué el español se obstina en vivir anacrónicamente consigo mismo? ¿Por qué se olvida de su herencia germánica? Sin ella—no haya duda—padecería un destino equívoco . . ." (*O.C.*, I, 356), and again: "Los alemanes tienen una virtud que a nosotros nos falta, a despecho de las apariencias, el respeto y el amor al pasado" (*O.C.*, I, 426). Among other advantages adduced by Ortega was German clarity as opposed to Mediterranean imprecision where grotesque combinations of concepts alternated with "un defecto de elegancia mental" (*O.C.*, I, 345). Ortega often spoke scornfully of the Mediterranean and his culture and thought of himself as spiritually a German.

Nevertheless, scattered throughout Ortega's works are uncomplimentary references to Germany. He cites the lack of personality of the German who, unlike the Spaniard, has submerged himself completely and delivered up his personal existence to an organized collective life. In 1935, in a series of essays for *La Nación*, Ortega repeated that the German is almost a puppet or automaton. "Las personas viven automatizadas, y cuando el Reglamento público que regula su comportamiento no determina lo que deben hacer, se quedan perplejas, sin saber qué gesto, qué acción ejecutar" (*O.C.*, V, 204). He admits that much earlier he had seen only the magnificence and efficiency of German organization without realizing that it had progressed at the cost of disindividualizing those who made it up. Ortega even mentions his spontaneous antipathy to German culture. "Puede creérseme si digo que nadie habrá sentido y seguirá sintiendo mayor antipatía espontánea hacia la cultura germánica que yo" (*O.C.*, I, 209). Ortega struggled against the German idea which presented culture and thought as something justifiable in itself. He combated the doctrine of intellectualism which for him isolated one from the mainstream of life, and chastised his German university professors for their attitude. "Sobre todo en los alemanes . . . en los que fueron mis maestros . . . vino la cultura, el pensamiento a ocupar el puesto vacante de un dios en fuga. Toda mi obra, desde sus primeros balbuceos ha sido una lucha contra esta actitud. . . ." (*O.C.,* V, 309–310).

As early as 1908 Ortega had sought to explain his contradictions. "El imperio alemán, como esas viviendas lacustres asentadas sobre el légamo enfermizo y movible está construído sobre lo culturalmente falso. La labor educativa alemana es hoy—no hablo de ayer—una fábrica da falsificaciones" (*O.C.,* I, 96). There are really two Germanies, the Germany of today as opposed to the Germany of yesterday, of tomorrow, of always. The latter Germany will never die, because with its death would perish the only European possibility of a future worth living. In his *La Nación* essays he tried again to explain the contradictory Germanies. "Quien conozca la importancia permanente que Alemania ha tenido en mi vida podrá aforar la fuerza de choque que la impresión ahora recibida ha tenido sobre mí . . . Por una espontánea operación de mi retina, el presente, en lo que tiene de tal, ha sido rechazado por ella. . . . ¿Cómo se explica esta ceguera para lo inmediato, para lo que debía haberme sido más patente?" (*O.C.,* V, 184–186). For him, what he saw was not what had happened in three or four years but the product of twenty-three long and important ones.

From 1949 to 1951 Ortega lectured in Switzerland and Germany, and his greatest triumph in Germany came in the summer of 1951. "Fue recibido en triunfo por la Universidad y las organizaciones estudiantiles de Munich, por la 'Bayrische Akademie der Wissenschaften und Schönen Künste' . . . Las eminencias de la sociedad homenajearon al huésped de honor en numerosos actos y durante toda una semana Ortega concentró con sus conferencias en la más amplia sala académica de Munich a miles de oyentes cultos de todas las edades." [8]

Of all German subjects, that of Goethe interested Ortega most. Writers on Goethe have been plentiful in Spain. Manuel de Sandoval considered Goethe as one of the "genios de primer orden . . . que a la vez que honran la patria en que nacieran, enaltecen y glorifican la humanidad a que todos pertenecemos." [9] He hailed the German as the guide for all European youth and considered him almost a demigod, an attitude to which Ortega objected in his analysis. José Miguel Sacristán, on the other hand, denies Goethe's spiritual and mental health.[10] Most of Goethe's works had been translated into Spanish by 1921.[11] Juan Valera and Marcelino Menéndez y Pelayo had written of Goethe, both with some reservations, but the work "más extenso y de más tenaz esfuerzo que se ha escrito en España sobre Goethe" [12] was that of Urbano Gonzáles Serrano, professor of philosophy and student of Sanz del Río.

Egon Schwarz says that one should expect Ortega's image of Goethe to be part of the Leibniz-Herder-Kant tradition, but that it does not fail to exhibit the ambiguity of Ortega's vision. "On the one hand 'Goethe is eternally deserting his innermost destiny,' on the other hand he is the giant within our Western civilization 'in whom for the first time dawns the consciousness that human life is the individual struggle with his most intimate and personal destiny,' i.e., that human existence is made up of the problem itself." [13] One must agree that Ortega's interpretation and concern is with the spiritual meaning of Goethe's existence in general, as his continual preoccupation was always with the meaning of existence and living one's life. "Nuestra vida pues . . . no es una cosa cuyo ser está fijado de una vez para siempre sino que es una tarea, algo que hay que hacer; en suma un drama" (*O.C.,* V, 123). Ortega repeats this refrain countlessly. "Pero el hombre no sólo tiene que hacerse a sí mismo, sino que lo más grave que tiene que hacer es determinar lo que va a ser" (*O.C.,* VI, 33).

Ortega wrote his essay "Pidiendo un Goethe Desde Dentro" for the Berlin magazine, *Die Neue Rundschau,* in a number dedicated to Goethe, but references to Goethe abound in all of Ortega's works. Ortega commented that Goethe biographies, elaborated on the principle of creating a statue for a public place or Goethian tourist guide, treat the exterior Goethe, but he postulates a Goethe "desde dentro." This *dentro* is hard to define, for it is neither body nor soul, conscience nor character, for these are as much outside one as the countryside is around one's body. Life is not abstract but rather signifies the "inexorable forzosidad de realizar el proyecto de existencia que cada cual es" (*O.C.,* IV, 400). This vital project, or what one is to become, is called *Bestimmung,* as equivocal a word for Ortega as destiny or *Schicksal.* Life is a drama because it is a frantic struggle with things and even with our characters to try to be in fact what we are potentially. The reason he chose to attempt Goethe from inside, in addition to refuting the exterior view, was that he felt Goethe was the man in whom for the first time there arose the concept that human life is the struggle of man with his individual destiny and that life is made up of the problem of itself, that is, "que su substancia consiste no en algo que ya es . . . sino en algo que tiene que hacerse a sí mismo" (*O.C.,* IV, 403).

Ortega's principal concern in his treatment of Goethe is the theme of existence which represents Ortega's struggles to find his own essence and the meaning of his own existence. In "Adán en el Paraíso," for Adam life exists as a problem, and man is the problem of life, the essence of each thing being a relative matter. This says Ortega, "no existe, por lo tanto esa supuesta realidad immutable y única . . . hay tantas realidades como puntos de vista" (O.C., I, 475). Ortega's interest in Goethe's attitude toward life, then, reflects his own eternal search and can be broken down into various headings such as the meaning of existence, the necessity for action, and the attempt to find one's essence.

According to Ortega, life is like a shipwreck. The poor human, feeling himself sink, moves his arms to keep himself afloat, a movement which might be termed culture. But when culture endures too long, man, becoming more sure of himself, loses his sinking feeling, and culture becomes static and parasitical. Some discontinuity, then, is necessary to renew a sense of loss of support, so that his arms may thrash around once more in a saving gesture. Continuing his analogy, Ortega insists that all classics, among them Goethe, should be judged by a jury of the shipwrecked who would question one on authentic life.

Various interpretations of life are possible, but only with man "llega a ser vivido lo humano" (O.C., II, 19) according to Goethe. Man knows God only as man is and knows Humanity. Ortega agreed with Dilthey that we cannot transmit to our fellow man our experience of life, but added that "I do not think that anyone in Europe before Goethe had meditated upon the subject of human life to such an extent as he. There is lacking, to be sure, a single book wherein his reflections on human life are gathered together, analyzed, and studied in all their depth." [14]

For Ortega a man was cultured only when he had taken possession of himself completely. "Cultura es fidelidad consigo mismo, una actitud de religioso respeto hacia nuestra propia y personal vida. Decía Goethe que no podía estimar a un hombre que no llevase un diario de sus jornadas" (O.C., II, 161). A man who scorns his own reality cannot possess the truth, and his ideas, acts, and very words will have only an illusory quality, for a man who does not believe in himself cannot believe in God. He finds Goethe's insistence on a diary significant in terms of living and preparing for the future, reviewing that which we were and that which we aspire to be, and in this way only do we take possession of our lives during each fleeting hour. However, in the final analysis, he finds Goethe's insistence on symbolic actions but a way to conceal from himself the decisive character of his behaviour. Goethe's pagan ideal of life did not interfere with his idea that man's truth lies in the exact correspondence between gesture and spirit, the external and the internal. As Ortega quotes him: "Nada hay dentro, nada hay fuera; lo que hay dentro eso hay fuera" (*O.C.*, II, 85).

Yet Goethe underneath his official ideas seeks anxiously for the mystery of his authentic being, and Ortega quotes from *Truth and Poetry,* "Todos los hombres de buena casta sienten, conforme aumenta su cultura, que necesitan representar en el mundo doble papel, uno real y otro ideal y en este sentimiento ha de buscarse el fundamento de todo lo que es noble" (*O.C.*, IV, 405). But no matter how much man may search on earth or in heaven, in the present or future, for his fate, he remains always in a kind of perennial vacillation, subject to an external influence which perturbs him.

Goethe distinguished between real or effective fate and ideal or superior fate, but he traditionally confused the ego which each one has to become with what Ortega terms the generic ego that one ought to become. This duplicity to which tradition submits Goethe causes his perennial vacillation or "ewiges Schwanken." For Goethe life itself was ethical. If a man's entelechy is to be a thief he has to be it, even if his moral ideas are opposed to it and cause him to live lawfully. For the man who was to be a thief and by an effort of will succeeded in not being one, falsified his life. In any event, the important thing is not to confuse the "deber ser," a moral and intellectual preoccupation, with the vital imperative of the "tener que ser" which is the primary and profound essence of our being. Goethe finally emerges from his confusion with "lo recto es lo que es conforme al individuo" (*O.C.*, IV, 406). Man recognizes his vital program or entelechy through his unhappiness when he departs from it, though man knows not whence he comes, nor whither he goes.

Goethe preoccupied himself ceaselessly with his life because life is preoccupation with "self." Therefore Goethe was the first contemporary or romantic who saw that life is not a reality which confronts problems but that it consists of the problem of itself exclusively. Only man's joys and suffering instruct him, and the relationship between what he has to be and what he is may result in anguish and sorrow or in happiness.

Ortega emphasizes the constant contradiction between the ideas of Goethe the thinker about the world—for him the least valuable part of

Goethe—and his own life and work. The thinker, in his botanical image of life, views all as transpiring without anguish. For the plant and animal do not have to decide now what they are to be in the following instant. Life for them is not a drama but an evolution. Man's life is different, for he must decide at each instant what he is to do at the next one. Goethe, says Ortega, spent his life looking for his "self" or fleeing it, "que es todo lo contrario que cuidando la exacta realización de sí mismo. Esto ultimo supone que no existen dudas sobre quien se es, o que, una vez averiguado, el individuo está decidido a realizarse: entonces la atención puede vacar tranquilamente a los detalles de la ejecución" (*O.C.*, IV, 407). Much of Goethe's work presents us with tragic creatures like Faust and Meister who seek their real selves without knowing who to be. They reveal the contradiction between Goethe's optimistic concept of nature which marks all his relationships with the universe, and his constant preoccupation with his own destiny, his "self." Goethe was so unhappy, though his life seems to have turned out well, because he never really discovered his essence. Ortega visualizes Goethe's life as a series of flights, from the real loves of his youth, from his Weimar life as a writer, and from Weimar itself, and Ortega disputes those who defend the flights as Goethe's means of preserving himself more faithfully for his authentic vocation. He insists that Goethe felt his work and production to be merely symbolic and that he was basically indifferent to them (ziemlich gleichgültig). Man, in order to be what he is, needs first to find out what he is, ask himself what the things around him are, and what he is in the midst of things. Life is the basic "task," the thing to be made, to be lived, and to be realized, and it is this reality from which Goethe perpetually tried to desert. His life urged him always to be something irrevocably, but he came to hate anything which demanded irrevocable decisions, made no painful effort to determine his essence, and sought a favorable environment, like the Weimar cocoon, to protect him from the world. In spite of the contradictions, Ortega concluded that Goethe was the first modern who told us: "Libértate de lo demás hacia ti" (*O.C.*, IV, 419). Ortega, too, hated irrevocable decisions and showed the same contradictions he found in Goethe.

Ortega emphasizes the contrast between Goethe's naturalistic concept of life inherited from the Greeks and his existential feelings. The first concept belongs to what has been called his Naturphilosophie. Modern man is a being who has escaped from nature and separated himself from the mineral, plant, and animal world. Goethe, nevertheless, at times felt strongly that nature endowed man with a divine soul in which everything, mineral, plant, animal, and man, had its fitting and related part. Ortega explains Goethe's biological or botanical view as an external concept of life and continues: "Pero esto no significa sino que las ideas que un hombre se hace son superficiales a su verdad vital, preintelectual. Goethe piensa su vida bajo la imagen de una planta, pero la siente, la es como preocupación dramática por su propio ser" (*O.C.,* IV, 405). Goethe's answer to "who am I" smacks too much of the biological which reorients the question from the "who" to the "what am I." Ortega saw in Goethe's admiration for Shakespeare, because Shakespeare accompanied nature, Goethe's own effort to accompany her and his love for "circumstance."

But Goethe held another view of human life opposed to his botanical interpretation. Goethe the sufferer is not the same as Goethe the serene. Man possesses thought as an instrument, as he owns a body, and the former is no more the essence than the latter. As Goethe said: "Ja diesem Sinne bin ich ganz ergeben,/ Das ist der Weisheit letzer Schluss/ Nur der verdient sich Freiheit wie das Leben/ Der täglich sie erobern muss.[15]

Ortega admires Goethe, the fighter, who feels that he alone deserves liberty and life who daily must conquer them. Life cannot be repeated, though Goethe created in Faust the paradox of life which repeats itself. First one lives, and only thereafter does one philosophize. One must conquer life constantly, act it out, and possess it repeatedly. Goethe had learned by many a hard lesson that "at the most urgent crises the call to us is, 'Physician, heal thyself' . . . I tread the winepress alone." [16] The surest basis on which to build was his own creative talents, he felt, though he often neglected the sense or direction of his work. To aid man nature has endowed him with power, activity, and endurance, and especially volatility, "Leichtsinn," but the more Goethe thought on life the more apparent it became to him that it exists simply to be lived. It is time for men to stop living for religion, for science, for morality, or even for art or pleasure, but to live deliberately for the sake of living. Thus, says Ortega, "por esto decía genialmente Goethe que sólo todos los hombres viven lo humano" (*O.C.,* III, 292). Ortega reiterates his central thesis, that man must refute the idea that intelligence functions of itself, and that the problem is to discover what things are and to decide constantly what we are going to do and be at each instant.

The existential implications of Ortega's theories are obvious. As he himself claims: "Apenas hay uno o dos conceptos importantes de Heidegger que no preexistían a veces con anterioridad de trece años, en mis libros. Por ejemplo: la idea de la vida como inquietud, preocupación e inseguridad, y de la cultura como seguridad y preocupación por la seguridad, se halla literalmente en mi primera obra, *Meditaciones del Quijote,* publicada en 1914" (*O.C.,* IV, 403).

Heidegger's *Dasein* or human existence, concerned with its being as its own possibility, consists among other things of the things which are in existence in the ordinary sense of the word, *vorhanden*—literally at hand. The *vorhanden* category comprises "things" such as a tree which has a special quality and whose essence can be easily ascertained. *Dasein* gains its importance in connection with its relationship to the future, and thus the temporal problem of "being" is based on its *Geschichtlichkeit* or historicity. Ortega much earlier stated the proposition in almost identical language. Man cannot avoid his present or past "circumstance" or escape the future. The essence of human life is to determine the future, and even a decision not to act affects it. Ortega expresses the Sartrian thought that man, unlike objects, through present action to construct a future, creates a future which permits understanding and changing the present, and things teach him that he is in the world anything but a thing. "Porque esto es lo que verdaderamente diferencia al hombre de la piedra: no que el hombre tenga entendimiento y la piedra carezca de él . . . el ser piedra le es dado ya, hecho de una vez para siempre y no tiene que decidirlo ella. . . . El hombre, cada hombre, tiene que decidir en cada instante lo que va a hacer, lo que va a ser en el siguiente. Esta decisión es intransferible; nadie puede sustituirme en la faena de decidirme, de decidir mi vada" (*O.C.,* V, 21–23).

Goethe's concept of reality intrigues Ortega. Goethe thought of the world as a continuum of diversity composed of infinite but not absolute differences. In order not to lose ourselves in it, we have to mark off boundaries and establish absolutely differences which are only relative. Ortega quotes Goethe's "las cosas son diferencias que nosotros ponemos" (*O.C.,* II, 106) and "lo primero que el hombre ha hecho en su enfrente intelectual con el mundo es clasificar los fenómenos, dividir lo que ante sí halla en clases" (*O.C.*, V, 446–447). Goethe observed that Nature's humbler phenomena were often models which clarify the mystery of others of a more complex nature. He named these humble ones "proto-phenomena," and he once wrote to Jacobi on one of his botanical geological excursions that he was scouring the countryside, seeking the "divine" in plants and stones. Goethe sought divinity and "raison d'être" in many things and in different areas: "Goethe busca la pluralidad de formas vitales con vistas, no a su anulación, sino a su integración" (*O.C.*, IV, 285). Ortega repeats over a hundred favorite and often contradictory Goethian statements on a variety of matters such as: nobility, "symphronism," religious inspiration, love, the phenomena of nature, and the interpretation of the physical and psychological worlds.

Ortega feels that the critic's task is not to separate literary works into good and bad. "Cada día me interesa menos sentenciar: a ser juez de las cosas, voy prefiriendo ser su amante" (*O.C.*, I, 325). Nevertheless, he comments on Goethe's style which, influenced by Wincklemann, Diderot, and his own genius, paralleled that of painting, and on some of this themes.

Faust, like Don Juan, was once a tale of simple content, but Goethe carried the idea to its ultimate possibilities and transformed the common theme of a decrepit wise man who buys with his soul one more spring-time, to a "gigantesco poema filosófico." Precisely because we wish to be faithful today to the medieval story, we must tell it in another manner because the modern soul has become more complex, the words have taken on a new meaning, and the world which surrounds us reveals a different kind of joy.

Ortega sees Goethe as a literary liberator and contends that he and Chateaubriand "fueron los sensibilizadores del arte literario: abrieron heroicamente sus arterias y dejaron correr el vital flujo de su sangre por el caz del verso y el curvo estuario del período" (*O.C.*, II, 242). In a broader sense they are the first men who had the "audacia deliberada de adelantar como personajes que se supone decir su obra, un personaje que resulta ser su mismo autor" (*O.C.*, IV, 390). Goethe did not consider himself the master of the younger generation, but he felt he could call himself its liberator because it saw in him not only a man who lived from within but an artist who created and revealed from within. "La liberación de que se trata es, pues, la liberación hacia sí mismo" (*O.C.,* IV, 424–425). Goethe, in the last days of his life, summing up what he had been for the young poets, claimed, "podría muy bien llamarme su libertador, porque en mí han averiguado que . . . el artista . . . haga lo que quiera, solo logrará dar a la luz su propia individualidad" (*O.C.,* II, 242).

[From *Hispania,* vol. XLII, no. 3, 1960]

A Falangist View of
Golden Age Literature

THE NATIONALIST supporters who worked on the Madrid *ABC* staff fled to Seville with the outbreak of the Spanish Civil War and established a rival *ABC* there from July 23, 1936, to April 5, 1939. While the contributors concentrated on the contemporary period and criticized "enemy" writers such as Ramón Pérez de Ayala, they also devoted space to other literary epochs. Whenever possible the critics compared a classic work and the current scene. Thus Concha Espina found comfort in reading Alfonso el Sabio in the "tiniebla dura en que vivimos" (October 23, 1938), and Juan Pujol considered Franco as the modern Cid "valeroso y caballeresco" (February 13, 1937). Metaphorical comparisons between Fascist Spain and literary concepts abounded. F. Cortines Murube praised the profound originality of Pedro Mexía's *Silva de varia lección*. The action of bulls therein described recalls the actions of modern nations. "Pasce las yerbas este animal diversamente entre todos los animales, porque viene retrayéndose para atrás cuando anda pasciendo; todos los otros van delante." Spain, likewise unique, must withdraw from the somewhat showy displays of other countries and their democratic myths, and base itself on old traditions. "Pace la verdad y acude al peligro de todos con la nobleza de su valor, y retrayéndose—como los toros sementales cuando pastan, se llena España . . . de una bravía, segura, y firme inmortalidad" (May 28, 1937). An article of October 26, 1937, claimed: "Nuestros Garcilaso, Cervantes, Lope, Ercilla . . . así son miembros de nuestra Cruzada Nacional de hoy."

The *ABC* contributors considered Catholicism, *hispanidad*, tradition, and aristocracy as the positive virtues. José María Pemán, a leading spokesman for the Nationalists, defended the aristocratic nature of their movement and their literature. He claimed that the *pueblo* was incapable of high attainments. "Todos los demás poetas nacionales, todos los otros nombres máximos de la civilizacion estaban ya, más o menos, requisados por la aristocracia: Lope de Vega, teólogo, culto hasta con 'las torres' de que hablaba Góngora en su escudo. . . . El más cercano a la masa era Cervantes: el prototipo de la clase media del Renacimiento; el hidalgo de Esquivias, el amigo de duques y condes; el soldado de Lepanto." Obviously, said Pemán, to consider that a common man could create what Shakespeare did is communistic, for if a man of the people could write *The Tempest,* he could also govern well (May 26, 1938).

The *ABC* contained many discussions of the theater and its origins, especially concerning itself with the performances of *autos sacramentales* in the sixteenth century, the appearance of the *zarabanda,* the *loa,* the *mojiganga,* celebrated in the streets and plazas on public feast days, and the *entremés.* The Marqués de Quintanar felt that the autos sacramentales, "el género dramático que comenzó con Gil Vicente y siguió con Timoneda y Valdivielso y Tirso y Calderón fue creado para que en noches de Corpus, bajo el llanto de la Luna, se representase en el atrio de la Catedral de Segovia" (June 25, 1938).

In spite of a continuing censorship, dating from the time of Alfonso el Sabio, more and more autos were performed, and the secular note more noticeably entered other types of dramas. The Ataranzas, San Pedro, and Don Juan *corrales* were founded in Seville in 1568. Doña Elvira de Ayala maintained the most famous corral on the calle del Agua. *Los siete infantes de Lara* had its first performance there, as well as the works of Pedro de Saldaña, Alonso Rodríguez, and Alonso de Cisneros, who was praised highly by Lope de Vega and Felipe II's son Carlos. Juan de Morales and his wife Jusepa Vaca, the latter satirized by Góngora, headed the cast of actors. In 1600, with the appearance of the rival corral de Montería, companies started the custom of announcing plays on billboards (December 2, 1937).

Of all the Golden Age dramatists treated during the almost three years of the Seville *ABC,* Lope de Vega attracted the most attention. The Falangists found in him their concept of the state, nation, and religion, and his *Fuenteovejuna* came to be a symbol of their ideology. Performances of that drama given by the Republicans were proclaimed as perversions of what Lope meant to say and as dangerous to the Fascist cause. An editorial of December 22, 1936, stated: "Todos saben que existe un pueblo al que la pluma inmortal de Lope de Vega hizo famoso: Fuenteovejuna, *Fuenteovejuna,* obra clásica del teatro español, ha sido esgrimida criminalmente por las izquierdas para exaltar y enardecer a las muchedumbres, haciéndolas producir efectos y daños que jamás al autor pudo ocurrírsele." The editorial complained that the Marxists twisted an imaginary incident in Lope's drama to stir up the villagers. These Andalusian peasants, maddened by pernicious propaganda and led by the "Marxistas de Fuenteovejuna," performed atrocities of the worst kind. The Republic was responsible because of its crusade to bring culture to the masses and give twisted performances of Lope's work in its home town.

Concha Espina waxed vituperative as she considered how the "reds" were using works they deemed vulnerable for their own vile and vicious propaganda. She extolled Lope's virtues and his works for exemplifying the best kind of Catholicism in literature, as she excoriated the "reds" for trying to destroy his drama. "Así sucede con esa obra insigne que los rojos zarandean mutilada en perversa interpretación, el drama *Fuenteovejuna,* que en poder de los comediantes Marxistas extiende su patetismo como un inri más, clavado sobre la egregia cruz de España" (December 24, 1938). José Pemartín agreed that the two principal characteristics of the Spanish pueblo demonstrated in *Fuenteovejuna* were religion and monarchy. "En *Fuenteovejuna* el pueblo mata al tiránico comendador Fernán Gómez a los gritos de '¡Vivan Fernando e Isabel y mueran los traidores!', y 'nuestros señores son los reyes católicos'" (August 7, 1937). Francisco Quesada recalled the August, 1935, performance of *Fuenteovejuna* on the three-hundredth anniversary of Lope's death. The organizing commission planned to have the play performed in the town square by Margarita Xirgu and Rivas Cherif, Manuel Azaña's brother-in-law. The play was to start at ten, but at eleven there was still no performance because Xirgu was receiving a commission of peasants. Rivas, meanwhile, gave all the workers free passes and told them to observe especially those passages in which the village takes justice into its own hands and kills the tyrant *comendador*. The drama as finally given, said Quesada, was Marxist propaganda and responsible for the death the "rojos" committed in that village in 1937 (August 4, 1937).

José María Pemán, major spokesman on such issues, attempted to ex-

plain what *Fuenteovejuna* meant to the Falangists. Commenting on a
Christmas Day performance of that play in Seville, put on in spite of
great difficulties in acquiring costumes, scenery, and other equipment, he
claimed:

> Sabido es que la gran tragedia de Lope ha sido impúdicamente secues-
> trada por el Soviet y representada en Rusia con intencionadas mutila-
> ciones, como la mejor expresión dramática de la rebeldía popular y de
> la justicia revolucionaria . . . Ni siquiera puede calificarse la tragedia
> lopiana de antiseñorial o antiaristocrática. El Comendador que en ella
> es asesinado por el pueblo, lo es por lo que tiene de cacique, de in-
> moderado poder ilegítimo. Es el drama de la absorción por el Estado
> de todos los sub-Estados o anti-Estados dispersos por el país. El pueblo
> enfurecido de Fuenteovejuna ayuda a la obra unitaria estatal y
> moderna de los Reyes Católicos. El pueblo no maldice de la Cruz
> Roja del Comendador, sino que quiere que pase al pecho del Rey.

Pemán felt it was a monarchical and national play in every sense of the
word. The pueblo wished no intermediate powers between the king and
the nation. Thus the Falangist movement does well in attempting to claim
for itself Lope's tragedy kidnapped by Russia. The National Movement
(Franco's rebellion) is another *Fuenteovejuna,* not against lords and com-
manders but against intermediate powers such as caciques and Marxists
interspersed between the pueblo and the state. The pueblo has revolted
against them, and this time the nobles are on its side as national forces.
Since the new comendadores are the Marxists, *Fuenteovejuna* supports
Franco for the "reintegro de España a su heredad tradicional." The play
points up that many timid souls don't recognize the wave of the future. As
the Comendador said to Flores, "El mundo se acaba, Flores . . . ," but the
world did not disappear, only "un cierto mundo." Pemán concluded that
some critics do not understand the nationalist elements in Lope's work
because it is *their* world which is ending and not *the* world (January 1,
1939).

Many foreign productions of *Fuenteovejuna* displeased the Falangist
journalists. On February 12, 1938, a critic complained that the Teatro del
Pueblo in Paris, using what formerly was Sarah Bernhardt's theater, gave
a performance of *Fuenteovejuna,* sponsored by Jewish money and translated by Jean Camps and Jean Cassou with the title of *Font aux Cabres,*

which suffered from suppressed passages and other distortions and deformations.

Adaptations of other Spanish plays also evoked the displeasure of *ABC*. Mariano Daranas took the Comédie Française to task for not recognizing the tricentenary of *Le Cid* by Corneille. He viewed this oversight as a plot of the Popular Front, for the Spanish play "como escuela de honor, nobleza y heroismo, como símbolo moral y sujeto de historia, es nuestro, exclusivamente nuestro. Todo un pueblo lo contó en su propia lengua a lo largo de los siglos y al cabo de novecientos años; el mismo pueblo reza ante su tumba todavía. Hasta tal punto que la resistencia del Frente Popular a celebrar la obra imperecedora, responde a un prejuicio antiespañol, no menos que a un prejuicio demagógico" (December 26, 1936). An editorial of February 23, 1938, examined a production of Corneille's *Le Menteur,* an adaptation of Juan Ruiz de Alarcón's *La verdad sospechosa,* which according to Menéndez y Pelayo was "la obra más perfecta del teatro castellano." The editorial ironically inquires whether the "reds" will now maintain the spiritual adhesion of Alarcón and Menéndez y Pelayo to the Soviet cause as they had already done with Lope in their Teatro del Pueblo.

Not all foreign performances of Spanish plays were criticized. Sigfrido Bürmann felt the Germans had done well by Lope and Spain. The *Estrella de Sevilla* and the *Caballero de Olmedo* had fantastic successes in Germany in 1936. This caused a renewed interest in Lope's works, and productions such as *La dama boba, Si no vieran las mujeres, Amor sin saber a quien, El castigo sin venganza, De cosario a cosario,* and *Los milagros del desprecio* received critical acclaim in various German cities in 1937. The year 1938 produced *Fuenteovejuna, Peribáñez y el comendador de Ocaña,* and *El niño diablo.* Therefore, wrote Sigfrido Bürmann, "en Alemania el autor dramático que en la temporada pasada ha tenido un número de estrenos mucho mayor que cualquier otro autor de teatro se llama . . . ¡Lope de Vega!" (October 20, 1938).

Calderón received much less attention than Lope, although quotations from the former's works are scattered throughout the journal. Typical is the article by Capitán Nemo. "Pues la peripecia de estos últimos años recuerda directamente a *La vida es sueño* cuando el áspero y brutal Segismundo se erige en príncipe y comete todas las barbaridades que su naturaleza primitiva le aconseja." Force overcame him, however, and Segismundo, the counterpart of the loyalists, will also be conquered and imprisoned

(March 19, 1937). An editorial of July 13, 1938, questions Calderón's "'No hubiera capitán, si no hubiera labrador.' Hoy habría que rectificar eso, diciendo que no habría labrador si no hubiera capitán." Calderón was "el mayor dramático de la poesía cristiana," and his concepts found an echo in the homogeneous religious pueblo that was the Spain of his time (January 26, 1937).

José María Salaverría, in an article dated November 4, 1938, insisted that the great national myths belonged to the Falangists. "Don Quijote no hay duda que pondría su lanza al servicio de Franco, dispuesto como nunca a pelear contra los malandrines rojos, y don Juan, el españolísimo, el de la terrible espada, haría completamente igual." One must never forget, said Salaverría, the origin of Don Juan in the Spanish Church. Don Juan feels himself profoundly superior, and in the consciousness of this superiority "por derecho de origen y de naturaleza, reside precisamente la explicación y el hecho psicológico del imperialismo." Don Juan is one of the brave adventurers who for honor, power, and glory helped the Spanish Empire.

While drama evoked the most critical response, other genres such as the novel were not neglected. Concha Espina claimed that Vicente Espinel demonstrated one of the best combinations of arms and letters, and she compared him to the noble Falangist warriors: "a veces parecidos . . . a los de esta guerra de apostasías y monstruosidades, vencidas milagrosamente, con el entusiasmo y la fe de los patriotas." *Marcos de Obregón* reveals a pure "estilo . . . alto vuelo de . . . metáforas y . . . sano orgullo." A cultivator of arms and letters, faithful to the laws of nobility, he devoted himself to the Catholic faith and thus calmed his spirit and found peace in an unhappy world (September 16, 1938).

Each April brought forth a large number of articles on Cervantes, which the writers used not only for adulation of Spain's greatest writer but also for attacks against the enemy, the "evil Republicans who allowed the true national treasure of the Golden Age to be lost." Juan de Castilla lamented the disappearance of Cervantes' remains from the convent of the Trinitarios, where both Cervantes' and Lope's daughters lived for many years and where a requiem mass was said for Cervantes every April 23. The San Sebastián Church where Lope was buried was destroyed "hace algunos meses por los bárbaros iconoclastas" (April 24, 1937). The *ABC* writers insisted on interpreting Cervantes politically. Mariano Daranas criticized a production of *Numancia* given in the Antoine Theater in Paris by Jean Louis Barrault because the latter put into the play a feeling of collective life, the suffering of the masses, and a plea for the dignity and love of humanity, sentiments which Cervantes never had (April 23, 1937). Capitán Nemo discussed the famous dispute between arms and letters (April 2, 1938), an adaptation of *El curioso impertinente* by Luc Dartain, and Cervantes' contribution to literature (May 16, 1937), while Concha Espina evoked Cervantes in his battles against the "apóstatas, renegados y gentiles, entre piratas y arraeces, por la fe de Cristo y el honor de España," and compared them to the fight of Franco's brave soldiers against the "patricidas, ateos, y masones" of contemporary Spain. Cervantes' virtues as a good Catholic should inspire the Spanish followers of Franco to defend the integrity and religion of Spain (November 2, 1938).

Aside from Garcilaso, claimed for the Fascist cause as a man of arms and letters, Luis de León and Luis de Góngora also merited acceptance. Ernesto Giménez Caballero compared the virtues of Fray Luis de León to those of Franco, his "héroe cristiano." He stressed Luis de León's line "a solas con Dios, ni envidiado ni envidioso," which is the cure for the "envidia hispánica" noted by so many, a defect which exists in modern Spain. At last Spain is fortunate enough to have its Caudillo, a Christian hero dreamed of by Fray Luis de León, the man who is neither "envidiado ni envidioso" (July 18, 1937). Pedro Sainz Rodríguez also claimed Luis de León for the Falangists and praised his *Nombres de Cristo* as "la más profunda sabia y eminente sabiduría de las cosas de Dios que acaso hayan escrito los hombres" (May 27, 1938).

Góngora, as a priest, inspired the *ABC*'s admiration, although his pagan themes were frowned upon. José Carlos de Luna felt that "Acaso se libró Góngora de la tempestad modernista, no ciertamente por españolismo, sino para, fusilándole en su Fábula de Polifemo, sentirse un poco ángel de las tinieblas y hacer de lo enrevesado piedra de toque para la intelectualidad al uso" (September 2, 1937). Concha Espina, on the other hand, thought that his critics "se iban rindiendo al hechizo de una desbordante inspiración," and she claimed that Góngora helped her as she prayed her rosary, for the Cordovan poet was, after all, a "sacerdote y gigante figura en el universo literario" (September 28, 1938).

A variety of other sixteenth and seventeenth century authors were discussed by the *ABC* critics. J. López Prudencio viewed Juan Luis Vives' work as the first "refutación acabada del comunismo" and saw in him the profound influence of Vitoria (February 1, 1939). Víctor Sánchez listed Luis Vives as one of the precursors of the New Spain. Sánchez recalled the work of don Carlos Riba and Marqués de Lozoya, two founders of a "vivista" society to publish Vives' works which Mayáns y Siscar had first made known in Latin in the eighteenth century, an effort which only the New Spain will vindicate, for it will not forget this "insigne polígrafo valenciano y que por todos los medios a su alcance procurará el estudio y expansión de sus doctrinas, tan llenas de vida para ella."

The *ABC* also commented on Diego Saavedra Fajardo, whose works, it said, bolstered the concept of a New Spain "imponente . . . invencible" (February 3, 1938), but Quevedo was its special favorite. J. Portal Fradejas in an article, "España y don Francisco de Quevedo," explained that Quevedo stressed the glory of arms over letters as had Cervantes, that he defended Spain against all attacks, and that he realized that Spain could be great only in its understanding of the infinite and the value of divine protection. Quevedo should serve as the current example for Spain instead of the so-called intellectuals "que firmaron para angustia de España la maldiciente generación del 98" (January 9, 1937). Concha Espina claimed that Quevedo found peace from the ills of the world in his *Política de Dios y gobierno de Cristo* as the only remedy "contra los desmanes inciviles y persecutorios del Frente Popular." In any event his multiple talents and his interesting personality continue to contribute to his favorite position among the Falangists (September 22, 1938).

The *ABC* critics, in their analyses of Spanish literature, reveal once more the polarization of Spanish literature and the dramatic dualism which one finds in almost all aspects of the Spanish scene, a polarity expressed in the struggles of Menéndez y Pelayo against the Krausists in the nineteenth century and by the Spanish Civil War in the twentieth.

[From *Hispania,* vol. XLIX, no. 2, May, 1966]

A Fascist View of
Nineteenth-Century Spanish
Literature (1936–1939)

SHORTLY after the Spanish Civil War started on July 18, 1936, Franco supporters who worked as staff members of the Madrid *ABC* escaped to Seville and established a rival *ABC* which existed from July 23, 1936, to April 5, 1939. Although the Seville journal devoted most of its space to war news, it also examined Spanish literature, especially of the twentieth century. It criticized "enemy" writers such as Antonio Machado, Pérez de Ayala, and Américo Castro at the same time it lauded the supporters of the "cause" such as Manuel Machado, Concha Espina, Ramiro de Maeztu, and José María Pemán.

The nineteenth century also preoccupied the contributors of the *ABC*, and although their study of its authors shows no startling surprises, it reveals the continuing controversy of the Spanish literary-political relationships between the foreign and the native, tradition and progress, a polemic which even today clouds Spanish critics' literary evaluations.

The first issue of *ABC* to mention literary matters was the July 28, 1936, number which started republishing Enrique Gil y Carrasco's historical novel, *El señor de Bembibre,* from the middle of Chapter 37 where it had broken off in the Madrid *ABC* of July 14, 1936. Thereafter every number contained literary evaluations.

José Zorrilla was the romantic who received the greatest acclaim. Larra was rejected as a suicide and liberal (March 20, 1937), and Espronceda, as José María Salaverría states, unlike Zorrilla, instead of joining the Franco movement would probably have been a "diputado del Frente Popular" (October 22, 1938). J. Mayoral Fernández praised the inspirational qualities of the "versos mágicos del poeta excelso (Zorrilla)"

(March 23, 1937). José María Salaverría commented on the incomparably patriotic aspect of José Zorrilla's poetry. He felt the poet's works should serve contemporary Spanish youth because of their classic concept of Spanish Catholicism and honor. "No puede darse nada tan español como esa obra que en su totalidad fue dedicada a cantar en versos de admirable belleza verbal las leyendas y tradiciones de nuestro pueblo" (October 22, 1938). Eduardo Marquina marked the lack of the traditional performance of *Don Juan Tenorio* in Seville on November 2, 1938, with "trazo negro de luto y nostalgia en su anuario sentimental y estético la inusitada ausencia del héroe españolísimo" (November 8, 1938). In response to Marquina's complaint, the Bassó-Nicolás Navarro company gave a special performance of *Don Juan Tenorio* in the Gran Teatro Cervantes on November twenty-sixth.

Gustavo Adolfo Bécquer was another favorite of the *ABC*. On February 16, 1937, the Bécquer brothers' remains were removed to a new tomb beneath a commemorative monument. Doña Virgilia Reparaz, Gustavo Adolfo Bécquer's godchild, attended the ceremony which revealed the affection with which Bécquer was regarded in Seville. For Manuel Siurot the poet was "el mágico prodigioso" (January 11, 1938). The Quintero brothers, perhaps Bécquer's most ardent admirers, turned his *narración, La venta de los gatos,* into a drama in July 1936 to commemorate the anniversary of his birth. On June 11, 1938, Carmen Díaz gave its first performance at the San Fernando Theater.

Most of the Falangist intellectuals viewed Menéndez y Pelayo as their spiritual guide and the most important nineteenth-century writer. For J. López Prudencio he was "aquel entendimiento gigante que, con sus erudición asombrosa, con su fe ardiente, con su laboriosidad incomparable, puso de manifiesto ante España y ante el mundo culto, la razón y los fundamentos sólidos que tiene España" (May 26, 1937). An editorial of August 26, 1937, recalled him as "maestro insuperable de la nueva, mejor dicho, de la renovada y eterna España." An editorial the following day labeled him "guardián de nuestros tesoros seculares." May 19, 1937, marked the twenty-fifth anniversary of his death, and the titles of the articles and lectures reveal the reasons for the Falangists' reverence for Menéndez y Pelayo: "Menéndez y Pelayo y el Imperio," "Menéndez Pelayo y Acción Española," and "La Tradición y el Estilo en Menéndez y Pelayo." Manuel Machado dedicated a poem to him: "Eras tú cuando toda nuestra gloria / en tu obra ingente revivir supiste / cuando del claro ayer fuiste el espejo." Manuel Artigas stated that Menéndez y Pelayo's books were indispensable guides for Spaniards who wished fully to understand the art, literature, and true beliefs of Spain, especially as the latter compared with the currents of European culture of modern times (May 19, 1937). José María Pemán found in the works of Menéndez y Pelayo the soul, substance, ideology, and logic of "este gran Movimiento de reivindicación española [Franco's] . . . en lo que tiene de pensamiento y en lo que tiene de heroicidad." Menéndez y Pelayo was a classicist, a Catholic, and a traditionalist, qualities which Pemán views as those of the Franco revolt. As Pemán interpreted him: "Para los más, la alegría, la tranquilidad y la satisfacción de obedecer. Para los mejores, el dolor, la inquietud y la responsabilidad de mandar." He agreed that European decadence stemmed from the rupture of Christian unity and that Descartes triumphed over the Scholastics because of his style. In the duel between truth and style the latter has won in modern times. Thus, current Spaniards should learn from the lessons taught by Menéndez y Pelayo, says Pemán. "Tenemos la verdad, pero es preciso arroparla con el estilo." Style without truth is valueless. Spain needs both and can find them through the teachings of Menéndez y Palayo (May 27, 1938). Capitán Nemo reflected on the shock Menéndez y Pelayo would have had on seeing his provincial land changed into a republic opposed to his ideas of "españolismo, de casticismo, de cristianismo." The key to the character of this Spanish paladin who justified Spain's actions was exactly this exaltation of "eterna España." Menéndez y Pelayo had renounced his possibilities as a potentially proficient poet to dedicate himself to the more difficult task of literary and historical criticism. For Nemo he merits both the title "divino" and, like Lope, "monstruo de la naturaleza" (August 25, 1937).

These *ABC* critics venerated Menéndez y Pelayo for his battle against the Krausists and the Institución Libre de Enseñanza which they saw as the precursors of the Loyalist government they were fighting. The Institución was "esclava de Francia y de Inglaterra" (December 21, 1937), an organization which lacked "orgullo en ser español (March 20, 1936), a "vasta red masónica y judía" (April 7, 1937). It and men like Joaquín Costa and his "anatema terrible" (about the *sepulcro del Cid*) were the enervating forces of Spain's spiritual strength which had led to the socialization of the Spanish Republic (May 17, 1938). If the Institución, Giner de los

Ríos, and Joaquín Costa had produced the enemy, by the same token Franco was heir to the philosophy of Menéndez y Pelayo.

Others who stressed Catholicism were revered as precursors. Jaime Balmes, whom Menéndez y Pelayo had called "el pensador más profundo del pasado siglo," said Alfonso Sala, should be read by all young Spaniards, especially his *El protestantismo comparado con el catolicismo,* "la apología más completa y acabada de la religión católica y el fundamento más preciado de la prosperidad y grandeza de España" (October 12, 1937).

Among nineteenth-century novelists Benito Pérez Galdós received only brief mention. Gabrielillo, young hero of *La batalla de los Arapiles,* today would not be following his beloved Inesilla's footsteps. Instead he would be fighting the French who have accepted undesirable Spaniards and Russians, "esclavos unos y otros de masones y judíos" (March 23, 1937). A December 12, 1937, article on Madrid, "víctima aherrojada del Soviet ruso y de unos millares de españoles indignos de serlo," cites Galdós' "españolismo" and love of Madrid. José María de Pereda and Armando Palacio Valdés were the Falangists' favorites. Pereda shared their ideas of *españolismo, casticismo,* and *cristianismo.* He was attached to his *tierruca,* but he viewed it as but a part of his total national pride. No aspect of his area or people, the landscape, the mountains, or the sea escaped him, and he treated them all with love. When one recalls Pereda's works, to think of the fighting and the republic in Santander is as difficult to accept as the thought of Avila, the home of Santa Teresa, sponsoring a world wide convention of atheists.

Palacio Valdés died on February 5, 1938, "un mártir más de la causa sagrada de España, por la cual han sido inmoladas tantas víctimas." Material and moral support was impossible under the rule of "bárbaros modernos," and this and his profound disillusion at the decomposition he saw around him caused his death (February 5, 1938). An editorial recalled Palacio Valdés' birthplace, the pleasant Asturian village of Entralgo, so well described in his novel, *La aldea perdida,* and the transformation of its simple customs at the hands of a materialistic government, the destruction by the "hordas bárbaras" of the theater named for him in Avilés, and his many famous novels, of which *La hermana San Sulpicio* was "la más perfecta . . . porque en ella y junto al humorismo innato, campean sus envidiables facultades de narrador y su acierto al arrancar de la realidad, tipos y personajes que se mantienen vivos, dentro de las páginas del libro" (February 5, 1938). His masterpiece, however, did not lend itself to the theater. The life and vigor of the novel's characters could not be transmitted to the stage. As Palacio Valdés himself admitted: "A la novela no le va el teatro. La luz de las candilejas la hace empalidecer, la amortigua y la mata" (February 6, 1938) .

Juan de Castilla, an intimate friend of Palacio Valdés, reminiscing over their relationship, described the latter's habits, hobbies, and home as pretty, peaceful, and correct. Palacio Valdés liked his family, children, friends, flowers, and the color blue. He disliked noise and turmoil. Generous to a fault, he was deceived by all kinds of swindlers and crooks. The last days of his life were saddened by a fall that broke his leg, which kept him from walking, his favorite pastime. He acquired a car, which he disliked, and his principal pleasure on warm days was to visit the Retiro. He set himself a quota of eight or ten pages a day of writing, and he always managed this limited amount. If one considers the works of Galdós as "corriente caudalosa," those of Pereda as "torrente que se despeña a veces en cataratas," then the work of Palacio Valdés is a "plácido arroyo, de manar incesante y tranquilo cuyas claras linfas . . . dejan ver con su transparencia, las menudas guijas del fondo." If one could sum him up in one word, that word would be *pulcritud* (February 10, 1938).

Castilla recalled that many years before Pereda wanted to meet Emilia Pardo Bazán, then a budding authoress. He enlisted Palacio Valdés' aid, and they visited her in her modest boarding house in Santa Ana Square. She discussed the *novela cortesana* as a separate genre requiring practice and a perfect knowledge of the *ambiente*. The bad-tempered Pereda attacked her; she in turn told him to "cultivar su huerto — las escenas de la montaña." Once outside, Pereda said a dirty word, and Palacio Valdés rushed him down the stairs, protesting that Pardo Bazán might be listening at the window. Palacio Valdés in later years said: "De aquella entrevista un poco accidentada, nació *La Montálvez.*" Pereda thus showed that one could write "una novela cortesana sin necesidad de estar avecinado en Madrid" (February 10. 1938).

According to J. López Prudencio, Palacio Valdés' novels lacked the success in Spain accorded those of Pereda, Galdós, Valera, Alarcón, Clarín, and Pardo Bazán. Even *La hermana San Sulpicio* needed four years to sell its first Spanish edition. Nevertheless, his novels gained greater success in the rest of Europe than those of the other authors. His style was clear and correct, but he never worried about an impeccable classicism. His works were as Spanish as the most Spanish of his contemporaries, but his depth of observation of human beings and life had a universal quality easy to translate, whereas the other novelists used langage or created figures hard to understand outside Spain. Palacio Valdés also exhibited a humor, often compared to that of Dickens, which was easily assimilated outside his country. With the occasional exception of works such as *La espuma* and *La fe,* in which Palacio Valdés experimented with French naturalism, this humor is the chief characteristic of his work. Surprisingly enough, with the appearance of new novelists such as Pío Baroja, Ricardo León, and Valle Inclán, Palacio Valdés' novels reached the height of their popularity in Spain.

Blasco Ibáñez, considered an "enemy" writer, did not fare so well. J. Miquelarena commented on him as "un tal Vicente que según dicen algunos escribía novelas en camiseta, con un botijo al lado. Yo sólo sé que murió en Mentón, rodeado en su 'villa' de la interpretación más bárbara del arte de vivir en climas azules que se conoce en el mundo" (April 23, 1938).

The contributors to *ABC* examined Spanish literature from both a historical and future point of view. Using Franco's *Movimiento* as their vantage point, they viewed it as the fruition of the moral bases they found in Menéndez Pelayo and others. In their perspective it presumably promised an even more appealing future, where writers like Ramiro de Maeztu and José María Pemán would emancipate that section of the Spanish public enslaved by the radical and revolutionary doctrines of the Spanish Republic and aggressively reaffirm the eternal ethical and spiritual qualities they found in the classic conservatives of the past.

[From *Romance Notes,* vol. VII, no. 2]

Culture and the Spanish Civil War—A Fascist View: 1936–1939

ALMOST from the inception of the Spanish Inquisition, which sought to stifle scientific investigation and philosophical speculation while rejecting foreign ideologies, contrary currents existed in Spain. The liberal humanistic movement headed by Erasmus preached intellectual freedom and a defense of interior religion. This ideology never disappeared in Spain in spite of the formation of the Company of Jesus by Ignacio de Loyola and the efforts of Spanish theologians who promoted the Counter Reformation at the Council of Trent. Under Felipe II foreign ideas were forbidden as heretical and interpretations independent of the Church were stifled. Nevertheless, criticism of the status quo continued. Reginaldo González Montano wrote the first attack on the Inquisition, *Sanctae Inquisitionis Hispanicae* in 1567. The picaresque novel, among other literary genres in the sixteenth and seventeenth centuries, revealed the dichotomy ever present in Spain between the conservative elements which supported the status quo and those who stressed change in the name of progress.

In the nineteenth century the struggle between the Catholic, traditional Spain of the Middle Ages and the progressive, European-oriented one of the Renaissance became sharply focused in the polemics between the supporters of the conservative writer, Marcelino Menéndez Pelayo and those of the Institución Libre de Enseñanza.[1] In the twentieth century, the two philosophies, in modern dress, clashed head on during the dictatorship of Primo de Rivera and under the second Spanish Republic.

The assassination of José Calvo Sotelo, the leader of the terrorist rightist elements, on July 13, 1936, triggered the tragic Spanish Civil War, begun on July 18, 1936, which was to turn family against family and brother against brother. On July 20, 1936, *ABC,* a conservative royalist daily journal which had been publishing since June 1, 1905, was taken over by the Loyalists. Franco supporters on the staff fled to Seville and started a rival *ABC* on July 23, 1936. From that date until April 5, 1939, two versions of *ABC* existed, a Nationalist[2] one in Seville and a Loyalist one in Madrid. The *ABC* was well known in Latin America. The Seville version had extremely limited circulation, but it had a contributing Latin American correspondent. With Franco's triumph the two journals again became one and continued as a Madrid publication.[3]

The Fascist *ABC,* which became one of the semi-official organs of Franco propaganda, adopted a historical approach to further both contemporary and future aims. It tried to justify Franco's revolt intellectually, and its contributors sought to provide the moral base, which they saw in Menéndez Pelayo and other classic conservatives of the past, for future writers. The latter, in their turn, would be the heirs of Ramiro de Maeztu, José María Pemán, and other contemporary conservatives. These authors, it was hoped, would emancipate that section of the reading public enslaved by the radical and revolutionary doctrines of the Spanish Republic and aggressively reaffirm the spiritual qualities of their right wing revolt. Not since the time of the Inquisition in Spain was such a deliberate attempt made in that country to determine the future course of Spanish literature. It resembled the efforts of the Russian writers, after the Russian Revolution, to shape literature to political ends, the favorite technique of the police state.

Among the Spanish contributors to the *ABC* were J. López Prudencio, Luis de Galinsoga who used the pseudonym SIUL, W. Fernández Flórez, Manuel Machado, José María Salaverría, Julio Camba, Eduardo Marquina, E. Giménez Caballero, Concha Espina, and José María Pemán. Its foreign correspondents were César González Ruano in Rome, Mariano Daranas in Paris, and El Bachiller Alcañices in Chile. Their articles were filled with virulent attacks against the Jews, the Loyalists, the United States, and the Russians, and with profuse praise for Hitler and Mussolini. If one was not with them, one was a "masón, rojo, o hereje." A defense by them of their point of view was understandable, although the rabid hatred expressed for the Jews, the Institución Libre de Enseñanza, and other supposed enemies of their way of life resembled psychotic fantasy rather than objective criticism. They occasionally revealed their lack of intellectual depth, but their consistent clarion call convinced or converted the wavering and the weak, the frustrated, the phobic, and the paranoid who sought a kind of intellectual justification for their new attitudes.

The *ABC* contributors, unlike their German counterparts, offered no so-called new philosophy of life, although they also constantly echoed the anti-Semitic and anti-Communistic themes of the Nazis. Instead, the *ABC* brought into sharpest focus the age-old conflict in Spain between the real and the ideal, the traditional and the progressive, the native and the foreign, themes so apparent in all Spanish literary works and movements from their very beginnings. The contributors insisted on *hispanidad,* tradition, and Catholicism. Indeed, said E. Giménez Caballero, "fascismo para España no es fascismo, sino catolicismo." [4]

Some of the critics in their new zeal questioned whether they had produced anything of value before the war. Melchor Fernández Almagro admitted that the civil war had completely changed his viewpoint. In the light of that "anguished and glorious war," "a esta luz purísima—terrible y prometedora—la literatura se nos ofrece mucho menos interesante que la vida misma y la crítica—con mayor motivo—como algo estúpidamente superfluo. Entiéndase: la crítica profesional" (January 18, 1939). New critical criteria meant for them the constant reiteration of a few simple themes. In their sometimes querulous attempt to bolster the righteousness of their position, the critics enlisted the aid of the great classic writers. José María Salaverría agreed that Nationalist Spain should try to incorporate into its cause the writers and thinkers of the past, most of whom would have joined the Falangist side and given "su adhesión incondicional a nuestro Caudillo." Garcilaso de la Vega, Hurtado de Mendoza, Ercilla, Lope, Calderón, Cervantes, and Quevedo would have joined Franco. The nineteenth-century authors such as Zorrilla, Valera, Pereda, Menéndez Pelayo, and Emilia Pardo Bazán would have belonged to the "Cause." Espronceda, on the other hand, "sería diputado del Frente Popular" (October 22, 1938).

Manuel de Lamberri contrasted what he felt were the differences in the writings of the Loyalists and the Nationalists. For him the Nationalists were the direct heirs of the Catholic sovereigns, Velázquez, Cortés, Pizarro, Santa Teresa, and San Juan de la Cruz. "El suyo (the Loyalist faction) no procede de los instintos profundos y no es jamás afirmativo. Viene de la crítica y de la duda. Su raíz hay que buscarla en la Enciclopedia y su tronco y ramas en las utopías económicas y en los círculos tristes y judaicos de los Engel y de los Marx." This, then, was the leitmotiv of much of the criticism in the *ABC*. The Nationalists were the owners of the strong biological creative drive. The Loyalists were the weak, the divided, and the confused, all elements reflected in their style. The opponents were hasty and superficial. The Nationalists were serene and profound. For the Nationalists Mars was the forceful symbol of the future, as they assigned to the Loyalists the support of Mercury and Venus, "espíritu judaico, de anónimo y de vitriolo, espíritu de Venus tarada y prostituida, ponzoña y bacterias, chismes de comadre, espíritu que chocará siempre, con impulso débil con nuestra proyección lenta, seguida y serena hacia el radiante porvenir" (February 11, 1938).

The critics felt that the best hope for creating a new literature which would serve their cause lay in the theater, and they evinced a constant concern over its current state. Joaquín Calvo Sotelo decided that what he termed the decadence of the Spanish theater stemmed from a lack of "autores capaces de vigorizarlo mediante la incorporación a la escena de obras de fuerte realismo." He expected that a future theater might replace old tired themes (November 10, 1936). José María Pemán viewed the theater as "la expresión y la conciencia de lo compartido y comunal. Un período histórico sin teatro sería algo mutilado, afónico, que ni se sentiría a sí mismo ni sería comprendido por los demás." The new Spain, he said, needed a new theater to promote a communion of collective ideas (April 8, 1937). José Antonio Álvarez organized such a theater in 1937 to promote the future New Spain under Franco. His war theater, TAC, *teatro ambulante de campaña,* offered a kind of reactionary counterpart to the Republic's La Barraca group. The actors traveled in a bus and used a truck, one side of which was movable, for the stage. Luis Escobar, discussing the performance of TAC, compared its equipment to that in the famous description Cervantes gave of Lope de Rueda's theater (November 16, 1937).

Throughout 1938 Manuel Machado called for renovation of the theater based on tradition, for, he claimed, in art "lo que no es tradición es plagio" (January 28, 1938). On March 19, 1938, he pleaded for union of all groups interested in the theater, for the formation of a commission to award special prizes for performances, and for the reading of Golden Age plays, "con el castellano de los siglos de Oro, tan venido hoy a menos."

On June 1, 1938, the Ministry of the Interior announced the establishment of a special literary prize for the production of *autos sacramentales*. Machado was greatly pleased for he felt the revival of the theater lay in constant reemphasis of Spanish "tradición gloriosa. . . . El teatro español que comienza en Lope y termina en Calderón es, en gran parte—y acaso la mejor—teatro religioso" (August 4, 1938). La Tarumba, a university theater of the Falange, listed officially as the "teatro nacional de Falange Española Tradicionalista y de las Jons," under the direction of Luis de Escobar, performed *Las bodas de España,* a sixteenth-century anonymous auto, *El Hospital de los Locos,* an auto sacramental by Valdivielso, and a series of classical dramas by Lope de Vega, Juan Ruiz de Alarcón, and others.

Other critics reiterated the same double theme of the need for tradition and the necessity for a new theater which would promote the New Spain under Franco. As María Matilde Belmonte said: "Hay que hacer un teatro grande, magnífico, fuerte, digno de la Nueva Patria. Tienen que nacer nuevos autores de entre aquéllos que hoy se juegan la vida por España. . . . Qué ocasiones tan únicas ofrece la guerra para la imaginación del escritor moderno . . ." (July 2, 1938). Eduardo Marquina blamed the absence of good theater on the movies. He sought to equate the theater with national service and pleaded for the coordination of the activities of all professionals to try to avoid the "colapsos como el que hoy paraliza del todo la vida normal del teatro en la ciudad de Sevilla. Y en tantos otros de España." For him Spanish theater was history, relived and projected in new dimensions in a present-day context. The theater as a way of life could help maintain pride in Spanish honor, theology, and the Catholic religion. It represented action, the yoke and the arrow, but it needed to free itself from European heresies and represent once more "el alma nacional española" (November 8, 1938). Wenceslao Fernández Flórez stressed the sad state of the Spanish stage and praised the patriotic efforts of Marquina and his committee to elevate the Spanish theater to a pure and lofty stature suitable to the New Spain (December 3, 1938).

One might gather from the above that Falangist Spain was living in a complete cultural vacuum filled only by the movies. Such was not the case, although a partial listing of the best dramas performed in Seville from 1936 to 1939 reveals reasons for concern. No major production of worth was written or performed during the war years. Emphasis lay almost exclusively on the farcical and light productions of Pedro Muñoz Seca, the Quintero brothers, and their imitators. Among the dramatic companies were Concha-Catatá-Juan Calvo, Fernando Burgos, Tina Gascó-Fernando de Granada, Bassó-Navarro, and the Company of Carmen Díaz, the latter a friend of the Quintero brothers who specialized in their comedies.

The critics acclaimed plays by Fascist authors and attacked any adverse criticism. On May 15, 1937, an editorial boasted that while a work such as *Julieta y Romeo* by Pemán could be given in Seville, the theater of "reds" in "el Madrid marxista están cerrados o sólo se abren para emporcarse con mitinescas blasfemias." The *ABC* reacted violently to bad reviews which *El Divino Impaciente* by José María Pemán received in Argentina and attributed them to corruption and politics, "ese conglomerado de apetitos, concupiscencias y claudicaciones . . . esa Prensa, vergüenza de toda una nación, esa Prensa vendida representada por *Crítica,* el diario más inmundo de todos los países" (September 22, 1937). In Spain, *El Divino Impaciente* elicited: "En sus escenas está el alma de España, el alma de la España que no muere" (October 9, 1937). A January 14, 1939, article gleefully commented that *El verdugo de Sevilla* by Pedro Muñoz Seca, one of their supporters, was to be performed in Barcelona to help make up the tremendous deficits which the "reds" had run up by giving their revolutionary works.

The films which had been blamed for the lack of good theater in Seville were largely of United States origin. In 1937 and 1938 more and more German, Italian, and Spanish productions were presented, but American films still outnumbered the others. A partial list of actors taking part in these United States films presented at the eight or nine Sevillian theaters reads like a Hollywood *Who's Who*: Preston Foster, William Powell, Joan Crawford, James Cagney, Maureen O'Sullivan, Shirley Temple, Eddie Cantor, Ginger Rogers, George Brent, Alice Faye, Boris Karloff, John Wayne, Miriam Hopkins, Joel McCrea, Dick Powell, Jean Harlow, Franchot Tone, Robert Taylor, Irene Dunne, Greta Garbo, Warner Baxter, Lionel Barrymore, Harold Lloyd, Cary Grant, Clark Gable, George Raft, Carole Lombard, Jeanette MacDonald, Robert Montgomery, Edward G. Robinson, Myrna Loy, Claudette Colbert, Katherine Hepburn, Fred McMurray, and Richard Dix. Yet the Spanish critics remained unsatisfied and unimpressed.

On January 3, 1937, the Lloréns theater, whose Vicente Lloréns first brought talking pictures to Seville, stated: "La escasez de buenas películas, originada en el actual estado de cosas, obliga a las empresas de los habituales espectáculos cinematográficos a abrir alguna tregua en sus programas de proyecciones sustituyéndolas de vez en vez por otra índole de atracciones." The movies had been unable to avoid the consequences of the Spanish Civil War "creando dificultades para la adquisición de buen material extranjero con que proveer los programas; obstáculos que en cierta manera se han derivado, en la esfera moral, del mismo elevado espíritu que nutre la ingente empresa por la España del Caudillo acometida. En servicio y amor de ella importaba mucho el excluir, en la selección de firmas y películas cuanto no estuviese inspirado en los Cristianos sentimientos que el glorioso alzamiento de julio vino a restaurar." This lack, announced the Coliseo and Lloréns theaters, would henceforth be filled by UFA, a German company which offered aid with gallant disinterest and solidarity, "la noble y gloriosa Alemania . . . un nuevo testimonio altísimo de esa amistad leal y calurosa con que la grande Alemania se inclina solícita hacia las inquietudes de nuestra Patria" (March 21, 1937).

In addition to the German films about heroic Nazis, on January 15, 1939, it was announced that José María Pemán's *El Divino Impaciente,* to be filmed by Cine Cittá in Rome, was to be the first of twelve to be based on his works, which it was hoped would show "el espíritu y las grandes gestas de la verdadera España" (January 15, 1939).

The Institución Libre de Enseñanza proved to be the most consistently criticized historical scapegoat. J. López Prudencio attacked its members as unpatriotic descendants of the Encyclopedists who never knew the noble pride of being Spanish. The Falangists, on the contrary, without the hollow intellectual pretensions of the members of the Institución, promote a proud vision of a new and glorious Spain (March 20, 1937). The *ABC* declared that vanguard movements in art and literature originated from that "infecta Institución Libre de Enseñanza . . . y en toda la vasta red masónica y judía de Patronatos y Comisiones, a cuya mantenencia subvenían con estúpida esplendidez que hasta tenían a veces la humorada o la perversidad de llamarse conservadores" (April 7, 1937).

Franco supporters bitterly attacked the teachers at the Institución. Joaquín Costa was doubly penalized by being of humble Aragonese peasant origin and by being the leader of a group which fought for the Europeanization of Spain. Capitán Nemo derogates Joaquín Costa for having said,

"Hay que cerrar el sepulcro del Cid con doble vuelta de llave," a sad concept in which Costa and his followers were influenced by pernicious foreign influences, since pacifism is foreign to the Spanish nature. Only under such an influence "puede un intelectual español menospreciar al soldado, porque nuestra tradición literaria está henchida de reverencia marcial." He quotes Quevedo's "El español es por naturaleza soldado, que ha nacido para serlo," and insists that Spain must be always armed to the teeth. Spain will then not suffer the disaster through which it is going and may once more take its rightful place as a military power (January 31, 1937). J. López Prudencio attacks Costa and the Generation of 1898 for gnawing away at the spiritual greatness of Spain. He views Costa's insistence on Spain's backwardness and his "anatema terrible" (about the *sepulcro del Cid*) as the beginning of the Republic, the socialization of Spain, and the rejection of true values, luckily remedied by the "glorioso 18 de julio en que el Cid rompió las cerraduras de su sepulcro" (May 17, 1938).

Especially does *ABC* repeat the refrain about the Institución's responsibility for the Spanish Republic. Along with the Krausists and the Ateneo of Madrid, which *ABC* viewed as the publicity agent for both (and therefore "tan despreciables y había que exterminarlos"), they were responsible for Ossorio y Gallardo, Pérez de Ayala, Marañón, Diez Canedo, Araquistáin, Madariaga, Alvarez del Vayo, Américo Castro, Moreno Villa, Ortega y Gasset, the Residencia de Estudiantes, and the Centro de Estudios Históricos, all viewed as carriers of dangerous Leftist philosophies. Agustín de Foxá sees the Institución as the direct precursor of Azaña and the hated Republic. "Así lo soñaba la Institución Libre de aquel Giner de los Ríos que iba a la sierra despechugado y se ponía debajo de una 'casta encina' para soñar con una España pedagógica y telegrafista, de clase media y de brasero, sin príncipes, ni santos, ni guerreros. Toda ella oliendo a lejía y a cocido modesto, esclava de Francia y de Inglaterra, folklórica y pintoresca para los Kodaks extranjeros" (December 21, 1937).

The Generation of 1898 and their presumed followers also shared responsibility for Spain's literary and political tragedy, according to the Fascists. Capitán Nemo attacked those who signed intellectual manifestos out of vanity, exhibitionism, or frivolous incomprehension. Men of letters might reach a great elevation in critical investigation of ideas and philosophy, "y luego se equivoca como un analfabeto en cuestiones políticas." Valle Inclán especially was characterized as a coward and a fool (May 23,

1937). José María Salaverría recalled with sorrow the attempts of the members of the generation to decree the literary death of José Echegaray by attacking him in "una especie de manifiesto irreverente y cruel. A la cabeza de los protestantes figuraba el primero Valle-Inclán, maestro en arbitrariedades, en vanidades, en celos. Firmaron el manifiesto todos los que quisieron." To Salaverría this represented the most vicious side of Spanish character, for Echegaray, for all his defects, had filled the Spanish stage for many years with his powerful dramas (December 2, 1938).

Rubén Darío belonged to their side, said the Fascists. José Pemartín viewed Central American nations as supporters of the principles of Acción Española of which Rubén Darío was simply an earlier version. Pemartín saluted the poet who crossed the ocean to bring consolation to Spain in its sorrow (June 11, 1937). Some of the contributors, overlooking for the moment their normally ferocious moral strictures, were proud that Avila helped inspire Rubén with "una de las serranas típicas de Avila, Francisca Sánchez" (March 23, 1937). Pablo Aragonés, in his *Evocación de Rubén,* felt that all young Nationalist combatants should have on their lips Darío's "Sangre de Hispania fecunda" from his "Salutación del optimista," for the poem announces a new kingdom and resurrection of high virtues of the Spanish progeny, "consagración de afectos legítimos, los nacidos de dependencias de la sangre común, patricias decisiones, de concordias, y reanudación de lazos que reinstalen sobre firmes e inconmovibles asientos, las viejas prosapias" (January 12, 1838).

The Fascist writers held ambivalent viewpoints about Unamuno and attempted to claim him as a supporter of their cause. They praised him for "el alto valor cultural que representa en las letras hispanas" when news came of his removal as rector of the University of Salamanca (August 23, 1936). In September he apparently gave them cause to announce his support of their movement, but they carefully refrained from publicizing his later rejection. On December 10, 1936, the *ABC* quoted from a letter in Latin, attributed to Unamuno, to all universities protesting the atrocities and murders committed by the Spanish "gobierno rojo" in Valencia. However, unqualified praise for one so controversial from the Fascist point of view was too much to expect. César González Ruano agreed that Unamuno loved his country, but he did not serve it. He found in him an "atroz polémica entre lo que tenía de místico y de hereje, de clásico y de romántico, de hereje civil y de funcionario." In another historical period, he said,

Unamuno might have been burned at the stake. He was like so many other Miguels—Miguel Prisciliano, Miguel Servet, and Miguel Cervantes, and perhaps even a bit like Miguel the Archangel, dressed in the coat of a Protestant minister. Unamuno, both revolutionary and conservative, had influenced the sentiments but not the thoughts of the younger generation. In any event he is a symbol which youth must avoid, for his "honesto genio rebelde" has harmed Unamuno. His books will honor him, and the *Cristo de Velázquez* may even carry him to heaven, but one hopes that Spain's youth will be freed from "Unamunismo: del alboroto callejero y la pedrada en nombre de la cultura y la libertad" (February 17, 1937).

News of Unamuno's death was reported briefly on January 1, 1937. *ABC* claimed that about six in the evening while he was talking with friends, he died suddenly without any previous indication of illness. The church service at his burial received more attention. The church was completely filled, and his two sons, Rafael and Fernando, were present for the eleven A.M. service. At the four o'clock burial the bearers were Miguel Flela and Víctor de la Serna, Antonio de Oregón and Salvador Díaz Ferrero. One of the many newspapermen present said a few words at Unamuno's grave to the assembled professors and the rector of the university. On the second anniversary of Unamuno's death a Fascist editorial claimed that at the end of his life he became one of the worst enemies of the Republicans. He had believed in a democratic republic, a utopian dream, but the sad reality of his degraded country made him repent of his past errors, for "Unamuno, espíritu selecto, apasionado, creyente hasta el misticismo, no podía transigir con los sectarios cerriles y concupiscientes que hicieron de la ruina de España pingüe granjería." His death, said the editorial, "provocó groseros comentarios y denuestos en la zona roja" because his former friends could not forgive his stand "en favor de nuestro glorioso Movimiento y en contra de la anti-España" (December 31, 1938), a position which of course neither the facts nor the last three months of his life in virtual house arrest completely justify.

The Spanish intellectuals who supported the Spanish Republic or who failed to support Franco drew the bitterest, most violent, and most personal attacks. Juan de Castilla attacked the signers of a letter who supported the Republic, including writers such as Ramón Menéndez Pidal, Antonio Machado, Gregorio Marañón, Ramón Pérez de Ayala, Juan de la Encina, Antonio Marichalar, and José Ortega y Gasset (October, 1936). Yet Ortega y Gasset, whom the Falangists sought inferentially to claim as spiritual kin, escaped their full wrath. They especially liked to quote phrases from his works such as "La fuerza de las armas no es fuerza bruta, sino fuerza espiritual" (July 13, 1937).

Other enemies of the state received little mercy. The poets Antonio Machado and José Moreno Villa were accused of having stolen rare manuscripts from Madrid libraries. The Marqués de Quintanar referred to them and their friends as Communists who formed part of "aquella miserable caverna de la calle del Prado" (October 13, 1936), and J. López Prudencio accused the intellectuals who escaped from Madrid of having "sabios propósitos de atarla (España) al carro triunfal del judaísmo bolchevista. Siempre fue para ellos tan amable el judaísmo" (December 8, 1936).

Julio Camba, attempting to downgrade the opponents' literary merits, claimed that many of the criminal tendencies and the hate that "impulsa a las hordas rojas en sus crímenes desatentados salió de cierto patio que había en la calle Espartero de Madrid. Allí vivía el llamado Araquistáin, escritor muy por debajo de lo mediocre, que no lograba jamás obtener el menor triunfo literario. . . . Allí vivía Álvarez del Vayo, cuñado del anterior, y quien, según Unamuno, tenía la cabeza rellena de la misma sustancia que aquél, sólo que esta sustancia, que en la cabeza de Araquistáin ostentaba la forma del serrín, en la de Vayo había pasado al estado gaseoso y no era ya nada más que un puro vapor. Allí vivía Ramón Pérez de Ayala." According to Camba, Araquistáin attempted and failed in all literary genres. Unable to sell his works and in despair and frustration he abandoned socialism for communism to take revenge on others for his own deficiencies, "y este torvo, zafio y soez Araquistáin, a pesar de su mediocridad irredimible, constituyó uno de sus hombres más tristemente representativos" (August 4, 1937). For César González Ruano, Araquistáin was "la bestia parda número uno" (August 18, 1937).

The *ABC* rejoiced in reporting the enmity among literary rivals on the other side. An editorial, quoting from Azaña's secret memoirs, claimed he hated Ortega y Gasset because the latter had closed the doors of *El Sol* to him "cuando el monstruo (Azaña) las aporreaba pidiendo entrada." Azaña referred to Ortega y Gasset only as "el filósofo," and intended the quotation marks to convey Ortega's lack of stature. Azaña was bitter because Ortega had made a pact with the Jesuits of Bilbao, but his incompetence as a writer for *El Sol* led to his rejection, said the editorial. It quoted from *El jardín de los frailes* to show Azaña's failure as a writer and his empty soul. In the Ateneo in November 1932 Unamuno criticized Azaña in revenge for a critical article by Azaña. Pérez de Ayala and Azaña also hated each other, an enmity of many years' standing. "Cuando los amigos de Azaña querían encandilarle, le nombraban a Pérez de Ayala" (October 10, 1937).

Martín Andreu Valdés in an article titled "Los intelectuales responsables" wonders if "se ha pensado suficientemente en la culpable responsabilidad de nuestros seudointelectuales? . . . De todas las traiciones, ésta de los intelectuales ha sido la más repugnante y la más antipática." He cites as a pernicious example of the "virus moscovita" the theatrical success achieved by *Nuestra Natacha*, "obra de ambiente bien conocido," popular because of its timing and not because of any merits in the play. People like Casona, even if they repent, will always carry their "sins" with them (November 6, 1937). Agustín de Foxá criticized Casona's theater as "tablado ambulante—así ha terminado la barraca laica de los autos sacramentales—recorre las ciudades representando aquellas baladas de osos y zorros astutos de *Nuestra Natacha,* mezcla repugnante de laicismo, socialismo romántico y cursilerías pedagógicas" (January 1, 1938).

The most vicious attacks were reserved for Fernando de los Ríos. Juan Pujol insisted that Israel was directing the activities of the Marxists in Spain and viewed Fernando de los Ríos as one of the principal architects of the conspiracy. "Por casualidad también es un judío español—Fernando Ríos, y no de los Ríos como el muy farsante suele firmar" (December 30, 1936). José Carlos de Luna castigated Fernando de los Ríos for his connection with the "misiones pedagógicas babeando hiel por los pueblos de España. Aquel carro de La Farándula hacinamiento de polvos de talco, clámides de retor y coturnos de purpurina . . . [a reference to the traveling theatrical troupe, La Barraca, with which Lorca had been associated]" (April 1, 1937). Throughout the year, especially during August and September of 1937, reiterated attacks on Fernando de los Ríos included epithets such as *fanático, pedante, cursi, hazmerreír, afectado, vanidoso,* and *farsante.*

Américo Castro earned their ire also. An editorial commenting on his role as Ambassador to Berlin called him "la barba más hermosa de la República . . . una barba rizada como la escarola y con un sendero en el medio, que recorriéndola de arriba a abajo la partía por gala en dos. . . . Lo inexplicable es que la pasión antisemita, imponiéndose a la apreciación estética, hubiese hecho fracasar en su gestión a una barba tan distinguida" (August 14, 1937).

García Lorca posed a special problem for the Fascist writers. Accusations of his assassination by the Falangists touched them in a sore spot. No mention at all was made of him in 1936. On May 27, 1937, his character was analyzed in a quotation from his work: "Además Satanás me quiere mucho./Fue compañero mío/En un examen de/Lujuria." On August 31, 1937, El Bachillar Alcañices criticized Berta Singerman, reciter of theatrical pieces and Spanish poetry, for rejecting the support of rich and aristocratic Spaniards and devoting her time to "el populacho marxista, inestético, ineducado." She made the mistake of choosing to recite the poetry of García Lorca, "como emblema de hostilidad a la España nacional." Spain should be shut to her and Margarita Xirgu, "glorificadora también de García Lorca, no a título de valor literario, sino como símbolo de la antipatria, representada por el conjunto demagógico entronizado en Valencia" (August 31, 1937).

By 1938, however, the official line for García Lorca's death had been set. Thus, an article dated January 6, 1938, quotes an earlier interview with Joaquín Calvo-Sotelo about the poet's death. "Joaquín Calvo-Sotelo . . . me había dicho que el fusilamiento de García Lorca, en Granada, afirmación propalada desvergonzadamente, por Margarita Xirgu y su adlátere, Rivas Cherif, era una simple invención de la comedianta catalana tan 'íntimamente unida' al poeta andaluz." The Bachillar Alcañices, author of the article, complained that her campaign bore fruit, and in Chile and Argentina the nonsense was promulgated. The Leftist and misguided press and intellectuals repeated this calumny.

Sáenz Hayes had an interview with Franco, reproduced in *La Prensa* of Buenos Aires and in *El Mercurio* of Santiago, in which Franco denied the execution of Lorca. Alcañices claimed, "El Generalísimo Franco ha destruido la patraña con el ariete formidable de sus declaraciones." Franco stated: "Se ha hablado mucho en el extranjero de un escritor granadino, el vuelo de cuya fama no puedo yo medir hasta qué fronteras hubiera llegado; se ha hablado mucho porque los rojos han agitado ese nombre como un señuelo de propaganda. Lo cierto es que en los momentos primeros de la revolución en Granada, ese escritor murió mezclado con los revoltosos. Son los accidentes naturales de la guerra. Granada estuvo sitiada durante muchos días y la locura de las autoridades republicanas repartiendo armas a la gente, dio lugar a chispazos en el interior, en alguno de los cuales perdió la vida el poeta granadino. Como poeta su pérdida ha sido lamentable y la propaganda roja ha hecho pendón de este accidente, explotando la sensibilidad del mundo intelectual." On the other hand, says Franco, they make no mention of their cold-blooded murder of José Calvo-Sotelo, Víctor Prades, José Polo Benito, Honorio Maura, Francisco Valdés, Rufino Blanco, Manuel Bueno, José María Abinana, Ramiro de Maeztu, Pedro Muñoz Seca, Pedro Mourlane Michelina, Antonio Bermúdez Cañete, Rafael Salazar Alonso, Alfonso Rodríguez Santamaría, and many others.

Other Falangists shared Franco's annoyance that their own dead had been ignored. On August 22, 1936, the false news of the assassination of Jacinto Benavente, the Álvarez Quintero brothers, and the painter Zuloaga caused consternation, not fully refuted even several months later. The Marqués de Quintanar reproached the intellectuals of the opposing side for failing to be moved "ante los cadáveres de Benavente y de los hermanos Quintero que han honrado nuestro teatro de los últimos 25 años. Y ante el del mejor prosista del idioma, Manuel Bueno. . . . Qué gestión realizaron para salvar de la prisión y tal vez de la muerte a Ramiro de Maeztu, ensayista y escritor insigne" (December 5, 1936). Mariano Daranas rebuked the Academy at Stockholm for ignoring the house arrest in Valencia of the seventy-year-old Benavente (February 23, 1937).

Non-Nationalist poets, other than Lorca, did not merit second thoughts. The Marquis of Quintanar chastised Rafael Alberti as a "poeta de la revolución, rimador de la UHP y demás fugas de vocales cuya responsabilidad legal se evidenciará en plazo no lejano." The former Christian poet had sunk to such depths of degradation because he had become a slave of the devil (May 27, 1937). José Carlos de Luna, reporting on an anti-Fascist reunion in Barcelona and a speech given there by Alberti, commented on his fall from grace. "Alberti era un buen chico. Se dejó una melenita ondulada, y un buen día cayó en Madrid vestido de color de caramelo, y lleno de infinitas ambiciones, con sus poemitas bajo el brazo. . . . Surgió en reducida popularidad cuando el Sanhedrín de culteranos vanguardistas lo armó poeta, dándole el espaldarazo con la espada de Bernardo, y cuando se recitó ante público aquella su 'Chuflilla de Niño de la Palma,' toda saltitos, puchentos y desplantes de marioneta." These poems, a kind of guava paste, do not upset one's digestion too much, but he soon attempted more exotic flavors and became a grotesque acrobat, because of his stay in a New York of Broadway, whiskey, and blondes, if one can trust Alberti to have been there at all. Then he became a Communist and went to Russia, returning "con el corazón lleno de piojos semitas y mascando la palabrota sucia y el concepto de repulsiva crudeza." Worst of all, he became an atheist and rejected his earlier religious poetry. Luna calls on all to show their collective scorn for this "poetastro sin Dios, sin Patria y sin talento" (July 24, 1937).

Another Christian poet had also fallen from grace. Ernesto Giménez Caballero recalled his first meeting with Miguel Hernández: "Por el otoño de 1931 se elevó en Orihuela un busto a Gabriel Miró, por ser su ciudadano natal y en recuerdo de su muerte. Como todos los intelectuales republicanos andaban buscando enchufes, nadie de ellos quiso ir a conmemorar al poeta de las *Figuras de la Pasión.* Yo tenía un grupito de amigos—de fascistizantes—en aquel rincón levantino y me invitaron a hablar. . . . Formaba entre aquel grupito un malogrado muchacho, Ramón Sijé, que murió. Un magnífico poeta que acababa yo de descubrir en mi Robinson Literario, José (sic) Hernández, pastor de Orihuela. A ése le pasó algo peor que malograrse. Descarriarse como uno de sus más tontos borregos, en brazos de Bergamín, en venenosa *Cruz y Raya,* en el comunismo del Frente Popular" (July 30, 1937).

The writings of Falangist party members and their supporters drew much attention in the *ABC.* Book reviews excessively lauded works dealing with the war effort, for example, *Armas de Caín y Abel* by José Andrés Vázquez, a novel set in Badajoz and propagandizing for the Falangist cause; *Diario de una bandera* by Francisco Franco, a series of prophecies about the war and Spain's future; and Francisco de Cossío's *Manolo,* dedicated to his son who had died in the civil war and which Víctor de la Serna called "el mejor libro de la guerra: es toda una guía espiritual, una especie de Kempis para las almas doloridas" (December 23, 1937).

Much was made of the decree Franco signed on December 7, 1937, calling a reorganization meeting of all academies for January 6, 1938, at the University of Salamanca. On that date the academies were incorporated into the Instituto de España. Eugenio d'Ors and Sainz Rodríguez spoke. Among those present were Pemán, Eijo, Urquijo, Cabanillas, Azcue, the Marqués de Lema, Fernández Flórez, Pío Baroja, the duque de Maura,

and Manuel Machado. Asín Palacios sent his "adhesion," though he would
not attend. Manuel de Falla was ill and unable to attend. Manuel Machado
and Pedro Sainz Rodríguez were named to vacancies on the Academia de la
Lengua. SIUL, commenting on the event (January 7, 1938), lamented the
absence of Ricardo León, intimating that as a fighter against the Republic
this precursor of "The Crusade" had probably been murdered.

Those who merited most space in the *ABC* were Manuel Machado, César
González Ruano, José María Pemán, Ramiro de Maeztu, and José María
Salaverría, although Concha Espina, Wenceslao Fernández Flórez, whom
the Fascists always considered "figura cumbre del humorismo español" in
spite of Julio Camba's allegiance to the cause, and many others also received
encomiastic acclaim and space for their viewpoints. Manuel Machado in-
serted poems in many issues. His subjects, as might have been expected,
supported the reactionary viewpoint and stressed *hispanidad,* Spanish
Catholicism, and the glories of war. In a poem to San Ignacio de Loyola he
calls him "Soldado del amor Divino, ingeniero de la Fe," who can show
Spain the difficult road to heaven (November 24, 1936). Machado praised
the simple sacrifices of the traditional Spanish soldier for whom "bastaba
ser dueño del Mundo" (March 5, 1937). He evoked the eternal aspects of
Spanish history, the force of tradition, and love for one's parents, as he
wrote: "Ay del pueblo que olvida su pasado/y a ignorar su prosapia se
condena/ . . . Reniega de una vana pseudosciencia . . . /Vuelve a tu tradición, España mía./ ¡Sólo Dios hace mundos de la nada!" (November
10, 1936).

In a poem to the Virgin of Hope of Seville he concludes: "Ay, mi
Sevilla, que lo tiene todo,/cuando el Señor del Gran Poder le ofrece/la
Fe y la Caridad . . . ¡Tú,/la Esperanza!" (March 21, 1937). On June
12, 1937, he dedicated a poem to General Emilio Mola, a Fascist officer
who had died in a plane crash on June 4, 1937. His thesis is that "morir
por la Patria no es morir." In addition to his already cited work on the
theater, Manuel Machado uncompromisingly defended the Catholic church
(August 18, 1937) and virulently attacked the concept of democracy.
"Para mí los más no tendrán nunca razón contra los mejores. Democracia
. . . anarquía, confusión y canibalismo" (May 11, 1937). He lavishly
praised Franco as the man Spain had always needed: "Nuestro insigne
Caudillo tan querido, como admirado, y sus auxiliares más conspicuos"
(July 8, 1937); ". . . nuestro invicto Caudillo. El hombre de la guerra y

de la paz, el hombre de España. Franco, Franco, Franco" (December 7, 1937). For his labors he was rewarded with membership in the Royal Academy.

José María Pemán, named to the "presidencia de la comisión de Cultura en el Gobierno Nacional" (December 27, 1936), contributed poetry, much of it dedicated to defenders of the Cause such as Eugenio de Castro (May 15, 1938) and D. Tomas Domecq y Rivero (June 29, 1937), and to the war effort. His plays and poetry advocated an ardent Catholicism. Typical of his work in *ABC* is his poem "Madres." A mother sits next to her dead sons. She prays, but she does not cry, for she represents the best of Spain, and because of her and mothers like her, victory is certain. He concludes: "Sí para redimirnos y lavar nuestras culpas/fue preciso que en prenda del más alto dolor,/se unieran y juntaran, cual milagros gemelos,/ la pena de una Madre con la muerte de un Dios" (June 9, 1937).

Pemán's productions were accorded almost hysterical acclaim. M. Sánchez del Arco took other poets to task for not fighting more in the war effort. He claimed José María Pemán was the only poet who had truly used his art at the front to fight for the Cause. His verse, filled with war, revealed "la mística de la guerra." He alone expressed the truth as he sought to win the war with his art (January 2, 1937). Víctor María de Sola called Pemán the poet who moved a people and one worthy of the glorious movement which he defended as he filled hearts with patriotism. Pemán was the "excelso rapsoda que va de pueblo en pueblo, de campo en campo, glosando la épica y sublime grandeza del esfuerzo nacional, contándolo con sus arrebatadas palabras que encierran junto al lírico acento y la mágica inspiración de las más inflamadas arengas D'Annuncianas, el nervio y la energía de los más inspirados vates españoles." For, said de Sola, Pemán has the purity of Calderón, the facility of Lope, the delicacy of Garcilaso, the wit of Quevedo, the enthusiasm of Herrera, the sharp preciosity of Góngora, which make of him the "cantor de la raza, delante cuya Musa Castilla va ensanchándose como delante del corcel del Cid" (January 9, 1937). Manuel Machado called him "alto político, hondo pensador . . . orador de avasalladora elocuencia" and "el hombre de las profundas realidades" (April 30, 1937). An unsigned review of Pemán's *De ellos es el mundo* called him "inspiradísimo cantor de nuestra Cruzada" (April 17, 1938). J. López Prudencio compared his "El poema de la Bestia y el Angel" to Homer's poetry, amazed at the "asombroso e íntimo maridaje

que el poeta logra, entre lo subjetivo de su desbordado e incontenible
lirismo y la imponente majestad del realismo objetivo con que se ofrece al
lector la gesta inmortal, con todo su color trágico y sublime, con sus
aledaños de dolor, de ternura y de satisfacción triunfal, con su raigambre
negra en los senos malditos del mal y blanca en las virginales raíces de la
fe y de la hispanidad" (August 24, 1938). Pemán felt that one of his
plays, *Almoneda,* contained the "espíritu y razón" of the civil war in
Spain. The plot concerns a modern young Spanish lady who becomes Miss
Europe, has a Negro baby after an affair with her chauffeur, but finally
realizes the true eternal values of the old Christian virtues (April 8, 1937).

Pemán had strong ideas about intellectuals. In the old days he felt that
the intellectual was simply the herald or voice "de un pensamiento único;
que era unánime en la sociedad y oficial en el Estado." This changed in the
eighteenth century. Today the state reserves the right to treat harshly all
those who are betraying the nation, which means being a part of the "pacto
masónica, judío o internacionalista." "La democracia es ruido, y la inteli-
gencia no necesita ruido, sino paz. . . . La autoridad no es ya un recelo, sin
un beneficio." Spain will of course honor its true intellectuals (those who
supported Franco). The others by going through the proper purification
processes may become renewed because, says Pemán, "somos fuertes,
podemos ser generosos." Since intellectuals are no longer dangerous, they
are a luxury the state can afford. However, these reformed intellectuals
must walk softly (March 19, 1937).

José María Salaverría was much preoccupied with the future generations and the need for good books for children. This led him to republish
El muchado español which "se preocupaba de iniciarle [the Spanish
youth] en el culto del patriotismo." Children's books, naturally, had to
be morally and verbally clean, and thus a rigid censorship was necessary,
not only for the above but because it would be a crime to "turbar y com-
plicar el espíritu de un futuro carpintero o albañil con visiones de un
mundo como de Oscar Wilde, en el que nunca podrá penetrar, o con
problemas renanianos, que sólo han de servir para robarle la pureza y la
sencillez de sus convicciones" (January 18, 1939). The Spanish role in
America always preoccupied Salaverría. In *Los Conquistadores* and other
works he acclaimed the achievements of men like Cortés and Pizarro,
their bravery and personal attractiveness, their herculean force of will,

and their struggles against adversity. Their unpleasant characteristics, if there were any, were justified by the greatness of the undertaking. Salaverría thought that one should avoid writing literature which emphasized the terrible or depressing side of war, for the latter consists of talent, bravery, and sacrifice (May 6, 1938). While not displeased by the thought of fighting and war, he admitted he was unable to read police detective stories, for the fantastic thefts and murders of the Loyalist forces made fictional accounts pale to insignificance (March 25, 1939).

Ramiro de Maeztu, undoubtedly the most proficient writer of the group, awoke strong responses from others because of his unfortunate death in the Republican zone in 1936. Víctor Sánchez recalled that the Marqués de Lozaya had arranged a series of guest lectures in Valencia, where Maeztu, the first lecturer, had a great following who admired his theories on hispanidad. Maeztu had incurred the enmity of Vicente Blasco Ibáñez by questioning the latter's sincerity, and this was enough to shut the doors of Valencia to him forever. "*El Pueblo,* digno órgano de aquel partido que tanto daño hizo siempre a Valencia, publicó el ukasse, prohibiendo la entrada en Valencia de don Ramiro de Maeztu, bajo amenaza de producir un día de luto en la ciudad si no se actaba la orden" (February 15, 1938). Maeztu had to withdraw, and a substitute lecturer had to be found by the Marqués. Antonio Martín de la Escalera viewed Maeztu as the master of the concept of hispanidad, especially of the state. He remembered him as the martyr of "muero para que vuestros hijos sean mejores que vosotros," which applies not only to his executioners but also to good Spaniards (November 2, 1938). The Marqués de Quintanar felt that Maeztu's "prosa barroca y doctrinal" entitled him to a special place in the Nationalist hierarchy, for he was converted and not born to the Cause (July 4, 1937).

César González Ruano contributed to almost every issue with his essays from Italy on a variety of political and literary subjects. He chastised the Loyalists for the death of Emilio Carrère the poet of "pobres mujeres mal vestidas," a death caused not by politics but by the poet's association with the *ABC* and his refusal to continue after the Loyalists took over. Emilio Carrère's death had elicited especially bitter diatribes against the "horda infame" and "turbas criminales" who assassinated him, even though he had the reputation of being a "republican and liberal" (March 11, 1937). González-Ruano analyzed the futurism of Marinetti and its importance in Spain. Marinetti's movement led to the destruction of many bad things and showed not so much "de lo que se podía hacer en poesía, pero sí de todo lo que no se podía hacer más." Of more importance was Marinetti's "adhesión y profesión fascista." Marinetti was a poet who took joy in war, and as such González Ruano salutes him (April 21, 1937), for the latter believed that poetry should serve the war effort. The trenches needed verses dedicated to God and Spain. "La guerra la hacen los soldados, pero la cantan los poetas, y no hay guerra sin música" (April 14, 1937). His own volume of poetry, *Misterio de la poesía*, was most favorably reviewed by F. Bonmatí de Codecido on April 9, 1938, in *ABC*.

The glory of war occurs as a theme in most of the writers, among them Salaverría, González Ruano, and Eugenio Montes. Montes' thesis was that culture stems from the state and the power necessary to create values. Culture exists only because the state exists. The state, in turn, depends on an act of war from which it was born, for all states had their origin in this manner. War brings order and the defense of spiritual possibilities and thus culture. The mystics had their "anhelo de llegar a lo más allá," but it was a popular mysticism. In the same manner the true values of Spain depend on a higher spiritual ethic which is the motive behind the Falangists' fight (January 26, 1937).

Manuel Bueno, whose dawn attack against Valle-Inclán outside the Fornos Café cost the latter an arm, had also gained him a reputation. Bueno's death had proved a shock for most of the contributors, who claimed the "sayones de la judería" had killed him (December 15, 1936). An editorial of December 3, 1936, said that "ninguno de su generación o sea de la generación del '98—ni el desgarbado Baroja, ni el afectado Azorín, ni el bronco Unamuno, ni el premioso Maeztu—escribía un castellano tan fluido, ten elegante y castizo." Mariano Daranas called Bueno the prince of reporters, Benavente praised him, and the Marqués de Quintanar commented on the "maravilla de elegancia retórica y de agilidad espiritual de Manuel Bueno," while lamenting his lack of political prophecy (July 4, 1937).

Concha Espina, one of Franco's most ardent supporters, wrote many articles for the *ABC*, as did her son, Víctor. It is not surprising, therefore, that her works should have been so flatteringly reviewed and that she should have been considered eligible for membership in the Royal Academy, a membership Concha Espina modestly felt should go to Blanca de los Ríos whose "mano feble y aristocrática, henchida de tesoros intelectuales, ha debido franquear la puerta de la insigne Corporación" (January 30, 1938). Her son Víctor proudly wrote the prologue for her novel, *Retaguardia,* perhaps the first time in Spain that a mother wrote a novel prologued by her son. He examined her literary production, the patriotic and Catholic home she maintained, and the genesis of *Retaguardia* during the first year of the civil war. He called the novel, finished on August 22, 1937, a "continuo gemido" written in expectation of daily death and so a kind of testament of the painful civil war years. Its basic leitmotiv seems to be the fury and bloodthirsty evil of the Spanish "rojos." He considered *Retaguardia* the best of her works because of its youthful vigor and "una especie de 'superestilo' espiniano del que quedará *Retaguardia* como un canon" (May 5, 1938). J. López Prudencio felt the work had "ingenua lozanía vivamente natural . . . y llega holgadamente a donde quiere con un grato y fino son de limpia sencillez y diafanidad." He found that only in certain descriptive chapters of Gabriel Miró could the critic find something "que se le acerque en la literatura moderna" (August 5, 1938).

While Pío Baroja did not write for the *ABC,* its contributors considered him one of their own. He wrote a series of essays which apparently attacked the Loyalist viewpoint and praised the Nazis. For this and other support Ignacio Ramos, in an article on those who "integran la médula de nuestro Movimiento," includes Pío Baroja (March 22, 1938).

The 1936–1939 period has meaning for the contemporary critic in Spain and in America because it reveals that literature cannot be shaped permanently into a political mode by even the most persistent attempts to do so. For most literary historians who concern themselves with Spain the 1936–1939 period was a "silent" one which had produced no significant literature. It was significant, nevertheless, regardless of its intrinsic merit, for in spite of the energetic efforts of the Falangist authorities and intellectuals to intimidate not only "enemy" Spanish writers but their own, Cela and others reasserted their intellectual independence, an astounding manifestation of Spanish individualism when one considers the risks they ran in their reaction against the canons established during the Spanish Civil War. Even if one assumes that the emotional, extreme, and often vicious criticism can be explained as propaganda engendered by that tragic struggle, an analysis of the contributions and contributors gives us added insight into the relationships of Spanish politics and literature and a modern view of the eternal dichotomy which has plagued this land of "dos Españas" where the ideas of the Middle Ages, tradition, and national manifest destiny still fight those of the Renaissance, progress, and membership in the world community of nations.

[From *Journal of Inter-American Studies,* vol. VII, no. 4, October, 1965]

"Madrid" and
Spanish Literature

THE GENERAL feeling among Spanish scholars seems to be that little of literary value was produced during the Spanish Civil War. Yet a number of reviews such as *Hora de España,* of two years duration, and ephemeral ones such as *Madrid,* published twice (February and May, 1937) in Valencia, show that while the terrible was years had affected they had not desiccated either the creativity or the idealism of Spanish intellectuals. *Madrid* was the journal of the members of Casa de la Cultura of Valencia, supported by the Ministry of Public Instruction and Fine Arts. They chose the title *Madrid* because they felt "Madrid es lo que nos une a todos. Si de Madrid arranca nuestra labor, a ella y en homenaje a ella han de ir dirigidos todos los trabajos que aquí se publiquen." [1]

A rather unique journal, it might never have had its variety of contributors and subject matter except for the war. The critics, musicians, poets, painters, psychiatrists, and professors who wrote for it presented a wide range of literary and scientific articles to show they believed in the free development and historical continuity of culture which, they felt, ". . . sólo es compatible con la libre determinación política y social de los pueblos." [2] They wanted to contribute to the spiritual prestige of Spain, and although they evinced a demotic ideology, they sought to maintain cultural values by balancing past and present and discovering the one in the other. In their representation of Spanish culture they saw not an escape into abstractions or utopia, but a defense of the intellectual and moral values of their society. More irenic than irate in their view of current events and history, they could not escape completely the effects of the conflict, reflected more often than not by a consuming nostalgia or moral passion, but their sensitivity enabled them to evaluate professionally, even in the midst of obviously painful and destructive events.

Not all the writers, of course, could be equally objective. Juan de la Encina claims that he threw out the window "su pobre pluma de crítico la noche del 20 de julio de 1936, porque se dio melancólica cuenta de que en mucho tiempo—o tal vez para siempre— nada tenía ya que hacer en ese oficio y menester que venía cultivando con pasión, con espíritu de justica y desinterés, durante un cuarto de siglo. Dio por periclitada su labor y por infecunda su siembra. Sin embargo, todo esto, con ser mucho para su vida particular, le pareció nonada, bagatela, insignificancia sin remisión, cosa en fin despreciable, ante el dolor que en aquella hora amarga presentía para su patria." He claimed that only through the mirror of truth which the painter, Arturo Souto, held up to him could he return, if only for an instant, "a un oficio y a una acción que tenía por desuso casi olvidados." [3] In another article Encina evokes a Valencian bridge from which, after descriptions of water, sky, and countryside, he makes excursions into history and time. Caliban, the brute force of the earth, the first born of history, evolved not through literature but through blood; yet, perhaps, if Próspero lives, he may make Caliban offer more than sorrow and pain.[4] Only one other article deals with the civil war. In "Tres evocaciones de Madrid," Angel Ossorio y Gallardo recalls Madrid in 1933, 1936, and 1937.

The contributors treat a wide range of scientific subjects, among them chemical compounds, electrical conductivity, binocular vision, gases, and vitamins. The authors defended Spanish science, as Padre del Río Hortega elaborates in his analysis of the spiritual and scientific values of Spanish culture, for "los cien millones de españoles e hispanoamericanoes debemos aspirar a que nuestra literatura científica nos enorgullezca o, a lo menos, no nos sonroje." [5] The nonscientific writers include José Bergamín, who writes on Rousseau; Pedro Sanjuán, a musician; Ricardo de Orueta, who studies Visigothic sculpture; and José Moreno Villa, who deals with palace paintings in the Golden Age.

Four poets contributed literary articles. León Felipe attempts to define poetry in "Poesía integral," part of a course he once gave at the University of Panama and never before published. He feels that Spanish poetry may be viewed in a "línea paralela y congruente con la historia y política de España." [6] The poet of the future will differ from present ones whose poetry is only "un sistema luminoso de señales, hogueras que encendemos aquí abajo, entre tinieblas encontradas para que alguien nos vea, para que no nos olviden. . . . Poeta, para mí, es aquel hombre que tiene la virtud o la gracia de saltar rápidamente, en un momento determinado, de lo dómestico a lo épico, de lo euclidiano a lo místico, de lo contingente a lo esencial, de lo temporal a lo eterno, de lo sórdido a lo limpiamente ético." [7] He labels poetry not by schools (for him the principal error in literary history is the study of poets as anchored and unmovable islands without continuity), but as aristocratic, popular, or integral. Aristocratic poetry, the poetry of minorities, largely of foreign origin, is erudite, hermetic, and novel. Popular poetry is national, communal, clear, simple, human, and realistic. He finds in certain episodes in *Don Quijote* a key to the Spanish character, "los caminos bifurcados del poeta y del pueblo, de la épica y de la Historia." [8] The highest poetry, "poesía integral," is that of a known author who adapts the traditional efforts of his predecessors. An integral poet attempts to clarify and communicate a universal message to all mankind. Jorge Manrique is such a poet in his *Coplas,* a general integration of disarticulated and diverse elements, which is the final triumph of a series of traditional efforts. A real poet destroys both time and space by overcoming the barriers imposed on him by historical man. In the final analysis a poem cannot be explained: "Un poema no se explica nunca. Un poema se explica él mismo y explica muchas cosas. No hay que tener una llave para abrir un poema. Un poema debe ser una llave, él mismo que abra algo que estaba cerrado u olvidado en el mundo." [9] Life, as poetry reveals, is a consequential process, not a tale told by an idiot full of sound and fury, and the poet, therefore, reflects optimistic idealism at the possibility of a morally, socially, and intellectually free society.

Antonio Machado attempts to interpret Spain as more than history and tradition. Man carries history within himself, both knowledge of the past and the hope and fear of the future, but his most essential characteristic is mortality, which only a true person can face. Machado praises Unamuno, "el que menos habló de resignarse a ella [death]. Tal fue la nota antisenequista original y españolísima, no obstante, de este incansable poeta de la angustia española." [10] He views Unamuno as a precursor of European existentialism.

Juan José Domenchina, yet another poet, cites the importance of distinguishing the characteristics of Valle-Inclán from his characterizations.

He refutes Valle-Inclan's reputation for virulence, condemnation, and "terrible absolutes," finding his statements lacking in "intención dañosa, tal vez constituyesen . . . unos generosos escapes de la generosidad valle-inclanesca, que tendía a enaltecer, paradójicamente, monstruosamente, la insignificancia o la pobre significacion de sus prójimos." [11] The creator of the *esperpento,* which consists of contradictions, Valle-Inclán in his attacks carries no conviction, refusing to accept anything seriously. Rather than slander he offers a special kind of heroic, inoffensive truth. "Don Ramón jamás se propuso ofender o denigrar con sus barrocas y espléndidas calumnias. Por el contrario, el designio que le movía . . . era un designio de altura: magnificar con hipérboles de sevicia, con graciosas y generosas atribuciones de perversidad—en las que nadie, y él menos que nadie, podía creer—la insignificancia de sus semejantes." [12]

José Moreno Villa finds, in the buffoon and the palace fool, the mysteriously simple and monstrous aspects of nature which have always attracted mankind. Golden Age dramatists included these "locos de Palacio" in their works, but we do not know what they were really like and how they talked. Only through the theater, whose gracioso tried to make Spaniards laugh, can we glimpse this aspect of courtly life. Dwarfs do not appear in the dramas, probably because appropriately realistic actors were unavailable. Moreno Villa feels certain that Lope de Vega would have loved to have them in his plays, for in a theater like his, ". . . animado y coloro, esencialmente pintoresco, los enanos hubieran puesto su nota de contraste, tan esencial para las grandes figuras como la del gracioso u hombre de placer." [13] He wonders whether Cervantes was not influenced by the court jesters in portraying Don Quijote as a loco and Sancho Panza as a kind of dwarf.

Elsewhere Moreno Villa recalls Lorca, his "alegrías y perfumes," his fabulous stories, and his folklore. He sees him as "un manojo de cintas de colores, pero también una honda guitarra y un chato de manzanilla." [14]

Tomás Navarro Tomás examines the literary relationships involved in the intonation and physiognomic aspects of the voice. An emotional tone may convey understanding without meaningful words. In *La hermana San Sulpicio,* Puig's companions were unable to understand him, but "Sólo por la entonación y por las furiosas miradas que alguna vez nos dirigía, sabíamos que nos estaba poniendo como trapos." In *La ruta de don Quijote* Juana María's voice, rising above the crowd, elicits "Quien tiene esta entonación tan dulce, tan suave, tan acariciadora . . ." In *El tablado de Arlequín,* Pío Baroja's sick man cannot move his audience because he cannot find "la inflexión de voz propia del momento." [15] The voice tone often reveals the true emotional state that words seek to hide or, on the other hand, helps feign what one does not feel, common techniques among the picaresque heroes of the Golden Age. At times the intonation itself disguises the emotion (firmness and calmness during an emotional scene or irritation hidden beneath soft words), a technique employed by Padre Coloma, Palacio Valdés, Juan Valera, Valle-Inclán, and especially Blasco Ibáñez. Among older writers Cervantes evinced great interest in voice properties, seeking to specify the exact emotional degree with expressions such as, "voz turbada o alterada," "voz turbada y temerosa," "voz turbada y alta," or "voz turbada y lengua presurosa." [16] One must admit, nevertheless, that, in the broad panorama of Spanish literature, allusions to voice intonation are comparatively rare.

Physiognomic values are more commonly employed by Spanish authors. Belarmino tries to hear the voice of his beloved Angustias among the chorus of those at the convent, ". . . hacía esfuerzos por desenredar la voz azul de Angustias de entre la madeja polícroma del coro." The voice represents personality, as blind men in *Pedro de Urdemalas* by Cervantes and in *Flor de Santidad* by Valle-Inclán testify. Navarro Tomás examines briefly the relationship of man and animal voices in literature, citing Quijote's recognition of Sancho through the braying of his ass, "Famoso testigo . . . el rebuzno conozco como si lo pariera, y tu voz oigo, Sancho amigo." [17] Although other Golden-Age writers like Céspedes y Meneses, Lope de Vega, Vélez de Guevara, and Tirso de Molina adjectivally described voices as "soft" or "sweet," only Cervantes recognized the full measure of importance of voice quality in its real and human aspects and for the development of literary action. Modern writers more easily understand the evocative power of the voice, especially Azorín, Pérez de Ayala, and Valle-Inclán.

The civil war intellectuals of *Madrid* avoided manifestos. Elsewhere they repudiated the to them repugnant beliefs of the Fascists, but neither antipathy toward Franco nor justification or vindication of the Republican political position played a significant part in *Madrid,* in spite of its government subsidy. Without turbulence or tragic pose, vanity or naïveté regarding their importance in the scheme of things as exclusive defenders of culture, they continued their scholarly activities, certain of the necessity of cultural continuity as the beginning of wisdom for man, in his hope for a free society where human aspiration need not be defeated.

[From *Revista de Estudios Hispánicos*, Spring, 1969.]

The Pueblo, the Intellectuals, and the Spanish Civil War

Hora de España, a monthly review published from January 1937 through October 1938 initially in Valencia and then in Barcelona, contains perceptive essays on all the literary genres, discussions of the war, philosophy, painting, and the theater, and original poetry and fiction. The contributors include some of the brightest stars in the galaxy of twentieth-century Spanish literature, among them Antonio Machado, Rosa Chacel, José Bergamín, José Moreno Villa, Manuel Altolaguirre, Dámaso Alonso, Rafael Alberti, Jacinto Grau, Max Aub, León Felipe, and Luis Cernuda. The journal's subheading, "Al servicio de la causa popular," stems from the artists' contention that they were "viviendo *una* hora de España de trascendencia incalculable. Acaso *su* hora más importante. . . . Quede, pues, en *Hora de España,* y sea nuestro objetivo literario reflejar esta hora precisa de revolución y guerra civil. . . . España prosigue su vida intelectual o de creación artística en medio del conflicto gigantesco en que se debate." [1] The contributors wished to show Spaniards and the world that Spain's intellectual life was still flourishing.

From the first number on, the intellectuals established that although they were instruments of the people who represented a new kind of culture in the twentieth century, they were also the heirs of long tradition which was finally achieving a new dimension. As an editorialo f August 1938 points out, "Pueblo y literatura corren juntos, en todos los tiempos españoles, por un mismo cauce." [2] Antonio Machado concedes that to write for the pueblo is his highest ambition. "Escribir para el pueblo es escribir para el hombre de nuestra raza, de nuestra tierra, de nuestra habla, tres cosas inagotables que no acabamos nunca de conocer." [3]

Throughout most of the numbers of *Hora de España,* Antonio Machado insists on this identification with the pueblo. He cites the strange logic of the Fascists which claims that the masses can neither be educated nor saved. Machado feels this involves "la malicia que lleva implícita la false-dad de un tópico que nosotros, demócratas incorregibles y enemigos de todo señoritismo cultural, no emplearemos nunca, por un respeto y un amor al pueblo que nuestros adversarios no sentirán nunca." [4] Gentlemen invoke and sell liberty, but the pueblo buys it with blood. Machado considers himself on the side of the pueblo, the side of Spain, regardless of the ab-stract mottoes its banners may proclaim. "Si el pueblo canta le marsellesa, la canta en español; si algun día grita: ¡viva Rusia! pensad que la Rusia de ese grito del pueblo, si es en guerra civil, puede ser mucho más española que la España de sus adversarios." [5] In a letter to David Vigodsky of Leningrad, Machado, old and sick by his own admission and suffering from an incapacitating eye disease, continues to be a supporter of young and healthy Spain, that is, the pueblo, which is ". . . lo mejor. . . . Siempre ha sido lo mismo. En los trances duros, los señoritos—nuestros barines—invocan la patria y la venden; el pueblo no la nombra siquiera, pero la compra con su sangre y la salva. En España, no hay modo de ser persona bien nacida sin amar al pueblo." [6]

Machado's sympathy toward Russia has nothing to do with Marxism. He believes that both Spain and Russia discovered the true essence of Christianity when they shook off the yoke of the Church. This Christianity, one of love, follows the Cervantine and not the Calderonian tradition, for the former is truly popular, Yet in ages of hypocritical pragmatism, cynicism becomes necessary, and Marxism, "por muy equivocado que esté, en cuanto pretende señalar una verdad en medio de un diluvio de mentiras, tiene un valor ético indiscutible." [7] Machado considers Russia to be the active focal point of history, hoping that she will renounce im-perial ambitions and recognize the free personality of all peoples. In any event, the Russians, the only ones helping Spain, have won the sympathy and love of the pueblo. One can understand that the Slavic soul is pro-foundly human and although" . . . la Rusia actual . . . es marxista . . . es mucho más que marxismo . . . que . . . está al alcance de todos los pueblos . . ." [8]

Emilio Prados, Miguel Hernández, and others, acknowledging that each artist and writer must follow his own personal style, feel that the duty of all is to interpret the thoughts and feelings of the youth fighting in the trenches, hoping to express in their works the same human values which the young men affirm with their sacrifice. Neither pure art nor revolutionary propaganda satisfies them. The former seems false, and the latter, stressing workers with fist lifted or holding a red flag, is not art. They hope that the revolution may produce an art of the same intensity and passion which all great spiritual movements in the past have had, allowing them to see men in their moments of passion, suffering, and joy, rather than workers good or bad. They want to express a reality which they can support both poetically and philosophically and through the total human content of its dramatic dimension, avoid a conflict between objective reality and their interior world. To defend propaganda as an absolute value of creation would be as demagogic as to defend art for art's sake. Without rejecting tradition they wish to approach creativity in a new way. Yet "con todo, y por instinto tal vez, más que por compresión, cada vez estábamos más del lado del pueblo. . . . Porque, efectivamente somos humanistas, pero del humanismo éste que se produce en España hoy." [9] Humanism for these writers is that which seeks to understand man and restore him to the consciousness of his value, impossible in a capitalistic and dehumanizing state. They wish to give meaning to their time and their youth, to interpret the pueblo, to have the right thereby to interpret their generation, and by winning the war, define and realize themselves as men.

Along with Antonio Machado, most of the writers, of varying shades of political persuasion, although they called themselves anti-Fascists, recognized that Spanish reality demanded a solution which was different from the Marxist one in Russia. Some, in later years, radically altered their initial position or tempered their revolutionary zeal. Nevertheless, between fascism and Marxism there could be no choice. The former, aside from its intolerance, represented "no avanzar en el derrotero tomado por el pensamiento, no continuar la especulación y sus albures disolventes, no asomarse al vacío de ese punto final que avalora el porvenir." [10] The latter, as a social movement, attempted to establish conclusions of human thought with an aim to the future. The pueblo, unsatisfied with the status quo, its creativity unchecked, must demand that culture face the future unafraid, whatever the consequences. Moral force unifies culture and the people, and the intellectuals, creators of culture, must fulfill their responsibilities.

Rosa Chacel defines the pueblo as "ese yacimiento que hoy busca la cultura para vivificar sus raíces." [11] The pueblo cannot study itself in the manner of an intellectual who romantically and nostalgically studies folkloric origins and primary cultural sources. Young intellectuals, while favoring the pueblo, may fall victim to a pseudoculture of historical interpretation when what is needed is a living reality. In a revolution the moment counts. Later, with peace and tranquility, one can study history, but an intellectual cannot be a man of the people without partaking of street life and knowing about anarchy and realism. Juan Gil Albert, more specifically oriented toward Marxism, feels that the intellectual and artist are magic interpreters of the day. After the war both pueblo and artists will enjoy tranquility. Meanwhile the intellectual, without having to live or feel things, may think and reason them and analyze the social state even if it does not exist.[12]

María Zambrano also rejects the historical approach. In order to discover Spain's reality, one needs a temporal and objective perspective, but the self-styled traditionalists, tragically, have declared themselves the sole heirs of the Spanish world. "Ellos eran España y toda su obra en el pasado." [13] And since they had achieved greatness in the past, they feared the future, for them only a grotesque screen of deformed and nightmarish figures of a glorious history. Thus this nightmarish past for others not only causes a perpetual terror but also destroys the future. The generation of 1898 confused the ghost of history with history itself, but the pueblo, as distinct from the intellectual, did not. Traditionalists considered the pueblo as their object, as did certain intellectuals. While the pueblo furthered a life of true history for the future, traditionalists and liberal intellectuals, both movers of cardboard figures in frightening masks, fought bloody, blind, and directionless battles. The former hoped to make their grotesque figures real with their blood; the latter took refuge in a heroic individual fate without currency, space or perspective. Each intellectual made value judgments which led him to identify himself with Spain itself. "Caso típico, Don Miguel de Unamuno; creía que él era España y por eso no temía equivocarse ni creyó que tendría que dar cuentas a nadie; él mismo era el tribunal y el pueblo." [14] Now the Republic fights the grotesque

cardboard figures of the past, seeking an ever fresh tradition to reincarnate
in the present, giving Spain its history once more, and escaping the labyrinth of false mirrors.

The Spaniards, poor in theories, thoughts, and concepts, substituted
almost superhuman activity for ideas and philosophical systems. "El hacer
naturalmente lo que llega a parecer sobrehumano, es una de las cualidades
maravillosas que está poniendo de manifiesto nuestro pueblo. Virginal,
divina naturalidad de un pueblo que, habiendo permanecido casi al margen
de la cultura europea, la salva hoy en lo que de salvable tiene." [15] Spanish
thought, paralyzed through the petrification of the state, found no relief
in Christianity. Catholicism served to forge a national unity but admitted
no questioning of the present or past. History became a mystical process
not subject to reason, thought became paralyzed, a unitary dogmatic
monarchy eliminated doubt about existence and destiny, Spanish life became ossified, and the pueblo had to support the centuries of reiterated
disasters on its unbreakable will to live. Literature, from Cervantes to
Galdós, reflects this popular will, "a la base misma virginal de nuestro
pueblo, firme voluntad que ya no suena con asuntos tan altos como los de
Don Quijote, sino que confundida con el instinto es vocación materna en
la divina Fortunata . . . celtíbero amor de independencia en el Madrid del
Dos de Mayo. Es lo único que nos queda; el último elemento insobornable:
voluntad que es ya instinto; lo único vivo bajo la destrucción de la
sociedad y el desmoronamiento del estado." [16] The pueblo through its
will and life's blood may save Spain from disaster and help create a new
state. This realism expressed by Galdós and others reveals the instinctive
knowledge of the pueblo in which present day culture finds its deepest
roots. If a Spaniard penetrates the world of *Misericordia,* he immediately
discovers his affinity with the pueblo, knowing that he must suffer
Benigna's fate and hope, for in the "entrecruzado mundo de culturas y
linajes, Benigna es la pureza popular, tan pura como indiferenciada; es
decir, tan libre de partidismo, tan apta para toda comprensión." [17]

Rafael Dieste sees man, surrounded by death, living in a historical
dramatic reality called Spain. In this framework some have substituted
spiritual works for responsibility, as if spiritual considerations and life
were opposites. This error is compounded by those who classify men, by
aptitude or profession, into two groups, those who work in order to live
and those who "se interesan por las cosas objetivamente, es decir, espiri-

tualmente; llegando luego, por acomodación psicológica, a convertir los intereses del espíritu en intereses de clase." [18] Spaniards, real men surrounded by a real death, cannot live a dehumanized life.

José Bergamín, the editor of *Cruz y Raya* and an ardent Catholic, nevertheless attacks the clergy for their support of the Fascists. Without denying that violence had been perpetrated against churchmen, he insists it was triggered by their own acts in defense of corrupt right-wing political activity. Furthermore, they are completely indifferent to social problems, identifying with the rich to the detriment of the pueblo. While the Republican government bears some responsibility for attacks on the Church, its blame is minor when compared to that of men like the bishop of Madrid who aided Franco in attacking old women and children. In Spain national Catholicism belongs only to the rich and is a visible corruption of the true Christian church: ". . . Es peor que una mentira cuando con una mano entrega dinero para comprar armas al odio y con otra las bendice." [19]

In a criticism of *Hamlet* Bergamín views the prince of Denmark as a pure intellectual who, betraying the very truth of the intelligence he incarnates, is alienated and isolated, blinded to all proof of communion and human communication. For Bergamín, this "hamletismo" or intellectual personalism is the worst ill of all because personal consciousness is only a mask for a more profound human consciousness. The former must relate to the latter, for the only preoccupation worthy of writers is the human communion within which their own existence and work has meaning. Words and time, the raw materials a writer employs, serve either to affirm solitude or deny isolation. All true Spanish literature, written in the blood of the pueblo, incarnates the principle of solitude which leads to communication but not that of isolation. In Spain, "toda nuestra riqueza cultural es expresión viva y verdadera de nuestra pueblo . . . sólo con el pueblo se salvarán ahora todos los valores humanos de la cultura y, sobre todo, el de la generosidad contra el egoísmo." [20]

The intellectuals engaged in mild polemics with each other. Rosa Chacel feels that the only true Spanish philosophy is anarchistic. Although her initial essay in *Hora de España,* "Cultura y Pueblo," had elicited praise, Chacel proposes the formation of an anarchistic seminary to work with the some of her fellow intellectuals now attacked her as anti-revolutionary. popular movement, but she defines anarchism as identical with Christianity and humanity. Moreover, she believes that "Anarquía no es desorden ni

resentimiento. No es desorden, porque orden . . . es un concepto mera-
mente ordinal, anárquico. No hay nada más anárquico que el edificio de
los números en el que entra la pesadumbre de su extensión inconcebible,
la unidad es siempre real y absolutamente una. . . . Y, al fin, después del
diluvio de sangre, es amor. Amor de nada abstracto. Amor del que nace
en la sangre ante la sangre." [21]

Arturo Serrano Plaja, among others, attacks Rosa Chacel's arguments.
He denies that her concept of "anarquismo-cristianismo" and "hispanis-
mo" are identical and points out that individualism is a word much used
by the Falange to combat what they term "Asiatic communism." Anarchy,
prevailing in the Spanish condition, is a defect of the past with which one
must break. "En este sentido . . . hay que romper con el pasado para poder
continuar la tradición . . ." [22] Only in this way will the pueblo as a totality
reincorporate itself into history.

Some intellectuals overwhelmed by the war and their love for Spain,
exclaim, as does José Moreno Villa, "Ya no valen literaturas." [23] Others
feel that a social realism may serve if the author applies his passion and
fantasy to the popular cause. Only in aiding man toward his ultimate destiny can art serve, for it is "verdad, poesía, drama y no juego; es hombre,
libertad." [24] Still others, like Dámaso Alonso, stress the importance of
literature as a social factor from the Middle Ages to the present. The
Dance of Death reflects a defense of the poor and disinherited, a constant
in Spanish literature. Only the poor worker replies in a noble manner, and
death answers him without the sarcasm utilized in responding to others.
Beyond this kind of Christian literature, evoking sympathy for the poor,
other works such as *El libro de buen amor* protest against the unequal economic conditions under which men live. Dámaso Alonso views it as a cry
of rebellion against the social order of the day, an attack on the rich and a
defense of the poor: ". . . él entrega su obra al pueblo, invitándole a ser su
colaborador. . . . Sí: Juan Ruiz, hijo del pueblo por su nombre de escueta
castellanía lo mismo que por su inspiración y su expresión, entrega su obra
al pueblo." [25] Sixteenth-century Erasmian literature, stressing a kind of
Christian communism with its strictures against private property and its
defense of the rights of the underprivileged, left seeds which blossomed
later, especially in the nineteenth-century novel.

Many of the intellectuals thought that valuable literature might evolve
from the war itself, feeling that the "crisis of thought" was linked to the

hunger and oppression of the workers with whose salvation would come that of thought. The intellectual, facing a decisive moment of possible fulfillment of past intellectual activity, at times of a remote world, may see the literary movements in which he is involved disappear. However, men and artists live on, and some will encounter their salvation through a union with the world forged by workers and an effort to know "sus ocultas lágrimas para comprenderlos bien, y comprender sus últimos deseos de salvación." [26] The civil war, rejecting the immediately preceding classic forms and content, may help reorient poets toward realistic man, his joys and sorrows. Distinctions between epic and lyric poetry become vaguer as new poetry, both intensely personal and social, relates human heroism in humanistic fashion. Humanism involves action, not ideas, and the poet, by turning again to the people, will save himself and his deepest lyric vein.[27]

The pages of *Hora de España* are filled with the poetry of León Felipe, Emilio Prados, Rafael Alberti, Manuel Altolaguirre, and most of the other great poets of the day, all identifying themselves with the popular cause. Federico García Lorca, one of the most oriented toward the pueblo, brought the classic theater to poor peasants in all corners of Spain, suffering with them their misery and hunger. The peasant, understanding Lorca, gave him authentic costumes which had been tucked away in coffers for centuries. Everything Lorca touched, however esthetic or mysterious, "todo . . . se llenaba de profundas esencias, de sonidos que llegaban hasta el fondo de las multitudes." [28] Luis Cernuda agrees that no other contemporary poet was as popular or loved and understood the pueblo as well as Lorca: "Nadie . . . como Federico García Lorca para ser pura y hondamente popular, mucho más en tierra como la nuestra donde todo es pueblo, y lo que aquí no es pueblo no es nada . . . por comprenderle y amarle no sea ya pueblo, sino fuerza suya ejemplar, poeta, o dramaturgo, según su sino." [29]

Antonio Machado reiterates that a poet writes for the pueblo and that "señoritismo," profoundly anti-Christian, is anti-Spanish in ignoring the dignity of man which the pueblo affirms. The Cid represents the pueblo; the Infantes de Carrión, the señoritos. Poets who wish to write for an exclusive minority or for the "best" will find it only in the pueblo. Culture is for man and not the reverse: ". . . para todos los hombres, para cada hombre. . . . El hombre masa no existe; las masas humanas son una invención de la burguesía, una degradación de las muchedumbres de hombres, basada en una descualificación del hombre que pretende dejarle reducido a aquello que el hombre tiene de común con los objectos del mundo físico." [30] To write for the masses is not to write for anyone, but to write for the pueblo is to write for fundamental man, perhaps the universal and eternal man. Those who love the pueblo will never call its members masses.

According to Luis Cernuda, war poetry shows continuity, as each poet uniquely expresses the tragic reality of the conflict. Even Juan Ramón, the poet supposedly only in search of purity and beauty, extols the pueblo; for "Juan Ramón Jiménez ha estado desde el primer momento al lado de los poetas, lo cual equivale ahora a decir al lado del pueblo." [31] Antonio Sánchez Barbudo finds the poetry of Rafael Alberti an affirmation of the just cause of the pueblo, and Bernardo Clariana considers some *romances* of Emilio Prados on the civil war as among the most militant, not only in defense of liberty but in support of "nuestro pueblo." [32] Romances of the civil war are indeed difficult to write because the *juglar* must rely on the crude truth of painful small events removed from the grandeur of heroic projection. Although the anonymous can be truly popular, the war romances are nevertheless ". . . la verdadera voz del pueblo. Son los romances que responden a una verdadera necesidad de cantar. No a la vanidad de cantar." [33] One of the most ethical poets, Antonio Machado, sees his difficult destiny as a poet inextricably interwoven with the pueblo which, in turn, needs the word of a poet, "cuando la palabra del poeta, en efecto, nombre ese destino, lo alude y lo testifica, cuando le da, en suma, un nombre. . . . Para Machado la poesía es cosa de conciencia. Cosa de conciencia, esto es, de razón, de moral, de ley. . . . El poeta, dentro de la noble unidad del pueblo, no es uno más, es . . . el que consuela con la verdad dura, es la voz paternal que vierte la amarga verdad que nos hace hombres. . . ." [34]

Other arts in their relationship to the pueblo were analyzed from time to time, including a number of discussions on the need for a new Spanish theater for the pueblo and Enrique Casal Chapi's lament in the March 1938 issue over what he felt was Manuel de Falla's betrayal of the pueblo because of his alliance with the Fascists. Goya was looked upon as the portrayer of the most profound popular truths of Spain—"la revelación revolucionaria de nuestro pueblo. . . . Por eso ahora la vemos tan claramente." [35] Goya to Picasso involves only a simple revolutionary step, for parallels exist between the Spanish Civil War and the famous uprising of May second. Pablo Picasso, like Juan Ramón Jiménez, produced for a minority, but included the pueblo—which did not always understand or like his work—in his audience. No true artist writes or paints only for those with special culture or preparation; he writes for man, "desnudo de todo cuanto pueda ser en la vida social, para el hombre humano, para el hombre en su significación más limpia y profunda." [36]

The intellectuals of the day saw themselves as the heirs of a long tradition which started with Seneca, perhaps the most philosophical Spaniard of them all. His name lives in the memory of the pueblo which, as a creature of the past, has ancestors with permanent historical categories. If one views these categories statically, one finds that tradition prevents a meaningful future and oppresses rather than liberates. The Spanish pueblo in the twentieth century, while recognizing the wisdom of Seneca, cannot elect his "camino de la resignación porque el hacerlo deja vacía la escena donde se juega la tragedia del destino humano. Algo así como si Cristo se hubiera escapado de la cruz, donde murió sin resignarse." [37] Juan Ruiz, on the other hand, begins the live tradition of contemporary Spain, representing a "precursor agudo y fuerte de los reintegros y restituciones debidos al hombre, y que sólo habían de conseguirse en tiempos recientísimos, hasta el punto de que ello es una de las facetas, y no la menos interesante, de nuestra lucha actual. . . . Este hombre no es uno que se divierte con sus rimas . . . de espaldas a la lucha de sus días ni al pueblo. La participación en la lucha de su tiempo queda anotada en lo anterior. Su amor al pueblo, en la singularidad, pregonada por él únicamente que yo sepa, de desear y autorizar la popular colaboración anónima en su obra." [38] This vital spontaneity continues through many other works to the present and is needed for the creation of an authentic political state, to be won only through freely uniting man in a common elevated undertaking. A state without projects in common is not viable, a fact known instinctively by the pueblo, "sin saber que lo sabe, biológicamente diríamos, con sabiduría recibida por vía de sangre, que es en lo que se conoce una vieja y consolidada cultura que da el producto humano de un analfabeto, v.gr., más, inteligente a veces, que un sabio de otro pueblo sin esa tradición cultural. Y es por esta razón que nuestro pueblo ha tenido ánimo y alegría. . . . Esa vitalidad que en la práctica viene denotando nuestro pueblo, corresponde exactamente a la teoría de la razón vital. . . . Nuestra razón de hoy viene de un frente de seis siglos." [39]

While some of the original works and critical essays in *Hora de España* do not deal directly with the intellectual and the pueblo, undoubtedly their relationship is the leitmotiv of the journal. The intellectuals, as temporal humans, identified themselves in their world with its specific realities, re-affirming or rediscovering the age-old Spanish social search for human solidarity. More than as objects of compassion because they were victims of injustice, the pueblo was viewed by them as the essence of what they were trying to achieve in their writing. The intellectual, a man, became one with his fellow man, destined like him to live and die, but not alone, for the cause of liberty, justice, and universal brotherhood.

[From *Kentucky Romance Quarterly*, vol. XIV, no. 4]

Notes

NOTES TO "THE SEA AND MACHADO"

1. León Felipe, *Antología rota* (Buenos Aires, 1957), pp. 71, 185. Felipe cites the sea in twenty-eight different poems in this anthology alone.
2. Vicente Aleixandre, *Poesías completas* (Madrid: Aguilar, 1969). One hundred and forty-nine different poems contain sea symbolism.
3. Carlos Bousoño, *La Poesía de Vicente Aleixandre* (Madrid, 1955), pp. 233–236.
4. Pedro Salinas, *Poesías completas* (Madrid, 1955), p. 244. Other references are to this edition.
5. Concha Zardoya, *Poesía española contemporánea* (Madrid, 1961), p. 601.
6. Rafael Alberti, *Poesías completas* (Buenos Aires: Índice Autobiográfico, 1961), p. 11.
7. Ibid., p. 1012.
8. José Martínez Ruiz, "El paisaje en la poesía," *Clásicos y modernos* (Madrid, 1919), pp. 99–105.
9. Alice Jane McVan, *Antonio Machado* (New York, 1959), p. 76.
10. Richard Lionel Predmore, "El tiempo en la poesía de Antonio Machado," *PMLA*, LXIII, 2 (June, 1948), 696–711.
11. Ricardo Gullón, "Lenguaje, humanismo y tiempo en Antonio Machado," *Cuadernos Hispanoamericanos* (Madrid, September–December, 1949), pp. 567–581.
12. Juan López-Morillas, "Antonio Machado's Temporal Interpretation of Poetry," *The Journal of Aesthetics and Art Criticism*, VI, 2 (Baltimore, December, 1947), 161–171.
13. Bartolomé Mostaza, "El paisaje en la poesía de Antonio Machado," *Cuadernos Hispanoamericanos* (Madrid, September–December, 1949), pp. 623–641.
14. Richard Lionel Predmore, "La visión de Castilla en la obra de Antonio Machado," *Hispania*, XXIX (November, 1946), 500–506.
15. Dámaso Alonso, "Fuente y jardín en la poesía de Machado," *Cuadernos Hispanoamericanos* (Madrid, September–December, 1949), pp. 375–381.
16. Julián Marías, "Antonio Machado y su interpretación poética de las cosas," *Cuadernos Hispanoamericanos* (Madrid, September–December, 1949), pp. 307–321.
17. Luis Rosales, "Muerte y resurrección de Antonio Machado," *Cuadernos Hispanoamericanos* (Madrid, September–December, 1949), pp. 435–479.

18. José María Pemán, "El tema del limonero y la fuente en Antonio Machado," *Boletín de la Real Academia Española,* XXXII, cuad. 136 (May–August, 1952), 171–191.
19. Ramón de Zubiría, *La poesía de Antonio Machado* (Madrid, 1955).
20. Ramón F. Ruiz, "El tema del camino en la poesía de Antonio Machado," *Cuadernos Hispanoamericanos* (Madrid, 1962), pp. 52–76.
21. Alejandro Ramírez, "La tierra en la poesía de Antonio Machado," *Revista Hispánica Moderna,* XXVIII (1962), 276–286.
22. *Obras completas de Manuel y Antonio Machado* (Madrid: Plenitud, 1957), p. 917. All references to Machado's poetry, unless otherwise noted, are from this edition.
23. Pedro Laín Entralgo, *La espera y la esperanza* (Madrid: Revista de Occidente, 1958), p. 430. Originally his discussion of Machado formed part of his entrance speech at the Royal Academy in 1954, "La memoria y la esperanza."
24. G. Pradal Rodríguez, *Antonio Machado, vida y obra* (New York: Hispanic Institute of the United States, 1951), p. 28.
25. Alice Jane McVan, op. cit., p. 77.
26. Pedro Laín Entralgo, op. cit., p. 423.
27. Alice Jane McVan, op. cit., p. 77.
28. José Luis Aranguren, "Esperanza y desesperanza de Dios en la experiencia de la vida de Antonio Machado," *Cuadernos Hispanoamericanos* (Madrid, September–December, 1949), p. 389.
29. Luis Felipe Vivanco, "Comentario a unos pocos poemas de Antonio Machado," *Cuadernos Hispanoamericanos* (Madrid, September–December, 1949), pp. 551–552.
30. Ramón de Zubiría, op. cit., p. 35.
31. Alice Jane McVan, op. cit., p. 7.
32. José Martínez Ruiz, *Obras completas* (Madrid: Aguilar, 1947–1954), II, 806.
33. Bartolomé Mostaza, op. cit., p. 641.
34. Alice Jane McVan, op. cit., p. 226.
35. Dámaso Alonso, "Poesías olvidadas de Antonio Machado." In his *Poetas españoles contemporáneos* (Madrid, 1952), p. 122.

NOTES TO "GARCIA LORCA AND VERMONT"

1. Angel del Río, "Introduction to *Poet in New York,*" tr. by Ben Belitt (New York, 1955), p. xvii.
2. Gil Benumeya, "Estampa de García Lorca," *La Gaceta Literaria,* no. 98 (January 15, 1931).
3. Conrad Aiken, "The Poet in New York and Other Poems," tr. by Rolfe Humphries, *The New Republic,* CIII (1940), 309.
4. Letter to Philip Cummings, July, 1929.
5. See Federico García Lorca, *Obras completas* (Madrid: Aguilar, 1955), pp. 1602–1603. Citations from Lorca are to this edition—hereafter cited as *O.C.*

6. Information in a letter to the author from Philip H. Cummings, Woodstock, Vermont, May 9, 1957.
7. Guillermo Díaz-Plaja, *Federico García Lorca: estudio crítico* (Buenos Aires, 1948), p. 185.
8. Ibid., p. 189.
9. Edwin Honig, *García Lorca* (Norfolk, Connecticut, 1944), p. 86.
10. Alfredo de la Guardia, *García Lorca: persona y creación* (Buenos Aires, 1952), pp. 198–199.
11. Honig, op. cit., pp. 212–213.

NOTES TO "THE SEA, LOVE, AND DEATH IN ALEIXANDRE"

1. Sigmund Freud, *The Standard Edition of the Complete Psychological Works of Freud* (London, 1961), XIX, 42.
2. *Psychoanalysis Today,* ed. by Sandor Lorenz (New York, 1944), p. 66.
3. C. G. Jung, *Modern Man in Search of a Soul,* tr. by W. S. Dell and Cary F. Barnes (London, 1945), pp. 194–195.
4. Sigmund Freud, "Formulations on the Two Principles of Mental Functioning," *The Standard Edition* (London, 1958), XII, 224.
5. Sigmund Freud, *Delusion and Dream—An Interpretation in the Light of Psychoanalysis of Gradiva,* tr. by Helen Downey (London, 1921).
6. Sigmund Freud, *Leonardo da Vinci, A Study in Sexuality,* tr. by A. A. Brill (New York, 1947).
7. Lawrence Kubie, *Neurotic Distortion of the Creative Process* (Lawrence, Kansas, 1958).
8. Ibid., p. 143.
9. *Psychoanalysis Today,* p. 38.
10. Juan José Domenchina, *Antología de la poesía española contemporánea* (Mexico, 1947), p. 391.
11. Max Aub, *La poesía española contemporánea* (Mexico, 1954), pp. 156–159.
12. Dámaso Alonso, *Poetas españoles contemporáneos* (Madrid, 1952), p. 323.
13. Luis Cernuda, *Como quien espera el alba* (Buenos Aires, 1947), p. 44.
14. Vicente Aleixandre, *La destrucción o el amor* (Madrid, 1945), p. 17.
15. Carlos Bousoño, *La poesía de Vicente Aleixandre* (Madrid, 1950), p. 10.
16. Eleanor Turnbull, *Contemporary Spanish Poetry* (Baltimore, 1945), quotes Pedro Salinas on Aleixandre on pp. 17, 299.
17. Gerardo Diego, *Poesía española contemporánea* (Madrid, 1962), p. 649.
18. Federico Carlos Sáinz de Robles, *Panorama literario, 1954* (Madrid, 1955), II, 170.
19. Carlos Bousoño, op. cit., p. 11.
20. Vicente Aleixandre, op. cit., pp. 17–18.
21. Vicente Aleixandre, *Poesías completas* (Madrid: Aguilar, 1960), pp. 99–100. all future citations from Aleixandre's poetry, unless otherwise noted, are from this edition.

22. C. G. Jung, *Psychology of the Unconscious* (New York, 1944), p. 237.

23. Karl Abraham, in *Selected Papers on Psychoanalysis* (London, 1948), p. 203, relates darkness to womb fantasies. As the symbol of the mother it signifies both birth and death.

24. Bertram D. Lewin, *The Psychoanalysis of Elation* (New York, 1950), p. 111.

25. *Psychoanalysis Today*, p. 317.

26. Bertram D. Lewin, "Phobic Symptoms and Dream Interpretations," *The Psychoanalytic Quarterly*, XXI, no. 3 (July, 1952), 313.

27. Bertram D. Lewin, *The Psychoanalysis of Elation*, pp. 107–108.

28. Karl Abraham, op. cit., p. 176.

29. Other sea poems in this collection that relate the sensual to death and decay and show the sea as both love and death, involving a continuing symbolism of "bocas redondas," "peces podridos," "una dulce pasión de agua de muerte," and the like, are: "La muerte o antesala de consulta" (pp. 153–154), "Víspera de mí" (pp. 163–164), "El mar no es una hoja de papel" (pp. 182–183), and "Sobre tu pecho unas letras" (pp. 184–185).

30. Melanie Klein, *The Psychoanalysis of the Child* (London, 1949), p. 211. Fish attacks represent an attack on the father's penis. C. G. Jung, *Psychology of the Unconscious*, p. 223, equates the fish with a libido symbol. The fish may be a phallic symbol or may, at times, represent the woman.

31. Dámaso Alonso, op. cit., p. 298.

32. Similar themes may be found in other poems of the collection such as "Circuito" (p. 224), where he seeks the love of "sirenas de la mar"; "Nacimiento último" (pp. 230–231), where he views the sea as eternal life and death; "Toro" (p. 240), which emphasizes autoeroticism and narcissistic enjoyment of self, for his need of love is not easily fulfilled by women; "Muñecas" (pp. 247–248), about the pleasant-unpleasant aspects of physical love and girls at whose breasts bronze beetles bite; "Madre, madre" (pp. 257–258); "Palabras" (p. 260); "Tempestad arriba" (pp. 267–268); and "Donde ni una gota de tristeza es pecado" (pp. 289–290), on destructive death imagery and the pleasure-pain involved in love.

33. Bertram D. Lewin, *The Psychoanalysis of Elation*, p. 104.

34. Ibid., p. 48.

35. Ibid., p. 111.

36. Sigmund Freud, *Standard Edition* (1959), XX, 67. The forest, like the tree, has been mythologically portrayed as a maternal symbol. The juxtaposition of the sea and forest symbols seem significant.

37. Otto Rank, *The Trauma of Birth* (New York, 1952), p. 149.

38. *Psychoanalysis Today*, p. 160.

39. Sigmund Freud, *The Basic Writings of Sigmund Freud* (New York, 1938), pp. 394–396. See also *Standard Edition* (1953), IV, V, 227, 399–401, 403n, 406.

40. The remaining poems in *La destrucción o el amor* that contain sea symbolism continue to identify it with sexual force and the love-death relationship. Among these are, "Unidad en Ella" (pp. 307–308), "El mar ligero" (pp. 309–310), "Sin luz" (pp. 311–312), "Junio" (pp. 319–320), "A ti viva" (pp. 331–332), "Orillas del mar" (pp. 333–334), "Quiero saber" (pp. 335–

336), "El frío" (pp. 370–371), where he becomes the sea—"océano absoluto que soy"—but continues to seek life, light, and love; "Soy el destino" (pp. 375–376)—"mar único al que vendrán todos los radios amantes"—"Que así invade" (389–390), "Cuerpo de piedra" (pp. 393–394), and "Total amor" (pp. 407–408).

41. Aleixandre reveals a desire to fuse with the ocean coupled with a resistance to rejoining it. The sea *no es* a bed, a shroud. The regressively attractive mother symbol, the sea, is said not to be the very thing he holds it to be: a mechanism of denial or negation.

42. Carlos Bousoño, op. cit., p. 7.

43. Dámaso Alonso, op. cit., p. 309.

44. Vicente Aleixandre, *Algunos caracteres de la nueva poesía española* (Madrid, 1955), p. 11.

45. Other poems that recall the sea as eternal, a far-off love, sexual passion, earlier paradise, and yet a continuing sea of both life and death are, "El río" (pp. 475–476), "Plenitud del amor" (pp. 519–521), "Mensaje" (pp. 529–530), "El aire" (p. 538), "El mar" (p. 539), "Cuerpo sin amor" (p. 550), "Adiós a los campos" (pp. 560–561), "Ciudad del paraíso" (pp. 546–565), and "Hijos de los campos" (pp. 566–567).

46. J. C. Flugel, *The Psychoanalytic Study of the Family* (London, 1935), pp. 67–69.

47. Patrick Mullahy, *Oedipus, Myth and Complex* (New York, 1948), p. 163.

48. Bertram D. Lewin, "Phobic Symptoms and Dream Interpretations." Aleixandre uses the sea as an archetypal motif. In the 336 poems of *Poesías completas* (op. cit.), the sea occurs 182 times and is used as a central theme in sixteen others. For archetypal motifs see C. G. Jung, *The Integration of the Personality* (New York, 1939), pp. 52ff.

49. J. C. Flugel, op. cit., p. 66.

NOTES TO "THE CONTEMPORARY NOVEL OF ECUADOR"

1. In 1918 in Córdoba, Argentina, a student convention published a manifesto speaking about the democratization of teaching and student representation. Gabriel del Mazo, *Estudiantes y gobierno universitario* (Buenos Aires, 1941), p. 135, calls the students "generación que fue avanzada de un movimiento general continental," and Argentine educator Juan B. Terán, *Al servicio de la novísima generación de la América española* (Buenos Aires, 1931), p. 25, calls it "el grito que lanza la revolución social a las puertas de la universidad de paso a su heroico destino."

2. *La casa de los locos* (Guayaquil, 1929), p. 59.

3. *Mapa de América* (Madrid, 1930), p. 222.

4. Mensaje de la *Biblioteca Nacional del Ecuador*, III (1936), 33.

5. *América, novela sin novelistas* (Santiago, 1940), p. 30.

6. Demetrio Aguilera Malta, *Don Goyo* (Madrid, 1933), p. 32.

7. *Atenea*, XXXII (1935), 135.

8. Arturo Torres-Rioseco, "La novela de tema indígena en el Ecuador," *Modern Philology,* XXI (1939), 233.

NOTES TO "ALFREDO PAREJA Y DIEZ CANSECO"

1. Albert Franklin, *Quarterly Journal of International Relations,* 1940, p. 34.
2. Arturo Torres-Rioseco, "La novela de tema indígena en el Ecuador," *Modern Philology,* XXI (1939), 235.
3. Adolfo Simmonds, in Pareja y Diez Canseco, *La señorita Ecuador* (Guayaquil, 1930), pp. iii–iv.
4. Alfredo Pareja y Diez Canseco, *La casa de los locos* (Guayaquil, 1929), p. 59.
5. Alfredo Pareja y Diez Canseco, *La señorita Ecuador,* p. 97.
6. Neftalí Agrella, *Atenea,* XXV (1939), 337.
7. Fernando Díez de Medina, *Atenea,* XXVI (1934), 36.
8. Antonio Montalvo, *América,* no. 53 (1933), p. 356.
9. José A. Portuondo, *Letras de México* (May, 1945), p. 68.
10. Ricardo Latcham, *Atenea,* XXIX (1935), 329.
11. Fernando Díez de Medina, loc. cit.
12. Luis Alberto Sánchez, in *La Beldaca* (Santiago de Chile, 1935), p. 19.
13. Alfredo Pareja y Diez Canseco, *El muelle* (Mexico, 1945), pp. 86–87.
14. Ernest Poole, *The Harbor* (New York, 1915), pp. 341ff.
15. Luis Alberto Sánchez, op. cit., p. 13.
16. Ricardo Latcham, *Atenea,* LII (1938).
17. Carl Van Doren, *The American Novel, 1789–1939* (New York, 1940), p. 350.
18. Ricardo Latcham, see note 16.
19. Jorge A. Díez, *Trópico,* no. 2 (1938), p. 29.
20. Alfredo Pareja y Diez Canseco, *Hechos y hazañas de Don Balón de Baba* (Buenos Aires, 1939), p. 86.
21. Ibid.
22. Angel F. Rojas, *La novela ecuatoriana* (Mexico, 1948), p. 196.
23. Alfredo Pareja y Diez Canseco, *Hombres sin tiempo* (Buenos Aires, 1941), p. 8.
24. *Casa de la Cultura Ecuatoriana,* no. 2 (April–December, 1945), p. 296.
25. Alejandro Carrión, *Letras del Ecuador* (May, 1945), p. 10.
26. Alfredo Pareja y Diez Canseco, *Las tres ratas* (Buenos Aires, 1944), p. 55.
27. Information in a letter from Pareja y Diez Canseco, April 27, 1956.
28. Alfredo Pareja y Diez Canseco, *La advertencia* (Buenos Aires, 1956), p. 8.
29. Ibid., p. 333.
30. Ibid., pp. 386–387.
31. Alfredo Pareja y Diez Canseco, *Vida y leyenda de Miguel de Santiago* (Mexico, 1951), p. 7.
32. Alfredo Pareja y Diez Canseco, *Historia del Ecuador,* IV (Mexico, 1955), 88.
33. Alfredo Pareja y Diez Canseco, "Defensa del trópico," *Panorama,* no. 21, p. 12.
34. Benjamín Carrión, *El nuevo relato ecuatoriano* (Quito, 1950), p. 179.

NOTES TO "THE FICTION OF RAMÓN SENDER"

1. Samples of his animal imagery are: "La viejecita gorjeó como un pájaro," *Epitalamio del prieto Trinidad* (Mexico: Ediciones Quetzal, 1942), p. 23; "En la puerta comenzaba a sonreir como una gatita," *Los cinco libros de Ariadna* (New York: Iberica Publishing Co., 1957), p. 326.
2. *Imán* (Madrid: Editorial Cenit, 1930), p. 96.
3. *Siete domingos rojos* (Barcelona: Colección Balague, 1932), p. 44.
4. Ibid., pp. 309, 410, 442.
5. Ibid., pp. 160, 236, 355.
6. *El lugar del hombre* (Mexico: Ediciones Quetzal, 1939).
7. *El rey y la reina* (Buenos Aires: Editorial Jackson, 1949).
8. *El verdugo afable* (Santiago de Chile: Nascimento, 1952), p. 46.
9. *Orden público* (Madrid: Editorial Cenit, 1939), p. 182.
10. *Proverbio de la muerte* (Mexico: Ediciones Quetzal, 1939), p. 197.
11. *Réquiem por un campesino español* (Buenos Aires: Editorial Proyección, 1961), p. 50.
12. *Mexicayotl* (Mexico: Ediciones Quetzal, 1940), p. 136.
13. *Mister Witt en el cantón* (Madrid: Espasa Calpe, 1936), p. 126.
14. *The Basic Writings of Sigmund Freud* (New York: The Modern Library, 1938), pp. 835–836.
15. For other samples of this type of relationship see: *Imán,* pp. 49, 118, 120, 128, 247, 266, 268; *Orden público,* p. 195; *Siete domingos rojos,* pp. 141, 446; *El rey y la reina,* pp. 47, 194; *El verdugo afable,* pp. 41, 61, 350, 370, 386; *Los cinco libros de Ariadna,* pp. 17, 27, 30, 59, 102, 126, 151, 184, 229, 279, 302, 305, 363, 450, 468, 469, 471–472, 482; *Réquiem por un campesino español,* p. 197; *The Sphere* (New York: Hellman Williams and Co., 1949), p. 226; *Mister Witt en el cantón,* p. 39.
16. *Crónica del alba* (New York: F. S. Crofts and Co., 1946).
17. *Emén Hetán* (Mexico: Libro Mex, 1958).
18. For other sexual and love references see: *Los cinco libros de Ariadna,* pp. 50, 51, 71, 86, 118, 226, 451, 481; *Mister Witt en el cantón,* p. 65.
19. For other references see: *Los cinco libros de Ariadna,* pp. 137, 464; *Mexicayotl,* pp. 119, 123.
20. See also: *Los cinco libros de Ariadna,* pp. 114, 383; *Siete domingos rojos,* pp. 305, 306, 308, 465.
21. *Hipogrifo violento* (Mexico: Colección Aquelarre, 1954), p. 113.
22. "The Black Cat," *The Texas Quarterly,* Spring, 1961.
23. *El mancebo y los héroes* (Mexico: Editorial Atenea, 1950), p. 55.
24. For other youth references see: *Epitalamio del prieto Trinidad,* pp. 180, 204; *Imán,* p. 12.
25. See also: *La quinta Julieta* (Mexico: Colección Panoramas, 1958), pp. 105, 108.
26. For other identifications see: *Los cinco libros de Ariadna,* pp. 10, 16, 20, 45, 93, 115, 130, 211, 219, 364, 384; *Proverbio de la muerte,* pp. 56, 185, 186; *El rey y la reina,* pp. 66, 71, 86, 248; *Crónica del alba,* p. 26; *Hipogrifo violento,* pp. 200–201; *Orden público,* pp. 96, 109, 125, 128, 144; *El ver-*

dugo afable, pp. 48, 270, 395; *Mister Witt en el cantón*, pp. 102, 109, 272; *Imán*, pp. 27, 40, 163, 168, 215, 258; *Siete domingos rojos*, pp. 123, 204; *El lugar del hombre*, pp. 28, 103, 106, 207; *Epitalamio del prieto Trinidad*, pp. 35, 42, 75, 89, 90; *The Sphere*, p. 9.

27. For other interludes see: *Los cinco libros de Ariadna*, pp. 358, 549; *Proverbio de la muerte*, p. 112; *El rey y la reina*, pp. 77–78; *El verdugo afable*, p. 119.

28. See also: *Los cinco libros de Ariadna*, pp. 22, 44, 53, 58, 362; *Emén Hetán*, pp. 56, 142; *Crónica del alba*, p. 17; *El lugar del hombre*, pp. 17, 27.

NOTES TO "BENAVENTE ON SHAKESPEAREAN CHARACTERS"

1. Kessel Schwartz, "Shakespeare's Influence on Benavente's Plays," *The South Central Bulletin*, XXI (Spring, 1961).
2. Kessel Schwartz, "Benavente and Shakespearean Drama," *Romance Notes*, I, no. 2 (Spring, 1960).
3. Jacinto Benavente, *Obras completas*, 11 vols. (Madrid: Aguilar, 1950–1958), XI, 488. Citations from Benavente are to this edition hereafter cited as *O.C.*

NOTES TO "SHAKESPEARE'S INFLUENCE ON BENAVENTE'S PLAYS"

1. Jacinto Benavente, *Obras completas*, 11 vols. (Madrid: Aguilar, 1950–1958). Citations from Benavente are to this edition hereafter cited as *O.C.*
2. Alfonso Par, *Shakespeare en la literatura española* (Madrid, 1935), II, 243.
3. Ibid., p. 136.

NOTES TO "SOME RECENT WORKS OF CALVO-SOTELO"

1. *Teatro Español 1949–1951* (Madrid, 1955), p. 161.
2. *Teatro Español 1956–1957* (Madrid, 1958), p. 269.
3. *Teatro Español 1950–1951* (Madrid, 1952), p. 419.
4. *Teatro Español 1954–1955* (Madrid, 1956), p. 164.
5. Ibid., p. 155.
6. *Teatro Español 1953–1954* (Madrid, 1959), p. 66.
7. *Teatro Español 1955–1956* (Madrid, 1957), p. 265.
8. Ibid., p. 231.
9. Joaquín Calvo-Sotelo, *La herencia* (Madrid: Alfil, 1958), p. 55.
10. *Teatro Español 1949–1950* (Madrid, 1955), p. 162.
11. *Teatro Español 1950–1951* (Madrid, 1952), p. 406.
12. *Teatro Español 1955–1956* (Madrid, 1957), p. 245.

NOTES TO "JACINTO GRAU AND THE MEANING OF EXISTENCE"

1. José Ortega y Gasset, *Obras completas* (Madrid, 1947), V, 21–23.
2. Jacinto Grau, *El mismo daño* (Madrid, 1921), p. 236.
3. Jacinto Grau, *El burlador que no se burla* (Buenos Aires, 1941), pp. 69–70.
4. Jacinto Grau, *En Ildaria* (Madrid, 1917), p. 171.
5. Jacinto Grau, *El caballero Varona* (Buenos Aires, 1944), p. 232.
6. Jacinto Grau, *Los tres locos del mundo* (Buenos Aires, 1953), p. 82.
7. Jacinto Grau, *La señora guapa* (Buenos Aires, 1953), p. 201.
8. Jacinto Grau, *Las gafas de don Telesforo o un loco de buen capricho* (Buenos Aires, 1954), p. 102.
9. Jacinto Grau, *Unamuno y la España de su tiempo* (Buenos Aires, 1943), p. 30.
10. Jacinto Grau, *La casa del diablo* (Buenos Aires, 1945), p. 52.
11. Jacinto Grau, *El dominio del mundo* (Buenos Aires, 1944), pp. 14, 43.
12. See *The Philosophy of Karl Jaspers*, ed. by Paul A. Schelpp (New York, 1957). pp. 177–208.
13. Jacinto Grau, *Destino* (Buenos Aires, 1954), p. 221.
14. Jacinto Grau, *Horas de vida* (Buenos Aires, 1944), p. 118.
15. Jacinto Grau, *Entre llamas* (Buenos Aires, 1947), p. 32.
16. Jacinto Grau, *Unamuno*, p. 7.
17. Jacinto Grau, *El hijo pródigo* (Madrid, 1918), p. 319.
18. Jacinto Grau, *El señor de Pigmalión* (New York, 1952), p. 48.
19. Jacinto Grau, *Don Juan de Carillana* (Buenos Aires, 1947), p. 205.
20. Marjorie Green, *Dreadful Freedom* (Chicago, 1948), p. 70.

NOTES TO "THE WORKS OF ALEJANDRO CASONA"

1. *Reality and the Poet in Spanish Poetry* (Baltimore, 1940).
2. *La sirena varada* (New York, 1951), p. 74.
3. *Otra vez el diablo* (Mexico, 1937), p. 40.
4. *Prohibido suicidarse en primavera* (Buenos Aires, 1941), p. 122.
5. *La sirena varada*, p. 66.
6. *La barca sin pescador* (New York, 1955), p. 20.
7. *La sirena varada*, p. 11.
8. *Prohibido suicidarse en primavera*, p. 171.
9. *La dama del alba* (New York, 1947), p. 9.
10. *La sirena varada*, p. 39.
11. *Los árboles mueren de pie* (Buenos Aires, 1950), p. 186.
12. *La dama del alba*, p. 144.
13. *Nuestra Natacha* (New York, 1947), p. 82.

246 Notes to pages 151–157

NOTES TO "BUERO VALLEJO AND TRAGEDY"

1. Antonio Buero Vallejo, "Cuidado con la amargura," *Correo Literario* June 15, 1950, p. 8.
2. Ibid., p. 9.
3. Antonio Buero Vallejo, "Palabra final," *Historia de una escalera* (Barcelona, 1950), p. 154.
4. Ibid., pp. 153–154.
5. Jean Paul Borel, *Théâtre de l'Impossible* (Paris, 1963), pp. 158–159.
6. Antonio Buero Vallejo, *La señal que se espera, Colección teatro,* no. 21 (Madrid, 1953), pp. 66–67.
7. Antonio Buero Vallejo, "Lo trágico," *Informaciones—extraordinario teatral del Sábado de Gloria,* Madrid, April 12, 1952; Juan Emilio Aragonés, "Buero Vallejo, autor del momento," *La hora,* Madrid, November 1, 1956.
8. Antonio Buero Vallejo, "El teatro de Buero Vallejo visto por Buero Vallejo," *Primer Acto* (Madrid, 1957), p. 6.
9. Jean Paul Borel, op. cit., p. 180.
10. Antonio Buero Vallejo, "Comentario," *Hoy es fiesta, Colección teatro,* no. 176 (Madrid, 1957), p. 98.
11. Ibid., pp. 99–100.
12. Antonio Buero Vallejo, "La tragedia," *El teatro—Enciclopedia de arte escénico,* ed. by Guillermo Díaz Plaja (Barcelona, 1958), p. 71.
13. Ibid., p. 76.
14. Ibid., pp. 74–75.
15. Ricardo Salvat, "Teatro en 1961," *Primer Acto* (Madrid, December, 1961–January, 1962), p. 10.
16. Arthur Miller, "Tragedy and the Common Man," *Aspects of the Drama,* ed. by Sylvan Barnet, Morton Berman, and William Burton (Boston, 1962), p. 67.
17. José R. Marra-López, "Conversación con Buero Vallejo sobre el teatro español," *Cuadernos,* no. 42 (Mayo-Junio, 1960), p. 56. Similar views on tragic hope may also be found in: Antonio Buero Vallejo, "La juventud española ante la tragedia," *Papageno,* no. 1 (Zaragoza, Spring, 1958) ; "Buero Vallejo nos habla," *Boletín de la Editorial Losada,* no. 12 (Buenos Aires, April, 1960) ; and "Me llamo Buero Vallejo," *La palabra* (Madrid: Discos Aguilar, 1964).
18. "Antonio Buero Vallejo Answers Seven Questions," *The Theater Annual,* XIX (1962), 5.
19. Jean Jacquot, "Les tragiques Grecs au goût du jour," *Le Théâtre Moderne, Entretiens d'Arras* (Paris, 1958), p. 89.
20. Ibid., p. 94.
21. John Mason Brown, *Dramatis Personae* (New York, 1963), pp. 25–26.
22. Antonio Buero Vallejo, "Sobre teatro," *Cuadernos de Ágora,* no. 79–82 (Madrid, May–August, 1963), p. 14.
23. Bernard Dulsey, "Entrevista a Buero Vallejo," *The Modern Language Journal,* L, no. 3 (1966), 154.
24. Ricardo Domenech, "Reflexiones sobre el teatro de Buero Vallejo," *Primer Acto* (Madrid, November–December, 1959), pp. 5–8.

25. Carlos Muñiz, "Antonio Buero Vallejo, ese hombre comprometido," *Primer Acto* (Madrid, December, 1962), p. 10.
26. Domingo Pérez Minik, *Teatro europeo contemporáneo* (Madrid, 1961), p. 388.
27. Alfonso Sastre, "Los autores españoles ante el teatro como arte social," *Correo Literario,* August 15, 1951, p. 5.
28. *Primer Acto* (December, 1961–January, 1962), pp. 5–6.
29. José R. Marra López, op. cit., p. 58.
30. *Primer Acto* (December, 1962), p. 8.
31. Carlos Muñiz, loc. cit.
32. George Steiner, *The Death of Tragedy* (New York, 1961), p. 8.
33. *Enciclopedia del arte escénico,* p. 68.
34. *Cuadernos de Ágora,* pp. 12–14.
35. Domingo Pérez Minik, op. cit., pp. 339–340, 393, 526.
36. Jean Paul Borel, op. cit., p. 154.
37. *Cuadernos de Ágora,* pp. 12–14.
38. *Cuadernos para el diálogo—extraordinario dedicado al teatro* (Madrid, June, 1966), pp. 44–45.
39. Ibid.
40. *The Theater Annual,* XIX, 5–6.
41. Pedro Laín Entralgo, *La memoria y la esperanza* (Madrid, 1954), p. 99.

NOTES TO "TRAGEDY AND THE CRITICISM OF SASTRE"

1. Alfonso Sastre, "Lo nuevo y lo viejo en el teatro español," *Primer Acto* (Madrid, March, 1964), p. 14. See also *Drama y sociedad* (Madrid, 1956), pp. 146–147.
2. Domingo Pérez Minik, *Teatro europeo contemporáneo* (Madrid, 1961), p. 409. "En cuanto a su técnica y a su estilo, debemos afirmar que una y otro son los más modernos con que contamos en nuestro país."
3. For the main points in the polemic see Alfonso Sastre, "Teatro imposible y pacto social," *Primer Acto* (Madrid, May–June, 1960), pp. 1–2; Antonio Buero Vallejo, "Obligada precisión acerca del 'imposibilismo,'" *Primer Acto* (Madrid, July–August, 1960), pp. 1–6; and Alfonso Sastre, "A modo de respuesta," *Primer Acto* (Madrid, September–October, 1960), pp. 1–2.
4. Alfonso Sastre, *Anatomía del realismo* (Barcelona, 1965), pp. 76–77.
5. Ibid., p. 25.
6. Alfonso Sastre, "Los autores españoles ante el teatro como 'arte social,'" *Correo Literario,* August 15, 1951, p. 5.
7. Ibid.
8. *Anatomía del realismo,* p. 21.
9. Alfonso Sastre in Angel Medina, *Cuaderno de arte del Ateneo de Madrid* (Madrid, 1959), p. 3.
10. *Drama y sociedad,* p. 50.
11. *Correo Literario,* August, 1952, p. 28.
12. Alfonso Sastre, "El teatro de Alfonso Sastre visto por Alfonso Sastre," *Primer Acto* (Madrid, November–December, 1957), p. 7.

13. *Drama y sociedad,* pp. 92, 143.
14. Alfonso Sastre, *Cuatro dramas de la revolución* (Madrid, 1963), pp. 7–8.
15. *Anatomía del realismo,* p. 7.
16. Ibid., p. 256.
17. Alfonso Sastre, "Hombres de teatro," *Yorick,* no. 11 (January, 1966).
18. *Cuatro dramas,* pp. 8–10.
19. Francisco García Pavón, *El teatro social en España, 1895–1962* (Madrid, 1962), p. 177.
20. *Correo Literario,* August, 1952, pp. 26–28.
21. Alfonso Sastre, "Le théâtre espagnol contemporain," *Preuves,* no. 124 (May, 1961), p. 28.
22. *Drama y sociedad,* pp. 128, 142, 155.
23. Alfonso Sastre, "Espacio-tiempo y drama," *Primer Acto* (Madrid, November–December, 1957), pp. 13–16.
24. *Anatomía del realismo,* pp. 24–44.
25. Ibid., p. 69.
26. Ibid., p. 223.
27. Ibid., p. 114.
28. See note 17.
29. José María de Quinto, "El teatro," in "Los cuatro ángeles de San Silvestre," *Almanaque para 1958 de Papeles de Son Armadans,* pp. 339–340.
30. Alfonso Sastre, "Siete notas sobre 'Esperando a Godot,' " *Primer Acto* (Madrid, April, 1957), p. 49.
31. *Drama y sociedad,* p. 25.
32. Ibid., p. 37.
33. Alfonso Sastre, "Brindis por Anna Christie," *Primer Acto* (Madrid, July–August, 1959), p. 7.
34. Alfonso Sastre, "Tragedia y esperpento," *Primer Acto* (Madrid, November, 1961), p. 16.
35. *Anatomía del realismo,* p. 129.
36. Ibid.
37. See note 34.
38. *Anatomía del realismo,* pp. 221–223.
39. See note 12.
40. Alfonso Sastre, "Primeras notas para un encuentro con Bertolt Brecht," *Primer Acto* (Madrid, March–April, 1960), pp. 14–15.
41. See note 38.
42. Alfonso Sastre, "Teatro épico, teatro dramático, teatro de vanguardia," *Primer Acto* (Madrid, 1965), p. 5.
43. *Anatomía del realismo,* p. 253.
44. See note 2.

NOTES TO "ORTEGA Y GASSET AND GOETHE"

1. E. R. Curtius, *Kritische Essays zur Europäischen Literatur* (Bern, 1950), pp. 273–274.

2. José Ortega y Gasset, *Obras completas* (Madrid, 1957), IV, 25. Citations from Ortega y Gasset are from this edition hereafter cited as *O.C.*
3. Juan Ramón Jiménez, "Yo recuerdo a José Ortega y Gasset," *Clavileño*, no. 24 (November–December, 1953), p. 44.
4. E. R. Curtius, op. cit., pp. 247–248.
5. Ibid., p. 271.
6. Franz Niedermayer, "Ortega y Gasset y su relación con Alemania," *Clavileño*, no. 24 (November–December, 1953), p. 73.
7. Ibid., p. 72.
8. Ibid., p. 68.
9. Manuel Sandoval, "El centenario de Goethe," *Boletín de la Academia Española*, XIX (April, 1932), 229.
10. José M. Sacristán, "Goethe según la psicopatología," *Revista de Occidente*, XXXVI (1932), 91.
11. Manuel G. Morente, "Goethe y el mundo hispánico," *Revista de Occidente*, XXXVI (1932), 131–147.
12. Ibid., p. 137.
13. Egon Schwarz, "Ortega y Gasset and German Culture," Monatshefte, no. 2 (February, 1957), p. 90.
14. *Concerning a Bicentennial Goethe*, ed. by Arnold Bergstraesser (1950), p. 353.
15. Ibid., p. 357.
16. Goethe, *Truth and Poetry*, II (London, 1872), 37.

NOTES TO "CULTURE AND THE SPANISH CIVIL WAR"

1. The Institución was founded in 1876 by Francisco Giner de los Ríos (1839–1915). He helped spread the liberal doctrine of krausismo, which was based on the theories of the German philosopher Karl C. F. Krause (1781–1832), a disciple of Kant. Giner hoped to build a school, free from partisan politics, which would be based on love, beauty, tolerance, and the scientific method. The Krausists were an important factor in the formation of the first Spanish Republic (1873–1874).
2. The terms Nationalist, Fascist, and Falangist are used interchangeably in this paper. The original Falangists belonged almost exclusively to the wealthy upper middle class or to the aristocracy. Their first public meeting, held in October, 1933, was presided over by José Antonio Primo de Rivera. His *encamisados* saluted in the Fascist manner and accepted the totalitarian philosophy of Germany and Italy. They were not typical Fascists because of their inability to group various classes into a national whole, but they believed they could reach a Fascist state in spite of a lack of broad based support. Although the Falangists joined other rightist elements, they disagreed with the latter on almost all issues, but they remained as a single party, under the firm control of Franco, dedicated to a permanent censorship and to the extermination of the left.
3. By 1951, the *ABC* had become the largest daily in Spain. Ironically, the in-

tellectual censorship for which the Seville version had so consistently fought between 1936 and 1939 was imposed on the *ABC* itself in 1951. The owner, the Marqués de Luca de Tena, was forced to accept a new director named by the general press office because the government was dissatisfied with the publisher's attitude.

4. *ABC,* Seville, June 26, 1937. All citations in the text are to the Seville *ABC.*

NOTES TO "*MADRID* AND SPANISH LITERATURE"

1. *Madrid* (February, 1937), preface.
2. *Madrid* (May, 1937), preface. Further citations are all to this journal.
3. Juan de la Encina, "Arturo Souto o la vocación" (May, 1937), p. 156.
4. Juan de la Encina, "En el puente de la Trinidad" (February, 1937), pp. 143–148.
5. Padre del Río Hortega, "La ciencia y el idioma" (February, 1937), p. 68.
6. León Felipe, "Poesía integral" (February, 1937), p. 119, n. 1.
7. Ibid., p. 119.
8. Ibid., p. 122.
9. Ibid., p. 125.
10. Antonio Machado, "Notas de actualidad" (February, 1937), p. 10.
11. Juan José Domenchina, "Genio y paradoja de Don Ramón del Valle-Inclán" (February, 1937), p. 59.
12. Ibid., p. 60.
13. José Moreno Villa, "Locos, enanos y negros en la Corte de los Austrias" (February, 1937), p. 117.
14. José Moreno Villa, "Recuerdo a Federico García Lorca" (February, 1937), p. 149.
15. Tomás Navarro Tomás, "Citas literarias sobre entonación emocional" (February, 1937), pp. 26–27.
16. Ibid., p. 31.
17. Tomás Navarro Tomás, "Datos literarios sobre el valor fisionómico de la voz" (May, 1937), p. 128.

NOTES TO "THE PUEBLO . . . AND THE SPANISH CIVIL WAR"

1. *Hora de España* (January, 1937), pp. 5–6. Further citations are all to this journal.
2. August, 1938, p. 33.
3. Antonio Machado, "Consejos, sentencias y donaires de Juan de Mairena" (January, 1937), p. 11.
4. Antonio Machado, "Sigue hablando Mairena a sus alumnos" (February, 1937), p. 10.
5. Ibid., p. 12.

6. April, 1937, p. 6.
7. July, 1937, p. 22.
8. Antonio Machado, "Sobre la Rusia actual" (September, 1937), pp. 9–11.
9. August, 1937, pp. 84–92.
10. Rosa Chacel, "Cultura y pueblo" (January, 1937), p. 14.
11. Ibid., p. 18.
12. June, 1937, p. 32.
13. María Zambrano, "El español y su tradición" (April, 1937), p. 24.
14. Ibid., pp. 26–27.
15. María Zambrano, "La reforma del entendimiento español" (September, 1937), p. 16.
16. Ibid., p. 27.
17. September, 1938, p. 45.
18. Rafael Dieste, "Desde la soledad de España" (January, 1938), p. 25.
19. José Bergamín, "Carta abierta a Madame Malaterre-Sellier" (January, 1937), p. 31.
20. August, 1937, pp. 32–36.
21. Rosa Chacel, "Carta a José Bergamín sobre anarquía y cristianismo" (July, 1937), p. 26.
22. Arturo Serrano Plaja, "A diestra y siniestra" (July, 1937), p. 42.
23. José Moreno Villa, "Frente" (January, 1937), p. 38.
24. July, 1937, p. 75.
25. February, 1937, pp. 17–18.
26. Antonio Sánchez Barbudo, "El surrealismo de Max Ernst" (January, 1937), p. 47.
27. Bernardo Clariana, "Humano trance de nuestra poesía" (January, 1937), pp. 56–58.
28. Pablo Neruda, "Federico García Lorca" (March, 1937), pp. 70–71.
29. September, 1937, p. 67.
30. Antonio Machado, "El poeta y el pueblo" (August, 1937), pp. 11–18.
31. Luis Cernuda, "Poetas en la España leal" (August, 1937), p. 73.
32. October, 1937, p. 75.
33. June, 1938, p. 64.
34. María Zambrano, "Las guerra" (December, 1937), pp. 69–74.
35. José Bergamín, "Pintar como querer" (May, 1937), p. 18.
36. Ramón Gaya, "España, toreadores, Picasso" (September, 1937), p. 28.
37. María Zambrano, "Un camino español, Séneca o la resignación" (May, 1938), p. 20.
38. Antonio Porras, "Nuestra razón de hoy" (April, 1938), pp. 62–63.
39. Ibid., pp. 64–65.

Index

Abinana, José María, 210
Abraham, Karl, 67
actors, American, 202
Aesop, 99
Agrella, Neftalí, 87
Aguilera Malta, Demetrio, 81, 82, 83, 97
Aiken, Conrad, 52
Alarcón, Pedro Antonio, 195
Alas, Leopoldo (Clarín), 195
Alberti, Rafael, 16–17, 37, 38, 210–211, 225, 232
Aldecoa, Ignacio, 163
Alegría, Ciro, 22, 93
Aleixandre, Vicente, 13, 18–19, 37, 62–77
Alfaro, Eloy, 96
Alfonso el Sabio, 183
Alonso, Dámaso, 13, 16, 38, 63, 68, 72, 225, 231
Altolaguirre, Manuel, 225, 232
Álvarez del Valle, 204, 207
Álvarez Quintero, Serafín y Joaquín, 202, 210
Andreyev, Leonid, 80
Apollinaire, Guillaume, 86
Aragonés, Pablo, 205
Aranguren, José, 42
Araquistáin, Luis, 204, 207
Arguedas, Alcides, 79
Arguedas, José María, 22
Aristotle, 99, 151, 168
Artigas, Manuel, 193
Asín Palacios, Miguel, 212
Asturias, Miguel Ángel, 23
Ateneo de Madrid, 204
Aub, Max, 63, 225
Ayala, Elvira de, 184
Azaña, Manuel, 185, 207, 208
Azuela, Mariano, 21, 79

Bachiller Alcañices, (El) 198, 209
Bacon, Francis, 120
Balmes, Jaime, 194
Barbusse, Henri, 80
Baroja y Nessi, Pió, 11, 24–25, 113, 196, 211, 216, 217, 223
Barraca (La), 200, 208
Baudelaire, Pierre Charles, 58
Beckett, Samuel, 156, 169
Bécquer, Gustavo Adolfo, 13, 192
Belmonte, María Matilde, 201
Benavente, Jacinto, 28, 29, 113–126, 210
Benedetti, Mario, 23
Benumeya, Gil, 52
Bergamín, José, 211, 220, 225, 230
Bergson, Henri, 15, 44
Bermúdez Cañete, Antonio, 210
Blanco, Rufino, 210
Blasco Ibáñez, Vicente, 215, 223
Bonmatí de Codecido, F., 216
Booth, Edwin, 115
Borel, Jean Paul, 153, 156
Borges, Jorge Luis, 23
Borja, Arturo, 80
Bousoño, Carlos, 18, 68, 69
Brecht, Bertolt, 156, 166, 167, 168, 169
Brémond, Henri, 16
Bueno, Manuel, 210, 216
Buero Vallejo, Antonio, 28, 31–32, 132, 151–161
Burbage, James, 115
Burmann, Sigfrido, 187
Caballero Calderón, Eduardo, 23
Cabanillas, Ramón, 211
Cabrera Infante, Guillermo, 23
Calderón de la Barca, Pedro, 10, 116, 117, 144, 184, 188, 199, 201, 213
Calvin, John, 108
Calvo, Juan, 202

Calvo-Sotelo, Joaquín, 127–132, 209
Calvo-Sotelo, José, 197, 210
Camba, Julio, 198, 207, 212
Camino y Galicia, León Felipe, 15, 16, 37, 220–221, 225, 232
Camps, Jean, 186
Camus, Albert, 134
Captain Nemo, 187, 189, 193, 203
Carpentier, Alejo, 23
Carrera Andrade, Jorge, 80
Carrère, Emilio, 215
Carrión, Alejandro, 94
Carrión, Benjamín, 80, 88, 98
Casal Chapi, Enrique, 233
Casona, Alejandro, 28, 30–31, 144–150, 208
Cassou, Jean, 186
Castellet, José María, 163
Castilla, Juan de, 188, 195, 206
Castro, Américo, 9, 11, 191, 204, 208
Castro, Julio, 49
Catatá, Concha, 202
Cela, Camilo José, 133, 217
Celaya, Gabriel, 20
Centro de Estudios Históricos, 11, 204
Cernuda, Luis, 16, 63, 225, 233
Cervantes, Miguel de, 144, 188, 189, 199, 200, 206, 221, 222, 223, 229
Céspedes y Meneses, Gonzalo, 223
Chacel, Rosa, 225, 228, 230–231
Charron, Pierre, 99
Cisneros, Alonso de, 184
Claudel, Paul, 156–157
Cohen, Hermann, 171, 172
Corneille, Pierre, 187
Cortázar, Julio, 24, 25
Cortés, Hernán, 199, 214
Cortés, Narciso Alonso, 49
Cortines Murube, F., 183
Cossío, Francisco de, 211
Cossío, Manuel Bartolomé, 10
Costa, Joaquín, 10, 194, 203–204
creacionismo, 13
criollismo, 21
Cuadra, José de la, 82, 83
Cummings, Philip, 52–53, 54, 55, 56, 57
Curtius, E. R., 171, 172
Daranas, Mariano, 187, 188, 198, 210, 216
Darío, Rubén, 13, 14, 41, 205
Dartain, Luc, 189
Delibes, Miguel, 27
Descartes, René, 99
Díaz, Carmen, 202
Díaz Ferrero, Salvador, 206

Díaz-Plaja, Guillermo, 57
Dicenta, Joaquín, 127
Diego, Gerardo, 13, 37
Dieste, Rafael, 229–230
Diez, Jorge, 91
Diez Canedo, Enrique, 204
Dilthey, Wilhelm, 172
Domenchina, Juan José, 63, 221, 222
Domenech, Richardo, 157, 158
Dostoevski, Fedor, 80
Dunbar, Flanders, 63
Duse, Eleonora, 115
Echegaray, José, 130, 205
Echeverría, Esteban, 21
Eucadorian novel, 79–98
Ehrenburg, Ilya, 86
Eliot, T.S., 58
Encina, Juan de la, 206, 220
Engels, Friedrich, 200
Erasmianism, 10
Erasmus, 197
Ercilla y Zuñiga, Alonso de, 183, 199
Escóbar, Luis, 200, 201
Escudero, Gonzalo, 80
esperpento, 28–29
Espina, Concha, 183, 185, 188, 189, 190, 191, 198, 212, 216, 217
Espinel, Vicente, 188
existentialism, 12–13, 15, 16, 17, 22–35
Falangists, 183–190
Falla, Manuel de, 212, 233
fascism, 191–218, 223, 226, 230, 233
Felipe II, 197
Fernández Almagro, Melchor, 199
Fernández de Moratín, Leandro, 117, 119
films, American, 202
films, German, 203
Flela, Miguel, 206
Foxá, Agustín de, 208
Franco, Francisco, 131, 183, 186, 188, 193, 196, 198, 199, 200, 201, 203, 209, 211, 212–213, 214, 216, 223
Franco, Jean, 22
Freud, Sigmund, 62, 63, 64, 70, 87, 103
Fuentes, Carlos, 24
Galinsoga, Luis de, 198
Gallegos, Gerardo, 81
Gallegos, Rómulo, 21, 22
Gallegos Lara, Joaquín, 80, 81
Galván, Manuel de Jesús, 21
Ganivet, Angel, 33
García Lorca, Federico, 13, 17–18, 28, 30, 37, 58–61, 208, 219–220, 222, 232
García Márquez, Gabriel, 23

García Pavón, Francisco, 165
Garcilaso de la Vega, 20, 183, 199, 213
Garmendia, Salvador, 23
Garrick, David, 115
Gasco, Tina, 202
Generation of 1898, 10–13, 14, 18, 25, 33, 204
Generation of 1927, 16
Generation of 1936, 19–20
Gide, André, 86
Gil Albert, Juan, 228
Gil Gilbert, Enrique, 84, 93
Gil y Carrasco, Enrique, 191
Giménez Caballero, Ernesto, 11, 198, 199, 211
Giner de los Ríos, Francisco, 10, 193–194, 204
Gironella, José María, 25
Goethe, Johann Wolfgang von, 35, 171–182
Golden Age, 183–190
Góngora, Luis de, 20, 184, 189, 213
González, Angel, 20
González Montano, Reginaldo, 197
González Prada, Manuel, 79
González-Ruano, César, 198, 205, 207, 212, 215, 216
Gorki, Maxim, 80, 86
Goya, Francisco, 233
Goytisolo, Juan, 27, 28, 36
Gracián, Baltasar, 10
Granada, Fernando de, 202
Grandmontagne, Francisco, 49
Grau, Jacinto, 29–30, 133–143, 225
Greco (El), 10
Guardia, Alfredo de la, 60
Guevara, Antonio de, 10
Guillén, Jorge, 16
Güiraldes, Ricardo, 21
Gullón, Ricardo, 38
Gutiérrez Nájera, Manuel, 13
Heidegger, Martin, 15, 34, 44, 140, 180
Herder, Johann Gottfried, 175
Hernández, Miguel, 20, 211, 226
Herrera, Frenando de, 213
Honig, Edwin, 61
Hugo, Victor, 119
Huidobro, Vicente, 13
Hurtado de Mendoza, Diego, 199
Icaza, Jorge, 81, 84, 91
Institución Libre de Enseñanza, 10, 11, 193, 197, 198, 203, 204
Jaspers, Karl, 139
Jensen, W., 63
Jiménez, José Olivio, 19

Jiménez, Juan Ramón, 14, 16, 37, 171, 233–234
Jones, Ernest, 66
Joyce, James, 22
Juan de la Cruz, San, 199
Jung, Carl, 62
Junta para Ampliación de Estudios, 11
Kafka, Franz, 22
Kant, Immanuel, 171, 175
Kierkegaard, Soren, 140, 141
Klein, Melanie, 62, 69
krausismo, 10, 11, 190, 193, 204
Laforet, Carmen, 27, 133
Laín Entralgo, Pedro, 35, 38, 40, 133, 161
Lamb, Charles, 113
Lamberri, Manuel, 199
Langtry, Lily, 116
Larra, Mariano José de, 191
Latcham, Ricardo, 90, 91
Leibniz, Gottfried W., 175
Leighton, Charles, 31
León, Fray Luis de, 189
León, Ricardo, 196, 212
Lewis, Sinclair, 86
Lezama Lima, José, 23
Linares Rivas, Manuel, 128
Llorens, Vicente, 202–203
López-Morillas, Juan, 38
López Prudencio, J., 189, 192, 195, 198, 203, 204, 207, 213, 217
Loyola, Ignacio de, 197
Luna, José Carlos de, 189, 208, 210–211
Machado, Antonio, 11, 12, 14–15, 16, 20, 37–51, 191, 206, 207, 221, 225–227, 232, 233
Machado, Manuel, 191, 192, 198, 200, 201, 212, 213
Machado Núñez, Antonio, 46
Madariaga, Salvador, 204
Maeztu, Ramiro de, 11, 191, 198, 210, 212, 215, 216
Mallea, Eduardo, 22, 24
Mallo, Jerónimo, 134
Mann, Thomas, 96
Manrique, Jorge, 9, 41, 221
Marañón, Gregorio, 204, 206
Marechal, Leopoldo, 24
Marías, Julián, 38
Mariátegui, José Carlos, 79–80
Marichalar, Antonio, 206
Marinetti, Filippo, 215–216
Mármol, José, 21
Marqués de Quintanar, 207, 210, 215, 216
Marquina, Eduardo, 192, 198, 201

Martí, José, 13
Martín de la Escalera, Antonio, 215
Martínez Moreno, Carlos, 23
Martínez Ruiz, José (Azorín), 11, 34, 47, 223
Marx, Karl, 200
Marxism, 226, 227
Matto de Turner, Clorinda, 21
Matute, Ana María, 27
Maura, Honorio, 210
Mayoral Fernández, J., 191
McVan, Alice, 38, 39, 46
Menéndez Pidal, Ramón, 206
Menéndez y Pelayo, Marcelino, 11, 174, 187, 190, 192–193, 194, 196, 197, 198, 199
Mexía, Pedro, 183
Meyer, Edward, 172
Meyer, Monroe, 70
Miller, Arthur, 156
Miquelerana, J., 196
Miró, Gabriel, 25, 211, 217
modernism, 13–14
Mola, Emilio, 212
Molière (Jean Baptiste Poquelin), 114, 117
Mommsen, Theodore, 172
Montaigne, Michel de, 99
Montalvo, Antonio, 88
Montes, Eugenio, 216
Morales, Juan de, 184
Moreno Villa, José, 204, 207, 220, 222, 225, 231
Mosquera Narváez, Aurelio, 85
Mostaza, Bartolomé, 38
Mourlane Michelina, Pedro, 210
Muñiz, Carlos, 158
Muñoz Seca, Pedro, 202, 210
Navarro Tomás, Tomás, 11, 222–223
Nazis, 203, 217
Nietzsche, Friedrich, 11, 15
Nineteenth-Century Spanish Literature, 191–196
Nora, Eugenio de, 20
Norris, Frank, 80
Obregón, Antonio de, 206
Oliver, Federico, 127
Olivier, Lawrence, 116
O'Neill, Eugene, 157
Onetti, Juan Carlos, 23
Onís, Federico de, 13
Ors, Eugenio d', 211
Ortega y Gasset, José, 12, 34–35, 133, 134, 171–182, 204, 206–207
Ortiz, Adalberto, 80
Orueta, Ricardo de, 220

Osorio y Gallardo, Angel, 204, 220
Palacio Valdés, Armando, 194–196, 222, 223
Panero, Leopoldo, 20, 151
Par, Alfonso, 121
Pardo Bazán, Emilia, 128, 195, 199
Pareja y Diez Canseco, Alfredo, 79, 81, 83, 85–98
Paz, Octavio, 14
Pemán, José María, 38, 183, 184, 185, 186, 191, 196, 198, 200, 202, 203, 211, 212, 213–214
Pemartín, José, 205
Pereda, José, 128, 194, 195, 199
Pérez de Ayala, Ramón, 25, 49, 191, 204, 206, 207, 208, 223
Pérez Galdós, Benito, 194, 195, 229
Pérez-Minik, Domingo, 158
Peterson, Julius, 11
Picasso, Pablo, 233
Pizarro, Francisco, 199, 214
Polo Benito, José, 210
Poole, Ernest, 89
Portal Fradejas, J., 190
Pradal Rodríguez, G., 38–39
Prados, Emilio, 16, 226, 232
Prados, Víctor, 210
Predmore, Richard, 38
Primo de Rivera, Miguel, 128
Prisciliano, Miguel, 206
Proust, Marcel, 22, 86
Pujol, Juan, 183, 208
Quesada, Francisco, 185
Quevedo y Villegas, Francisco Gómez de, 10, 190, 199, 204, 213
Quinto, José María de, 163, 167
Ramírez, Alejandro, 38
Ramón y Cajal, Santiago, 11
Ramos, Ignacio, 217
Rank, Otto, 69–70, 75
Reforma Universitaria (La), 79
Reparáz, Virgilia, 192
Residencia de Estudiantes, 204
Riba, Carlos, 190
Ridruejo, Dionisio, 19–20
Rimbaud, Arthur, 61
Río, Angel del, 52
Río Hortega, Padre del, 220
Ríos, Fernando de los, 208
Ríos y Lampérez, Blanca de los, 217
Rivas Cherif, 209
Rivera, José Eustasio, 21
Roa Bastos, Augusto, 24
Rodríguez, Alonso, 184
Rodríguez, Claudio, 20

Rodríguez Alvarez, Alejandro. See
  Casona, Alejandro
Rodríguez Santamaría, Alfonso, 210
Rojas, Angel F., 92
Rosales, Luis, 19, 38
Rossi, Ernesto, 115
Rueda, Lope de, 200
Ruiz, Juan, 231, 234
Ruiz de Alarcón, Juan, 187, 201
Ruiz, Ramón, 38
Saavedra Fajardo, Diego de, 10, 190
Sábato, Ernesto, 24
Sacristán, José Miguel, 174
Sáenz Hayes, F., 209
Sainz de Robles, Federico Carlos, 64
Sainz Rodríguez, Pedro, 211
Sala, Alfonso, 194
Salaverría, José María, 188, 191, 198,
  205, 212, 214–215, 216
Salazar Alonso, Rafael, 210
Saldaña, Pedro de, 184
Salinas, Pedro, 16, 37
Salvini, Tommaso, 115
Samain, Albert, 80
Sánchez, Francisca, 205
Sánchez, Víctor, 190, 215
Sanjuán, Pedro, 220
Santiago, Miguel de, 96
Sanz del Río, Julián, 172, 175
Sartre, Jean Paul, 34, 134, 135, 137,
  138, 142, 156, 169
Sastre, Alfonso, 28, 32, 162–170
Schwarz, Egon, 175
Sender, Ramón, 25–27, 99–111, 133
Séneca, 234
Serna, Víctor de la, 206, 211, 216–217
Serrano, Urbano González, 175
Serrano Plaja, Arturo, 231
Servet, Miguel, 206
Shakespeare, William, 99, 113–126,
  179, 184
Shaw, George Bernard, 117
Silva, José Asunción, 13
Silva, Medardo Angel, 80
Simmonds, Adolfo, 86
Sinclair, Upton, 80
Singerman, Berta, 209
social novel (The), 22
Sola, Víctor María de, 213
Souto, Arturo, 220
Spanish Civil War, 13, 15, 20, 27, 35–
  36, 190, 191, 197–218, 219–224
Stein, Gertrude, 86

Suárez y Romero, Anselmo, 21
Talma, Francois Joseph, 115
Teatro Ambulante de Campaña, 200
Téllez, Gabriel (Tirso de Molina), 10,
  116, 184, 223
Terán, Enrique, 80
Teresa de Jesús, Santa, 199
Timoneda, Juan de, 184
Tolstoi, Leo, 117
Torres-Rioseco, A., 86
Unamuno, Fernando, 206
Unamuno, Miguel de, 11, 12, 16, 24,
  29, 33, 37, 39, 43, 46, 133, 134, 140,
  161, 205, 206, 207, 221, 228
Unamuno, Rafael, 206
Vaca, Jusepa, 184
Valdés, Francisco, 210
Valdivielso, José, 184, 201
Valente, José Angel, 20
Valera, Juan, 128, 174, 195, 199, 223
Valéry, Paul, 16
Valle-Inclán, Ramón María de, 24, 28,
  29, 196, 204–205, 221–222, 223
Van Doren, Carl, 90–91
Vargas Llosa, Mario, 24
Vasconcelos, José, 79, 86
Vázquez, José Andrés, 211
Vega, Garcilaso de la. See Garcilaso de
  la Vega
Vega Carpio, Lope Félix de, 10, 116,
  183, 184, 185, 186, 187, 188, 199,
  201, 213, 222, 223
Velázquez, Diego de, 199
Vélez de Guevara, Luis, 223
Vera, Pedro Jorge, 80
Virgil (Publius Vergilius Maro,) 99
Vicente, Gil, 184
Vigodsky, David, 226
Villaverde, Cirilo, 21
Vivanco, Luis Felipe, 19, 42
Vives, Juan Luis, 189–190
Wade, Gerald E., 134
Weber, Max, 172
Whitman, Walt, 58
Wilde, Oscar, 116, 214
Wordsworth, William, 120
Xirgu, Margarita, 185, 209
Zambrano, María, 228
Zardoya, Concha, 38
Zola, Emile, 80
Zorrilla, José, 191, 192, 199
Zubiría, Ramón de, 38, 45
Zuloaga, Ignacio, 210